Law and Personality Disorder

CLARENDON STUDIES IN CRIMINOLOGY

Published under the auspices of the Institute of Criminology, University of Cambridge; the Mannheim Centre, London School of Economics; and the Centre for Criminology, University of Oxford.

General Editors: Mary Bosworth and Carolyn Hoyle
(University of Oxford)

Editors: Alison Liebling, Paolo Campana, Loraine Gelsthorpe, and Kyle Treiber
(University of Cambridge)

Tim Newburn, Jill Peay, Coretta Phillips, and Peter Ramsay
(London School of Economics)

Ian Loader and Lucia Zedner
(University of Oxford)

RECENT TITLES IN THIS SERIES:

Character, Circumstances, and Criminal Careers: Towards a Dynamic Developmental and Life-Course Criminology
Wikstrom, Treiber, Roman

Children in Police Custody: Adversity and Adversariality Behind Closed Doors
Bevan

Victims and Criminal Justice: A History
Cox, Shoemaker, and Shore

Rethinking Drug Laws: Theory, History, Politics
Seddon

A Precarious Life: Community and Conflict in a Deindustrialized Town
Willis

From Conflict to Modern Slavery: The Drivers and the Deterrents
Heys

Exporting the UK Policing Brand 1989–2021
Sinclair

Penality in the Underground: The IRA's Pursuit of Informers
Dudai

Assessing the Harms of Crime: A New Framework for Criminal Policy
Greenfield and Paoli

Power and Pain in the Modern Prison: The Society of Captives Revisited
Crewe, Goldsmith, and Halsey

Armed Robbers: Identity and Cultural Mythscapes in the Lucky Country
Taylor

Law and Personality Disorder

Human Rights, Human Risks, and Rehabilitation

Ailbhe O'Loughlin

Great Clarendon Street, Oxford, OX2 6DP,
United Kingdom

Oxford University Press is a department of the University of Oxford.
It furthers the University's objective of excellence in research, scholarship,
and education by publishing worldwide. Oxford is a registered trade mark of
Oxford University Press in the UK and in certain other countries

© Ailbhe O'Loughlin 2024

The moral rights of the author have been asserted

All rights reserved. No part of this publication may be reproduced, stored in
a retrieval system, or transmitted, in any form or by any means, without the
prior permission in writing of Oxford University Press, or as expressly permitted
by law, by licence or under terms agreed with the appropriate reprographics
rights organization. Enquiries concerning reproduction outside the scope of the
above should be sent to the Rights Department, Oxford University Press, at the
address above

You must not circulate this work in any other form
and you must impose this same condition on any acquirer

Public sector information reproduced under Open Government Licence v3.0
(http://www.nationalarchives.gov.uk/doc/open-government-licence/open-government-licence.htm)

Published in the United States of America by Oxford University Press
198 Madison Avenue, New York, NY 10016, United States of America

British Library Cataloguing in Publication Data

Data available

Library of Congress Control Number: 2023948499

ISBN 9780198839279

DOI: 10.1093/9780191875434.001.0001

Printed and bound by
CPI Group (UK) Ltd, Croydon, CR0 4YY

Links to third party websites are provided by Oxford in good faith
and for information only. Oxford disclaims any responsibility for the
materials contained in any third party website referenced in this work.

General Editors Introduction

The *Clarendon Studies in Criminology series* aims to provide a forum for outstanding theoretical and empirical work in all aspects of criminology and criminal justice, broadly understood. The Editors welcome submissions from established scholars, as well as manuscripts based on excellent PhD dissertations. The Series was inaugurated in 1994, with Roger Hood as its first General Editor, following discussions between Oxford University Press and Oxford's then Centre for Criminological Research. It is edited under the auspices of three centres: The Centre for Criminology at the University of Oxford, the Institute of Criminology at the University of Cambridge, and the Mannheim Centre for Criminology at the London School of Economics. Each supplies members of the Editorial Board and, in turn, the Series General Editor or Editors.

Ailbhe O'Loughlin's *Law and Personality Disorder* offers a thoughtful and detailed analysis of the legal, practical, and ethical challenges in criminal justice responses to 'dangerous' offenders. Through careful study of the Dangerous and Severe Personality Disorder (DSPD) Programme, an initiative established to develop techniques for treating and managing people in the DSPD category in prisons and secure hospitals in England and Wales in the early 2000s, as well as its successor, the Offender Personality Disorder (OPD) Pathway, she raises a series of difficult questions about how this particular group of people are treated, before suggesting some alternative possible approaches.

While under criminal law those diagnosed with personality disorders are treated as though they are fully responsible for their criminal actions, medical evidence suggests that not everyone may have been fully in control of their actions at the time of their offence. Once in prison, the logic of rehabilitation likewise suggests that they can transform themselves, even though that may not be possible. Such matters, O'Loughlin suggests, render this population at a disadvantage particularly those serving indefinite sentences.

In considering these complex matters O'Loughlin draws on a wealth of material from interviews and policy documents to a close reading of relevant ECtHR jurisprudence. Drawing them together in the conclusion, she presents some alternative principles and possible responses, founded on a plea of diminished culpability. In contrast to the current category of 'diminished responsibility', O'Loughlin argues, this new plea could potentially differentiate more effectively among offenders. She also calls for a more robust assessment of the likely impact of a prison sentence and whether a period of confinement could safely meet their needs. Sentencing courts, she suggests, could opt for non-custodial alternatives or a hospital disposal instead. Above all, she calls for a minimal use of preventive orders, arguing that the vast majority of those with personality disorders should be given determinate sentences.

This is an engaging yet troubling book which asks us to think about how best to identify and treat dangerous people. In so doing, O'Loughlin invites us to reflect on the role of the state, and the nature of liberty and security. We are pleased to include this challenging and novel study in the Clarendon Studies in Criminology.

Mary Bosworth and Carolyn Hoyle
General Editors
Centre for Criminology, University of Oxford
October 2023

Acknowledgements

This book is based on my doctoral thesis, which was made possible by generous funding from the Arts and Humanities Research Council and LSE. I am indebted to my PhD supervisors, Jill Peay and Peter Ramsay, for our stimulating discussions at LSE and their invaluable guidance and support. I have benefitted enormously from Jill's continuing mentorship, and my work has been much improved by her very generous advice and suggestions. I am grateful to my PhD examiners, Lucia Zedner and Peter Bartlett, for their encouragement and constructive feedback. Lucia also very kindly read and provided comments on draft chapters of this book.

Harry Annison has been a very supportive and encouraging friend and colleague throughout this project and provided comments on several drafts at various stages. Matt Matravers commented on drafts of every chapter and provided very helpful advice on framing the book. Magda Furgalska provided excellent research assistance. I am grateful to the peer reviewers for their thorough feedback on the manuscript. At Oxford University Press, I would like to thank Kate Plunkett for editorial support in the early stages and Lindsay Glick for helping me to bring the project to the final stages. I am also grateful to Lindsay and to Fiona Briden for their flexibility, and for their assistance with choosing the cover art and refining the title. Akila Mari at Newgen provided excellent production support, and Allan Hoyano undertook thorough copy-editing.

Specials thanks to the interviewees who generously gave their time to share their valuable insights with me.

This work has benefitted from generous comments, advice, and encouragement from academic colleagues at York and beyond. In this regard, I would particularly like to thank Jackson Allen, TT Arvind, Isra Black, John Child, Axel Dessecker, Tom Guiney, Simon Halliday, Caroline Hunter, Nicola Lacey, Natasa Mavronicola, Lawrence McNamara, Mattia Pinto, Nicolas Rennuy, Jenny Steele, Julie Trebilcock, and Sue Westwood.

An earlier version of Chapter 2 was published as 'Personality disorder in mental health and criminal law', in B.D. Kelly and M. Donnelly (eds) *Routledge Handbook of Mental Health Law*. Abingdon: Routledge.

Chapter 6 has been adapted from 'Risk reduction and redemption: An interpretive account of the right to rehabilitation in the jurisprudence of the European Court of Human Rights', *Oxford Journal of Legal Studies*, 41(2), 510–38. I am grateful to the peer reviewers and editors of these works for their suggestions, and I thank the publishers for permission to reuse this material.

Finally, for their love, encouragement, and fortitude, I would like to thank my husband, Ben; my parents, Mick and Fiona; my siblings, Clare and Paddy; and my friends. Finishing this book would not have been possible without them. This book is dedicated to the memory of my grandparents, Tommy and Attracta O'Loughlin.

Contents

Table of Cases xi
Table of Legislation xv
List of Abbreviations xvii

1 Introduction 1
   1.1 The Puzzle of the 'Dangerous' 1
   1.2 Introducing the Case Study 5
   1.3 Dangerousness, Risk, and Rehabilitation 11
   1.4 Preventive Justice and Coercive Human Rights 14
   1.5 Paradoxical Constructions of Offenders with Personality Disorder 16
   1.6 Methodology 18
   1.7 Structure 20

2 Personality Disorder: A Contested and Evolving Construct 24
   2.1 Introduction 24
   2.2 Defining and Diagnosing Personality Disorder 25
   2.3 Dimensions and Stigma 31
   2.4 Personality Disorder and Offending 35
   2.5 Treating Personality Disorder 39
   2.6 The Vagaries of Risk Assessment 46
   2.7 Legal Controversies 49
   2.8 Conclusion 54

3 The Origins of the Construct of Dangerous People with Severe Personality Disorder 56
   3.1 Introduction 56
   3.2 Advent and Uproar 57
   3.3 Explaining the Emergence of the DSPD Proposals 60
   3.4 Tracing the Origins of the DSPD Proposals 62
   3.5 Immediate Influences 70
   3.6 Conclusion 81

4 The Pilot DSPD Programme 83
   4.1 Introduction 83
   4.2 The Pilot DSPD Programme and the Problem of 'Warehousing' 84

x Contents

    4.3 Explaining the Outcomes of the DSPD Programme   87
    4.4 Competing Constructions of 'Dangerous' People with
          Severe Personality Disorders   100
    4.5 Risks of Harm and Disproportionate Punishment   106
    4.6 Conclusion   108

5 **The Offender Personality Disorder Pathway**   110
    5.1 Introduction   110
    5.2 The Advent of the Offender Personality Disorder Pathway   111
    5.3 The Traumatized Subject   122
    5.4 The Risks of the Trauma-informed Model   127
    5.5 Conclusion   130

6 **Preventive Detention and Human Rights**   132
    6.1 Introduction   132
    6.2 Two Concepts of Rehabilitation   133
    6.3 The Right to Security and the Limits of the Right to
          Rehabilitation   151
    6.4 The Duty to Engage in Rehabilitation   156
    6.5 Conclusion   158

7 **Culpability, Responsibility, and Personality Disorder**   160
    7.1 Introduction   160
    7.2 Law and Personality Disorder   161
    7.3 Sentencing and Mental Disorder   167
    7.4 Treatability at Sentencing and Post-sentence   183
    7.5 Sentencing and Human Rights   186
    7.6 Conclusion   190

8 **Reflections**   192
    8.1 Introduction   192
    8.2 The Survival, and Revival, of Rehabilitation   193
    8.3 Contradictory Constructions of the Dangerous Subject   196
    8.4 Responsibility, Dangerousness, and the Criminal Law   198
    8.5 Responsibility, Capacity, and Treatability under Mental
          Health Law   201
    8.6 Paradoxes of Human Rights   203
    8.7 Towards a Rights-respecting Framework   205
    8.8 Conclusion   214

Bibliography   217
Index   247

Table of Cases

EUROPEAN COURT OF HUMAN RIGHTS

Aerts v Belgium [1998] ECHR 64 81
Chahal v UK (1997) 23 EHRR 413 187–88
Gäfgen v Germany [2010] 6 WLUK 4; (2011) 52 E.H.R.R. 1 .... 187–88, 189
Grosskopf v Germany (2011) 53 EHRR 7 136
Hutchison Reid v UK [2003] ECHR 94.............................62, 80–81
James, Wells and Lee v UK [2012] ECHR 1706 .... 52–53, 135–36, 137–38, 139–40,
  142–43, 144–45, 148–49, 156, 159, 204
Keenan v UK (2001) 33 E.H.R.R. 38 .... 106–7, 187, 188
Khoroshenko v Russia, App no. 41418/04, ECtHR, 30 June 2015 ......138, 139, 152
M v Germany [2009] ECHR 2071.................................52–53, 136
Maiorano and others v Italy, App. no. 28634/06, ECtHR 15 Dec 2009 ..... 151, 152,
  154–55, 157–58, 159
Marcello Viola v Italy (No.2), App. no. 45106/04, ECtHR 13 June 2019 148–49
Mastromatteo v Italy [2002] ECHR 694......151, 152–55, 156, 159, 203–4, 210–11
Murray v Netherlands (2017) 64 EHRR 3...............136–37, 138, 139–40, 143,
  144–45, 148–49, 152, 204, 208–9
Nikolova and Velichkova v Bulgaria [2007] 12 WLUK 663; (2009)
  48 E.H.R.R. 40...189
Öcalan v Turkey (No. 2) [2014] ECHR 24069/03 ....138, 143
Öneryildiz v Turkey (No. 2) [2004] 11 WLUK 785; (2005)
  41 E.H.R.R. 20..188, 189
Osman v UK [1998] ECHR 101; (2000) 29 EHRR 245............ 80, 132, 151–53,
  154–55, 156, 187–88, 210–11
Pretty v UK (2002) 35 E.H.R.R. 1 106–7
Price v UK (2002) 34 E.H.R.R. 53 186–87
Renolde v France (2009) E.H.R.R. 42 .... 106–7, 187, 188
Rooman v Belgium [2019] ECHR 109..........................53, 54, 213–14
Tyrer v UK [1978] ECHR 2 187–88
Vinter and others v UK [2012] ECHR 61 (C); [2013]
  ECHR 645 (GC) 134, 144–51, 152, 156, 157–58, 159, 203–4, 208–9
Weeks v UK [1987] ECHR 3...135, 208–9
Winterwerp v Netherlands [1979] ECHR 4 ....53, 81
Z and others v UK (2002) 34 EHRR 3 .... 152, 187–88

GERMANY

Life Imprisonment case (1977) 45 BVerfGE 187 IV(c) 149
War Criminal case BVerfGE 72, 105 24 April 1986 — 2 BvR 1146/85 150

xii Table of Cases

ENGLAND AND WALES

DPP v Majewski [1977] AC 443. 167
Loake v DPP [2017] EWHC 2855 (Admin). 163–64
Queen v M'Naghten 8 Eng. Rep. 718 [1843]. 163–64, 165
R. (Bruton) v Parole Board of England and Wales and Secretary
    of State for Justice [2022] EWHC 1692 (Admin). .128–29
R. (Debono) v Parole Board for England and Wales and Secretary
    of State for Justice [2020] EWHC 655 (Admin). 128–29
R. (Falconer) v Secretary of State for Justice [2009] EWHC 2341 (Admin). 101–2
R. (M) v Secretary of State for the Home Department [2007] EWCA Civ 687. 171
R. (Michael Stone) v CCRC [2011] EWHC 3995 63–64
R. (on the application of Clarke) v Secretary of State for Justice [2022]
    EWHC 2577 (Admin) 104
R. (S) v Secretary of State for Justice [2009] EWHC 2168 (Admin) 101–2
R. (Samuel) v Parole Board for England and Wales and Secretary
    of State for Justice [2020] EWHC 42 (Admin). 128–29, 157
R. (SP) v Secretary of State for Justice [2010] EWCA Civ 1590; [2009]
    EWHC 2168 (Admin) 97
R. (Unwin) v Secretary of State for Justice [2021] EWHC 1503 (Admin) 128–29
R. (Wellington) v Secretary of State for the Home Department [2008]
    UKHL 72. 150
R. v Ahmed [2016] EWCA Crim 670; [2016] M.H.L.R. 282 182
R. v Birch [1989] 11 Cr. App. R. (S.) 202; (1990) 90 Cr App R 78 . . . . . . 171–73, 175, 178
R. v Codère [1917] 12 Cr App Rep 21 164
R. v Conroy [2017] EWCA Crim 81; [2017] 2 Cr. App. R. 26. 165
R. v Crerand [2022] EWCA Crim 962 182–83
R. v Drew [2003] 1 W.L.R. 1213. . . . . .173, 174
R. v Edwards and others [2018] EWCA Crim 595; [2018]
    4 W.L.R. 64; [2018] 2 Cr. App. R. (S.) 17. . . . . 169, 175, 176, 179–80, 182–83
R. v Fisher [2019] EWCA Crim 1066 182–83
R. v Fox [2011] EWCA Crim 3299 178
R. v Graciano [2015] EWCA Crim 980 . . . . .178, 179
R. v Hetherington [2009] EWCA Crim 1186 187
R. v Hoppe [2016] EWCA Crim 2258. . . . . 181–82, 184
R. v Howell [1985] 7 Cr. App. R. (S.) 360 172
R. v Johnson [2007] EWCA Crim 1978. 164
R. v Keal [2022] EWCA Crim 341. 164
R. v Khan [2017] EWCA Crim 174. . . . . .182, 187
R. v Lundy [2021] EWCA Crim 1922 . . . . 180, 182–83
R. v Martens [2015] EWCA Crim 1645 . . . . 178–79, 181–82
R. v Mbatha [1985] 7 Cr. App. R. (S) 373 172–73
R. v Miller [2021] EWCA Crim 1955 182–83
R. v Nelson [2020] EWCA Crim 1615. 182–83
R. v Qazi [2010] EWCA Crim 2579; [2011] 2 Cr. App. R. (S.) 8 187
R. v Skana [2022] EWCA Crim 186 180
R. v Staines [2006] EWCA Crim 15 178
R. v Stredwick [2020] EWCA Crim 650 182–83

R. v Turner [2015] EWCA Crim 1249 .... 181–82, 184
R. v Vowles and others [2015] EWCA Crim 45, [2015]
  1 W.L.R. 5131, [2015] 2 WLUK 161 .... 169, 173–75, 176–77, 178,
                                                  181–82, 183–86, 190, 191, 207
R. v Welsh [2011] 2 Cr. App. R. (S.) 68 173
R. v Westwood [2020] EWCA Crim 598 182–83
R. v Windle [1952] 2 QB 826 164
WH v Llanarth Court Hospital (Partnerships in Care) [2015]
  UKUT 0695 (AAC) 185, 213–14

SCOTLAND

Hutchison Reid v Secretary of State for Scotland [1999] 2 A.C. 512 .... 62, 80–81

USA

Kansas v Hendricks 521 US 346 (1997) 201, 202

Table of Legislation

UNITED KINGDOM

England and Wales

Coroners and Justice
    Act 2009 s 52(1) 164–65
Crime (Sentences) Act 1997
    s 28 .... 8, 144–45
Criminal Justice Act 2003 ..... 7–8, 78
Criminal Procedure (Insanity)
    Act 1964 163–64
Homicide Act 1957 165
    s 2 164–65
Legal Aid, Sentencing and
    Punishment of Offenders
    Act 2012 .... 9, 135–36
Mental Capacity Act 2005 169
    s 3 202
Mental Deficiency Act 1919
    s 1(1)(d) 65–66
Mental Health Act 1959 ..... 50, 56–57,
               67–69, 183–84, 193–94
    s 4(4) 50, 67
    s 60 70
Mental Health Act 1983 10–11,
        16–17, 54, 59–60, 67, 68, 72–73,
        74, 84–85, 93, 107–8, 129,
        160–61, 202, 213–14
Mental Health Act 1983 (as enacted)
    s1(2) 7, 58
    s 3 .... 58, 212–13
    s 37(2)(a)(i) 22–23
    s 47 58
Mental Health Act 1983 (as amended
    by the MHA 2007)
    s 1 7
    s 1(1) 162
    s 1(2) 169
    s 1(3) 38, 58

    s 3 .... 4, 5–6, 58, 185
    s 37 .... 4, 9, 51, 70, 166,
                  167–68, 169–70
    s 41 .... 168, 169, 170
    s 42(2) 170
    s 45A 4, 7, 168, 169, 170, 174
    s 47 .... 4, 58, 168, 170–71,
                     183–85
    s 49 170–71
    s 63 .... 162, 169
    s 50(1)–(2) 171
    s 56 169
    ss 57–58A 162, 169
    s 72(1)(b) 102, 170, 184–85
    s 73(1)–(2) 170
    s 145(4) 50, 54, 184–85
Mental Health Act 2007 ...... 7, 22–23,
              50, 73, 85, 97–98,
             103–4, 160–61, 170
Police, Crime, Sentencing and
    Courts Act 2022 9–10
Sentencing Act 2020 s 57 ..... 168, 179
    s 273 58–59
    s 275 169
    s 285 .... 9, 58–59, 158
    Sch 9, Pt 9 168
Trial of Lunatics Act 1883 163–64

Scotland

Criminal Procedure (Scotland)
    Act 1995
    s 57A(3) 51
    s 210B 50–51
    s 210E 50–51
Mental Health (Care and
    Treatment) (Scotland)
    Act 2003
    s 136 51

Table of Legislation

INTERNATIONAL INSTRUMENTS

European Convention on Human Rights 1950
- Art 2 .... 106–7, 132, 152–55, 157–58, 186–90, 191, 204–5, 207, 210–11, 213
- Art 3 ... 106–7, 132–37, 144–46, 149, 152, 157–58, 186–90, 191, 204–5, 207, 208–9, 210–11, 213
- Art 5 .... 132–33, 136, 213
- Art 5(1)(a) 52–53, 135–36, 207–8
- Art 5(1)(e) 6–7, 53, 58–59, 81, 212, 213–14
- Art 7 52–53
- Art 8 138

United Nations Convention on the Rights of Persons with Disabilities 2006
- Art 14.1 212

IRELAND

Mental Health Act (Ireland) 2001
- s 3 51
- s 8(2)(b) 51

UNITED STATES OF AMERICA

- 406 ILCS 5/1-129 52
- Kan. Stat. Ann. § 59-2946 52
- Kan. Stat. Ann. § 59-29a02 52

List of Abbreviations

ARAI	actuarial risk assessment instrument
ASPD	antisocial personality disorder
BPD	borderline personality disorder
CBT	cognitive behavioural therapy
CRPD	Convention on the Rights of Persons with Disabilities
CSC	close supervision centre
DBT	dialectical behaviour (or behavioural) therapy
DSM	*Diagnostic and Statistical Manual of Mental Disorders* (American Psychiatric Association)
DSPD	dangerous and severe personality disorder, or dangerous and severely personality disordered
DSPD Programme	The Dangerous and Severe Personality Disorder Programme
ECHR	European Convention on Human Rights
ECtHR	European Court of Human Rights
ICD	International Classification of Diseases (World Health Organization)
IDEA	Inclusion for DSPD: Evaluating Assessment and Treatment. An independent study evaluating the DSPD Programme in high secure services for men.
IMPALOX	research team from Imperial College, Arnold Lodge and the University of Oxford commissioned to evaluate the pilot DSPD Programme for men in its early stages.
IPP	imprisonment for public protection. An indeterminate prison sentence for 'dangerous' offenders introduced in England and Wales by the Criminal Justice Act 2003.
MAPPA	multi-agency public protection arrangements. A mechanism for coordinating the work of the Police and HM Prison & Probation Service in respect of offenders at risk of committing sexual, violent, or terrorist offences.
MEMOS	Multi-method Evaluation of the Management, Organisation and Staffing in high security treatment services for people with DSPD. An independent evaluation of the DSPD Programme in high secure services for men conducted by researchers at Imperial College and King's College London.

List of Abbreviations

MHRT	Mental Health Review Tribunal
NEON	National Evaluation of Offender Personality Disorder Pathway. An independent evaluation of the Offender Personality Disorder Pathway.
NICE	National Institute for Health and Care Excellence
NOMS	National Offender Management Service
OASyS	Offender Assessment System
OPD Pathway	The Offender Personality Disorder Pathway. Successor to the DSPD Programme.
PCL-R	Psychopathy Checklist Revised: a diagnostic tool for assessing psychopathic traits.
PIPE	psychologically informed planned environment
RC	responsible clinician
RCT	randomized controlled trial
RMO	responsible medical officer
RNR	risk-need-responsivity model of offender rehabilitation
SOTP	sex offender treatment programme
VRS	Violence Risk Scale

1
Introduction

1.1 The Puzzle of the 'Dangerous'

The concept of the 'dangerous' person presents society with a perennial and seemingly intractable puzzle. It is often taken for granted that the state has a duty to protect the rights and interests of the population within its jurisdiction. This duty becomes more complex when the risks to that population are presented by individuals within it, to whom the state owes the same duty. As a result, the population that claims the state's protection may at once be dismayed by the cruel acts that individuals perpetrate against others and by the coercive measures taken by the state against individuals on the grounds of what they might do. Those charged with fulfilling the state's duties to protect the population as a whole—from politicians and civil servants to police officers, parole board members, probation officers, and psychiatrists—are often on the receiving end of public blame when a person known to state agencies commits serious offences. While the costs of 'getting it wrong' are high, it is impossible to 'get it right' all the time in a context of limited state resources and unpredictable human behaviour.

This puzzle can be understood as an aspect of the 'paradox of liberty: that a major justification for taking preventive powers is to secure or enhance the liberty of individuals, but that one possible effect of such powers is to deprive some individuals of their liberty' (Ashworth and Zedner, 2014, 257). In response to this dilemma, a seemingly neat, but by no means new, solution has regained ground in the last two decades. What if society could offer something to the individual in exchange for removing or restricting their liberty that would benefit them as well as the population at large? What if people who are at risk of harming others could be cured and returned to society as productive citizens? Or what if they could be prevented from causing harm in the first place, avoiding the costs of both crime and punishment?

While the solution of identifying at-risk or risky groups and providing them with treatment, rehabilitation, or training is not new, it is

Law and Personality Disorder. Ailbhe O'Loughlin, Oxford University Press. © Ailbhe O'Loughlin 2024.
DOI: 10.1093/9780191875434.003.0001

increasingly gaining purchase in an ever-wider range of contexts. Examples include: deradicalization programmes for suspected adherents to certain political or religious ideologies; healthy relationships programmes for people convicted of sexual offences; parenting programmes; and domestic violence perpetrator programmes. These interventions have emerged alongside a barrage of psychological assessment tools that promise to target interventions at those who need them most.

This book unpicks the reasons why this solution has become so alluring for policymakers, legislatures, and courts as a response to a certain class of 'dangerous' people: those with a history of serious violent or sexual offending. It further aims to cast a light on how legal and political actors negotiate the competing demands of controlling crime and protecting the human rights of offenders and suspects against a background of uncertain scientific knowledge. It does so by tracing the creation of a new category—'dangerous people with severe personality disorders'—by policymakers in England and Wales in the late 1990s. 'DSPD' was not a medical diagnosis but a term for a small group of people who were presented as posing a significant risk to the public due to a serious form of personality disorder characterized by antisocial or psychopathic traits (Home Office and Department of Health, 1999). The New Labour Government, elected in 1997, proposed to create new powers to preventively detain the DSPD group by expanding the scope of mental health law and to allocate significant funding to develop better treatments for personality disorder.

The DSPD proposals reflected a common claim by politicians that the state has a duty to protect 'innocent' members of the public from crime and from the fear of crime (Lazarus, 2007; 2012a; 2012b; Ramsay, 2012a; 2012b, ch 7). Implicit in the proposals was another idea: that, in discharging its duty to protect the public by removing the liberty of the 'dangerous', the state incurs a duty to provide detainees with the means to regain their liberty. This idea has since been framed by the European Court of Human Rights (ECtHR) as the 'right to rehabilitation': a right for prisoners serving indeterminate sentences to be provided with risk-reducing rehabilitative interventions and frequent reviews of the grounds for their detention in the hope that this will allow them to eventually return to society (van Zyl Smit, Weatherby, and Creighton, 2014). A similar idea has driven calls for reform to mental health legislation since the 1980s: that people who are deprived of their liberty by the state on the grounds of mental disorder have a reciprocal right to suitable treatment and aftercare (Gostin, 1983; Department of Health, 1999).

While this solution may seem logical on its face, the idea that we can identify and treat 'dangerous' people raises more questions than it answers. How sure are we that crime really is the product of mental disorder? How accurate do our predictions of danger need to be before we can intervene? When it comes to people diagnosed with personality disorder, the solution of offering treatment in exchange for liberty is even less straightforward. What do we mean by 'treatment'? Curing the disorder or simply managing its symptoms? How can we be certain that the treatment is working? And, given that detained persons have an interest in regaining their liberty, how can we be sure that any positive changes in their behaviour are genuine?

The risks posed by supposedly 'dangerous' people are not the objectively quantifiable risks that we might find in the natural sciences. Rather, they are 'human risks' based on 'altogether more diffuse and non-quantifiable "facts"' (Zedner, 2006, 424). Humans are not machines but complex beings capable of independent thought and action. Perhaps unsurprisingly, our ability to predict what a given human will do, or when, is limited. Huge resources would therefore be required to identify and detain everyone who might go on to commit a serious crime. By attempting to do so, the state would inevitably draw into the net people who would not, in fact, have harmed anyone.

Misgivings have long been raised by psychiatrists, psychologists, and social scientists about the validity and legitimacy of the personality disorder construct. Antisocial personality disorder and psychopathy have both been criticized for their circularity as each diagnosis is based on evidence of offending behaviour (Wootton, 1981; Mullen, 1999; Howard, 2006). In short, 'the psychopath's mental disorder is inferred from his anti-social behaviour while the anti-social behaviour is explained by mental disorder' (Wootton, 1981, 90). A personality disorder diagnosis can be very stigmatizing as it suggests a whole host of undesirable traits, ranging from impulsivity and aggressiveness to dishonesty and manipulativeness. While improvements in the evidence base for the treatment of borderline personality disorder have contributed to an emerging consensus that personality disorders are not necessarily untreatable, the evidence is still not robust and therapeutic scepticism remains (Pickersgill, 2013). The idea that a person has an 'abnormal' personality has therefore been characterized as 'a clear moralistic position involving a long-term lack of confidence in those individuals who recurrently act in ways that others find offensive, disappointing and troublesome' (Pilgrim, 2007, 84).

These dilemmas played out in the Dangerous and Severe Personality Disorder (DSPD) Programme: an initiative established to develop techniques for treating and managing people in the DSPD category in prisons and secure hospitals in England and Wales in the early 2000s. The DSPD Programme's successor, the Offender Personality Disorder (OPD) Pathway, has drawn an even broader range of prisoners and people on probation into initiatives for individuals who show signs of personality disorder.

The DSPD Programme and the OPD Pathway demonstrate that the paradox of liberty also generates a paradox of security: by taking coercive measures to protect the public's 'right' to be safe and to feel safe, the state generates risks to the safety of the individuals it subjects to coercion. While the DSPD Programme was intended to reduce violent and self-harming behaviour amongst prisoners who were difficult to manage, treatment could also have the effect of increasing self-harm (de Motte et al, 2017).

As this book shows, offenders who are labelled as both dangerous and as suffering from a personality disorder are constructed in contradictory ways by law and policy, and this creates a double disadvantage. Individuals in this group are deemed sufficiently mentally well by the criminal law to be held responsible and punished for their offences but are not deemed sufficiently mentally well to escape detention and coerced treatment under mental health law. Similarly, prison regimes and interventions targeting offending behaviour tend to construct such individuals as responsible for their past offending and for their own rehabilitation. In addition, the sentencing case law considered in this book shows that judges can deny offenders with personality disorder entry to hospital through the front door on the basis of 'untreatability', even if their mental disorder puts them at a risk of serious harm in prison. But the same individuals can be admitted to hospital through the back door after serving their prison sentence for the purposes of preventive detention on the grounds that appropriate medical treatment is available to them. This is troubling as, according to the Mental Health Act (MHA) 1983, the same 'appropriate medical treatment' test ought to apply at sentencing and post-sentence.[1]

Ultimately, as this book shows, the response to these contradictions must be a project of law and policy reform. While it may be argued that the state owes a duty to the public to detain people who are 'dangerous', those powers must be limited by the rights of the 'dangerous' individual. Those rights

---

[1] See MHA 1983, ss 3, 37, 45A, and 47.

include the right not to be detained on an arbitrary basis, and the right to be protected from serious harm or death whilst in state custody. The empirical evidence considered in this book demonstrates that there is a strong argument for decoupling progress in treatment from progress towards release from detention. But the case studies of the DSPD Programme and the OPD Pathway also show that developing evidence-based and rights-respecting responses to the problem of 'dangerous' offenders is a perennial challenge. Broader cultural changes are needed to encourage greater public acceptance of the reality that not all untoward events can be prevented by the state.

Next, the case study underpinning this book will be more fully introduced. Then, the DSPD initiative and the OPD Pathway will be contextualized in light of two broader movements in penal practices. The first is the trend towards exclusionary practices of preventive detention for 'dangerous' offenders and seemingly more progressive or inclusive practices of rehabilitation. The second is the growth of legal mechanisms of 'preventive justice' (Ashworth and Zedner, 2014; Zedner and Ashworth, 2019; Tulich, 2017) and the development of a 'coercive human rights' doctrine that promotes punitive and precautionary policies towards 'dangerous' offenders (Mavronicola and Lavrysen, 2020). Then, the seemingly paradoxical constructions of people with personality disorder in mental health law and the criminal law will be unpacked.

1.2 Introducing the Case Study

In 1999, Tony Blair's New Labour Government published a joint consultation paper developed by civil servants at the Home Office and Department of Health. It described a group of 'dangerous and severely personality disordered' (DSPD) individuals who were at risk of falling through cracks in the mental health and criminal justice systems in England and Wales. The Government estimated that about 1,422 male sentenced prisoners, 400 male patients detained in psychiatric hospitals, and between 300 and 600 men in the community met the definition of DSPD (Home Office and Department of Health, 1999, 50). Only around 50 women were expected to meet the criteria (DSPD Programme et al, 2006, 8).

While the vast majority of the DSPD group in prisons were thought to have committed serious violent or sexual offences, most were thought to be serving determinate prison sentences. Once their sentences expired, the paper claimed that the authorities would have no choice but to release them despite the risk of 'serious anti-social behaviour resulting from their disorder' (Home Office and Department of Health, 1999, 12). At the time, the MHA 1983 only permitted the detention of individuals suffering from 'psychopathic disorder' in psychiatric institutions if it could be shown that treatment was 'likely to alleviate or prevent a deterioration' in their condition.[2] As personality disorders were considered untreatable by some psychiatrists, this treatability criterion was presented as a stumbling block to the detention of dangerous individuals to protect the public (Seddon, 2008, 304; Peay, 2011a, 176).

The plans were widely interpreted by the media as a response to the case of Michael Stone, who was convicted of the murders of Lin Russell and her six-year-old daughter Megan and the attempted murder of Lin's nine-year-old daughter Josie in October 1998. Lin, Megan, and Josie were attacked on a country lane in Chillenden, Kent in July 1996 and Stone was arrested one year later (Francis et al, 2006; Maden, 2007). Following his arrest, media reports described Stone as a 'psychopath' left free to kill after psychiatrists had refused to admit him to hospital on the grounds that he was 'untreatable' or 'too dangerous' (Francis et al, 2006, Table 1.14). While a subsequent inquiry found that these claims were false, the myths about Stone have proven persistent (Francis et al, 2006, para 1.8; see Lloyd and Bell, 2015, 2).

The 1999 consultation paper put forward radical proposals to establish new powers for the detention of individuals in the DSPD group in a dedicated institution, separate from prisons and secure hospitals, for as long as they posed a risk. Detention would not depend on a criminal conviction but would instead fall within the state's power to detain individuals 'of unsound mind' under Article 5(1)(e) of the European Convention on Human Rights (ECHR). The DSPD group would not merely be detained but would also be 'helped and encouraged to co-operate in therapeutic and other activity designed to help them return safely to the community' (Home Office and Department of Health, 1999, 9). By allocating significant funding to research into tailored treatments, the Government aimed to strike a 'balance' 'between the human rights of individuals [in the DSPD group] and the right of the public to be protected from these very dangerous people' (Boateng and Sharland, 1999, 7). If the risks posed by those in the DSPD group were found not to be reduced through treatment, however, there

---

[2] See, for example, MHA 1983 (as enacted), s 3(2)(b).

would be 'no alternative but to continue to detain them indefinitely' (Home Office and Department of Health, 1999, 9).

The plans quickly attracted vociferous objections from mental health practitioners, lawyers, patient groups, and civil liberties charities. Psychiatrists and legal commentators questioned the legitimacy of the DSPD construct, which was not a recognized diagnosis. Many argued that detaining the DSPD group in hospital in the absence of effective, evidence-based treatments was unethical as it was unclear how people labelled as 'DSPD' would ever be able to demonstrate their safety for release (Mullen, 1999; Peay, 1999; Buchanan and Leese, 2001; Maden and Tyrer, 2003). Others expressed the suspicion that the Government aimed to circumvent the provisions of the ECHR and to misuse mental health law to detain suspected offenders without trial (Eastman, 1999).

Plans to create a separate service and special powers to detain the DSPD group were eventually shelved in the face of sustained opposition. Instead, the New Labour Government focused its efforts on reforming mental health law to facilitate the detention of the DSPD group under existing powers. These efforts eventually resulted in the passage of the MHA 2007, which introduced a series of amendments to the MHA 1983. The MHA 2007 introduced a broad definition of 'mental disorder', defined as 'any disorder or disability of the mind',[3] to replace the old categories of psychopathic disorder, mental impairment, severe mental impairment, and mental illness in the MHA 1983 as originally enacted.[4] The treatability test was replaced by the much less stringent requirement that 'appropriate medical treatment' be 'available' to the patient in hospital.[5] Pending these reforms, a pilot DSPD Programme was established in 2000 to develop and test assessment and treatment processes for the DSPD group within existing legal frameworks (Department of Health, 2000). The Programme established a small number of specialist treatment units for men in prisons, secure hospitals, and in the community and a small prison unit for women.

A parallel development was the introduction of the sentence of imprisonment for public protection (IPP) under the Criminal Justice Act (CJA) 2003. Like the DSPD proposals, the IPP sentence was spearheaded by the New Labour Government as a solution to the perceived problem of 'dangerous' offenders being released prematurely from determinate prison

---

[3] MHA 1983, s 1 (as in force).
[4] See MHA 1983, s 1(2) (as enacted).
[5] MHA 1983, s 145(4) (as in force).

sentences (Annison, 2015, 31). Unlike the reforms to the MHA 1983, the IPP was prospective and applied after conviction to individuals who had a previous conviction for a listed offence.

The IPP is structured like a life sentence. A fixed period of imprisonment for the purpose of retributive punishment (known as the 'tariff') is followed by an indeterminate period of preventive detention in prison. A post-tariff IPP prisoner can only be released if the Parole Board is satisfied that his detention is 'no longer necessary for the protection of the public'.[6] A key means for IPP prisoners to progress towards release is by completing interventions that seek to reduce the risk they pose to the public. Prisoners serving such sentences were expected to be likely to be selected for the DSPD Programme. In a search of Offender Assessment System (OASys) data, 59 per cent of IPP prisoners required a clinical assessment for DSPD programme entry, compared with 34 per cent of life-sentenced prisoners and 29 per cent of the general prison population (Rutherford, 2009, S53).

Subsequent evaluations of the DSPD Programme for men suggest that it did not fully live up to the high expectations set by policymakers. Formal therapy took up an average of less than two hours per week in the high secure prison and hospital units for men (Burns et al, 2011, 237). Stays on the DSPD Programme were longer than expected and progress onwards from the units was slow (Trebilcock and Weaver, 2010b, 33). Nevertheless, successive governments have pursued plans to continue and even expand the programme under the new name of the Offender Personality Disorder (OPD) Pathway (Department of Health and Ministry of Justice, 2011; NOMS and NHS England, 2015; Skett and Lewis, 2019).

The OPD Pathway is a much broader and more diffuse initiative than the DSPD Programme. It incorporates a wide range of treatment, progression, and psychologically informed case management initiatives within prisons, psychiatric hospitals, and in the community. Surprisingly, the OPD Pathway does not require entrants to have a 'formal' diagnosis of personality disorder. Instead, it focuses on offenders who have 'complex needs consisting of emotional and interpersonal difficulties', who are difficult for agencies to manage, and who are thought to pose a high risk of serious reoffending (Department of Health and NOMS, 2011a, para 17). By December 2017, 31,090 men and 1,996 women were on the OPD Pathway (Skett and Lewis, 2019, 168).

---

[6] Crime (Sentences) Act 1997, s 28.

The IPP was abolished by the Legal Aid, Sentencing and Punishment of Offenders Act 2012. However, as the abolition was not retrospective, a significant number of prisoners continue to be subject to IPP. As of June 2022, 2,926 IPP prisoners were still in prison (House of Commons Justice Committee, 2022, para 3). Of these, 1,492 have never been released, and 1,434 are in prison after having been recalled from the community (House of Commons Justice Committee, 2022, para 3). Due to longstanding problems within the prison system, IPP prisoners struggle to obtain access to the interventions they need to demonstrate to the Parole Board that they are safe to release, and the uncertainty they live under is taking a toll on their mental health (House of Commons Justice Committee, 2022; Annison, 2018).

While ministers have acknowledged the injustices arising from the IPP sentence (Truss, 2017; Lidlington 2017), Conservative-led governments in England and Wales have continued to pursue sentencing policies that subject 'dangerous' offenders to lengthy prison terms on the grounds that they pose an unacceptable risk to the public (Ashworth and Kelly, 2022, ch 9.8). The IPP was replaced by new or reformed extended determinate and indeterminate sentences for dangerous offenders. The most onerous of these is the sentence of life imprisonment for 'dangerous' offenders aged 21 or over at the time of conviction. Under s 285 of the Sentencing Act 2020, where a court is sentencing an offender for an offence listed in Schedule 19 to the Act and is of the opinion 'that there is a significant risk to members of the public of serious harm occasioned by the commission by the offender of further specified offences' and that 'the seriousness of— (a) the offence, or (b) the offence and one or more offences associated with it, is such as to justify the imposition of a sentence of imprisonment for life' it *must* impose a life sentence.[7]

Over the past 20 years, sentencing policies have resulted in a significant increase in the numbers of prisoners serving indeterminate sentences, and therefore in the number of prisoners who are required to complete psychological treatment programmes to demonstrate to the Parole Board that their detention is no longer required to protect the public (Guiney, 2019). Prisoners are also spending longer periods in prison. In 2002, prisoners serving determinate sentences spent an average of 8.2 months in prison. By

---

[7] While the language of the statute is mandatory, it is still open to the court to make a hospital order under s 37 of the MHA 1983, with or without restrictions under s 41, as the sentence is not 'fixed by law'. See Sentencing Act 2020, s 285(4).

2022, this had increased to an average of 15.6 months (Ministry of Justice, 2023b, Table A3.2i). In 2002, prisoners serving mandatory life sentences for murder spent an average of 14 years in prison before release. By 2022, this had increased to 18 years (Ministry of Justice, 2023b, Table A3.3). For prisoners serving other life sentences, including IPP, the increase is even starker: from an average of 9 years in 2002 to 19 years in 2022 (Ministry of Justice, 2023b, Table A3.3). Even greater increases can be expected following the introduction of sentencing reforms under the Police, Crime, Sentencing and Courts Act 2022 that seek to ensure that offenders convicted of certain sexual, violent, or terrorism offences 'spend as much of their sentence behind bars as possible' (Buckland, 2020).[8]

Up to 96 per cent of IPP prisoners, including prisoners recalled from the community, have been found to meet the screening criteria for the OPD Pathway (House of Commons Justice Committee, 2022, para 72). While the OPD Pathway is intended to help prisoners to progress towards release, a recent independent evaluation of men's services found that referral to complex case consultation or treatment on the Pathway had no effect on actuarial risk scores, self-harm incidents, recalls to prison, and proven reoffending (Moran et al, 2022, 10). While referral for treatment seemed to reduce incidents of rule-breaking behaviour, this benefit did not offset the cost of treatment (Moran et al, 2022, 16). The qualitative data gathered by the study paints a much more optimistic picture, with both staff and offenders reporting improved relationships and more positive and supportive working and living environments (Moran et al, 2022, 17–24). However, the conclusion that treatment on the OPD Pathway was not associated with cost savings or a reduction in reoffending casts doubt on its future.

There is a concern that selection for the OPD Pathway may impede, rather than facilitate, the journey of prisoners serving indeterminate sentences, including IPP, towards release. Prisoners may be required to complete interventions that are not based in sufficient evidence to convince the Parole Board that their risk has been reduced. For prisoners serving determinate sentences, selection for the OPD Pathway may open the door to preventive detention in hospital under the MHA 1983. In the absence of robust evidence that current treatments for personality disorder are effective in reducing reoffending risk, patients detained on the grounds of

---

[8] For further details and discussion of recent changes to sentencing, see Wasik (2014; 2021); Beard (2021); and Padfield (2022).

personality disorder are likely to face a long battle to secure their discharge from hospital.

1.3 Dangerousness, Risk, and Rehabilitation

The DSPD initiative and the legal changes that followed it can be understood as part of a broader trend for governments in Europe, North America, and Australasia to enact preventive detention measures in response to public concerns about 'dangerous' offenders. These concerns gained significant political attention between the mid-1980s and early 2000s in the wake of the release of notorious offenders from prison and sensationalized media reports of violent or sexual crimes committed by individuals known to the authorities (Keyzer, 2011; La Fond, 2011; van der Wolf and Herzog-Evans, 2015; Brown, 2016). In the Netherlands and Germany, existing two-track systems of penalties and measures of preventive detention were repurposed to deal with violent and sexual offenders (van Marle, 2002; de Boer and Gerrits, 2007; Dessecker, 2009; van der Wolf and Herzog-Evans, 2015). Several US states introduced or revived powers to detain 'sexually violent predators' (La Fond, 2011). In Australia, courts were given the power to extend detention post-sentence for offenders convicted of serious violent or sexual offences (Keyzer, 2011). Such practices can result in individuals spending much more time in detention than would be required by principles of proportionate punishment. They therefore raise the concern that 'dangerous' individuals are being punished for who they are rather than for what they have done.

Legal commentators and criminologists have pointed to the tendency for such measures to blur the traditional boundaries between civil and criminal law, and to erode or circumvent due process and human rights guarantees (Hebenton and Seddon, 2009; Freckelton and Keyzer, 2010; La Fond, 2011). Promises by legislatures or governments to treat or rehabilitate 'dangerous' detainees are often characterized as mere rhetoric or as a cynical effort to avoid the safeguards associated with criminal trials and penal sanctions (see Keyzer, 2011 and La Fond, 2011). Such accounts fit well with the claim that the rehabilitative ideal, which David Garland (2001, 35) argues was the 'hegemonic, organizing principle' of criminal justice policy and practice in the post-war period, has been replaced by a focus on managing risk.

The rehabilitative ideal was premised on the assumption 'that human behavior is the product of antecedent causes', and that knowledge of these causes would facilitate 'the scientific control of human behavior' (Allen, 1959, 226). It further entailed that:

> measures employed to treat the convicted offender should serve a therapeutic function, that such measures should be designed to effect changes in the behavior of the convicted person in the interests of his own happiness, health, and satisfactions and in the interest of social defense (Allen, 1959, 226).

For Malcolm Feeley and Jonathan Simon (1992), the rehabilitative ideal was replaced by a 'new penology' that is not interested in transforming individual offenders but in managing risky groups using actuarial techniques of risk assessment. Drawing explicitly or implicitly on this thesis, some scholars argue that preventive measures targeting 'dangerous' individuals, including the DSPD initiative, aim to identify pathological 'monsters' and to permanently exclude them from society (Simon, 1998; Rutherford, 2006; Seddon, 2007; 2008).

Contrary to these accounts, the emergence of the DSPD Programme and its expansion and re-configuration under the OPD Pathway suggests a revival of the rehabilitative ideal and a seemingly genuine commitment on behalf of policymakers and practitioners to improving the mental health of 'dangerous' offenders. While one of the primary aims of the DSPD Programme was public protection, it has been praised for driving investment in research and in treatment programmes for a neglected, distressed, and socially excluded group (Mullen, 2007; Tyrer et al, 2015). The OPD Pathway has been cited as an example of good practice that stands out against a background of chronic under-investment in prisoner mental health in England and Wales (House of Commons Committee of Public Accounts, 2017, 17–18; Criminal Justice Joint Inspection, 2021b, paras 5.30 and 7.35). This raises the question of how criminological theory can explain the value that initiatives targeting mental health symptoms have for contemporary criminal justice policy.

The idea that the rehabilitative ideal dominated post-war penal policy and practice and that it suddenly fell from grace in the 1970s has been disputed by several commentators (Zedner, 2002; Bailey, 2019; Gendreau and Ross, 1987). While rehabilitation currently appears to be enjoying a revival in penal policy, scholars have shown that it never really ceased to be an aim of corrections in policy or practice (Genders and Player, 1995; Lynch, 2000; Hutchinson, 2006; Robinson, 2008; McNeill, 2012; McNeill et al, 2009).

Dangerous, Risk, and Rehabilitation 13

Rather than entirely displacing traditional welfarist strategies, risk technologies have been reshaped to meet ongoing political commitments to facilitate offender rehabilitation and reintegration (Hannah-Moffat, 2005). This can be seen in the proliferation of actuarial risk assessment tools and rehabilitative programmes that has accompanied the introduction of legal measures to preventively detain dangerous individuals (Monahan et al, 2000; Wong and Gordon, 2006; Bonta and Andrews, 2007; Ward and Fortune, 2013; Douglas et al, 2017).

Some studies have further shown that holistic practices of rehabilitation within prisons are valued for more than the promise that they will reduce reoffending (Sparks, 2002; Genders and Player, 1995; 2022). Such practices can also be valued for their contribution to improving institutional behaviour. However, where therapeutic regimes conflict with the priorities of the prison, including maintaining order and security, they are vulnerable to dilution, erosion, or being shut down (Sparks, 2002; Genders and Player, 1995; 2022).

Building on this literature, the case study of the DSPD Programme and the OPD Pathway demonstrates that treatment or rehabilitation is offered to prisoners not only with the intention of reducing the risks they pose to the public but also to manage the risks they pose within institutions and to the reputation of the state. As set out in this book, the survival of rehabilitative interventions in prisons despite a lack of clear evidence of their effectiveness in tackling recidivism may be attributable to their potential to reduce levels of distress, self-harm, and institutional violence amongst prisoners, allowing them to be managed in a safer, cheaper, and less physically coercive manner. While rehabilitative programmes and therapeutic environments generate conflict and tensions within criminal justice institutions, they can also complement the aims of the prison, which include maintaining external security; upholding internal order and control; and providing a safe and 'decent' environment for prisoners (Crewe, 2009, 26). In order to survive, therefore, initiatives with radical roots are likely to be forced to fall in line with the dominant culture of the prison system, which views prisoners as rational actors who must take responsibility for their own behaviour and be punished for any transgressions.

The longer history of the DSPD proposals further demonstrates that the plans were not a reaction to one high-profile case but were a response to a longstanding feeling within government that past attempts to tackle the problem of 'dangerous' people had failed. Policymakers considered that such attempts had not only failed to adequately protect the public but they also provoked public scandals, and threatened the reputation of the state as the guardian of safety and security within and beyond its secure institutions. Nevertheless, the use of psychological interventions with prisoners that aim to reduce risk to the public can also generate risks to participants. This issue is considered next.

1.4 Preventive Justice and Coercive Human Rights

Legal measures to preventively detain 'dangerous' offenders are based on a common premise: that some individuals have shown, by their past behaviour, a propensity for serious offending, and that the state has a moral or legal obligation to identify these people and to prevent them from harming members of the public. This argument is often couched in human rights terms, as can be seen from the justification for the DSPD proposals offered by Paul Boateng, then Minister of State at the Home Office:

> society has both a right and a need to protect itself from the actions of this small group of people who because of their disordered personality, pose an unacceptable level of risk of causing serious harm to others (Boateng and Sharland, 1999, 7).

The idea that the state has a duty to protect those within its jurisdiction from harm is not new. Rather, 'a central theme in classical political theory is the state's core function as guarantor of the safety of its citizens and defender of the nation's security' (Zedner and Ashworth, 2019, 430). This duty has, however, 'always been tempered by the risk that the state will exercise that authority excessively or arbitrarily' (Zedner and Ashworth, 2019, 430). As a result, the relationship between human rights and the criminal law can appear paradoxical (Mavronicola and Lavrysen, 2020).

On the one hand, human rights law affords individuals protection from coercion under the criminal law by requiring safeguards that place limits on coercive penal power. On the other hand, human rights are cited as a reason to coerce individuals who have committed, or who may commit, human rights violations. Human rights therefore act both as a 'shield' and a 'sword' in the criminal law context (Tulkens, 2011).[9] This raises the question of

---

[9] Tulkens (2011) attributes the terminology of 'sword' and 'shield' to Christine Van den Wyngaert, a judge at the International Criminal Court.

'how to properly balance the "shield" and "sword" functions, and how to address potential tensions between the human rights of (potential) victims and those of suspects and defendants' (Lavrysen and Mavronicola, 2020, 2).

The promise of rehabilitation has gained ground in human rights law as a means of addressing this balance. In the jurisprudence of the ECtHR, providing prisoners serving risk-based indeterminate sentences with opportunities for rehabilitation and regular recidivism risk assessments has been conceptualized as a safeguard against grossly disproportionate punishment and arbitrary detention (van Zyl Smit et al, 2014; Meijer, 2017; Annison and O'Loughlin, 2019; O'Loughlin, 2021a). However, the empirical claims implicit in this premise—that we can reliably identify those who will offend—are not supported by robust empirical evidence. Moreover, the parlous state of safety and the dearth of mental health support and constructive activities on offer in many prisons in England and Wales casts doubt on their ability to safeguard prisoners' basic rights and to provide them with adequate opportunities for self-improvement (National Audit Office, 2017; House of Commons Committee of Public Accounts, 2017; European Committee for the Prevention of Torture and Inhuman or Degrading Treatment or Punishment, 2020; HM Inspectorate of Prisons, 2019; 2023).

While the literature on coercive human rights has focused on the deployment of the criminal law, the preventive justice literature highlights that mental health law is also used to protect the security of the collective. As Tamara Tulich (2017, 18–19) notes, mental health law allows individuals to be deprived of their liberty in the interests of protecting others from harm, and this detention can be experienced as punishment (see also Stanton-Ife, 2012 and Ashworth and Zedner, 2014, ch 9). While the offer of rehabilitation can also curtail individual freedoms, this has not attracted sustained commentary in the literature on preventive justice (Tulich, 2017, 19).

As this book shows, while detention in a psychiatric hospital at the end of a prison sentence is not intended to punish, it may nevertheless be experienced by the detainee as an extension of the punishment imposed at sentencing. Similarly, extended detention on the grounds of risk may be experienced as punitive by prisoners but escape the notice of legal scholars. This book further highlights that engaging in rehabilitation has become a duty of prisoners serving indeterminate sentences under administrative law and human rights law. In order to have any chance of regaining their freedom, prisoners are obliged to cooperate with rehabilitative interventions and to demonstrate their trustworthiness to the Parole Board. Where a prisoner diagnosed with a personality disorder is serving a determinate sentence, they may be detained under mental health law if they are thought to pose a risk to the public. Such individuals must also cooperate with treatment if they wish to be discharged.

While there has been a revival in interest in rehabilitation both in criminal justice policy and in criminological scholarship over the past two decades, the meaning of rehabilitation itself remains under-theorized. There is a significant literature on the history of rehabilitation as a penal strategy (Garland, 1985; 2001; Rotman, 1990; Pifferi, 2016; Bailey, 2019) and a growing body of scholarship on the life-sentenced prisoner's 'right to rehabilitation' (van Zyl Smit, Weatherby, and Creighton, 2014; Meijer, 2017; Martufi, 2018; Annison and O'Loughlin, 2019). However, there have been few attempts to analyse what exactly the ECtHR means by 'rehabilitation'[10] and little scrutiny of what the 'right to rehabilitation' means in light of the competing right of the public to security.

This book shows that the jurisprudence of the ECtHR in respect of long-term prisoners is shaped by two distinct concepts of rehabilitation: rehabilitation as risk reduction and rehabilitation as redemption. The first concept takes for granted the disputed logic underlying the dominant risk–need–responsivity (RNR) model of offender rehabilitation: that an offender's risk of reoffending can be reliably assessed and reduced through targeted treatment programmes that are tailored to their needs. The second reflects the older idea that offending is a sign of bad character but that people can atone for their crimes by working hard to change themselves. Both concepts place the onus on prisoners to demonstrate that they have succeeded in achieving rehabilitation. Consequently, the ECtHR's case law on the right to rehabilitation risks legitimizing practices of preventive detention and fails to scrutinize the potential for preventive detention of the 'dangerous' to lead to disproportionate punishment.

1.5 Paradoxical Constructions of Offenders with Personality Disorder

'Dangerous' offenders diagnosed with personality disorders are constructed in contradictory ways by both law and policy. While offenders labelled as 'DSPD' were presented by policymakers as dangerous, disordered, and

---

[10] Notable exceptions are Rogan (2018) and Dagan (2020).

uncontrollable, they were also thought to be capable of learning to exercise self-control through participation in treatment. The idea that the risks posed by the DSPD group resulted from their disorders sits uneasily with the fact that most participants in the DSPD Programme had been held responsible by the courts for serious crimes and were given prison sentences rather than mental health disposals (Trebilcock and Weaver, 2010a, 30–31). Nevertheless, such individuals could be preventively detained under the MHA 1983 after serving determinate prison sentences.

The philosophical and legal literature on personality disorder or psychopathy and criminal responsibility is dominated by debates about how the criminal law, and particularly the law governing defences, ought to respond to the emotional and volitional deficits associated with these disorders (Fine and Kennett, 2004; Glannon, 2008; Morse, 2008b; Glenn and Raine, 2014; Pickard, 2015; Penney, 2012; Sisti and Caplan, 2012). Much less attention has been paid to the reasons why offenders are typically held accountable for their decisions by the criminal law despite these deficits.[11] Through a detailed examination of sentencing case law and mental health law, this book develops a deeper understanding of how the law deals with offenders who do not fit with the ideal, rational subject of the criminal law. It further shows that the combination of criminal law and mental health law creates a double disadvantage for offenders with personality disorders. They often do not enjoy the protections from punishment accorded to some of those who suffer from mental disorder, but nor do they enjoy the protections from coercion under mental health law accorded to those who have no mental disorder.

Both the DSPD Programme and the OPD Pathway initiatives further show the impact of the labels of personality disorder and dangerousness on the right to liberty. While prisoners and patients given these labels are unlikely to progress towards release from detention without engaging with treatment, doing so is not a clear path towards release. This is because the labels of personality disorder and dangerousness bring with them the implication that a person is unlikely to change and likely to seek release by deceiving the authorities into believing they have changed. This double bind is exacerbated by a paucity of evidence for the effectiveness of interventions with antisocial personality disorder and psychopathy in reducing serious offending.

---

[11] Notable exceptions are Peay (2011b) and Pickard (2015).

This unsatisfactory state of affairs is the product of historical attempts to reach a compromise between the competing values of safeguarding individual liberty and preventing future crimes. However, it is not inevitable or inescapable. This book sketches the outline of a more humane system based on principles of proportionate punishment and voluntary rehabilitation. This framework draws on the findings presented in this book along with insights from the literature on preventive justice, coercive human rights, and Egardo Rotman's (1990; 1986) rights-based model of rehabilitation.

1.6 Methodology

This book adopts a socio-legal and interdisciplinary approach to develop an explanatory and a normative critique of the current framework governing 'dangerous' offenders with personality disorders. It combines a criminological concern with exposing the assumptions that underlie practices of punishment and their effects in the real world with a legal or doctrinal concern for using the best interpretation of the law as the foundation for reform efforts. In so doing, it adopts a genealogical approach to tracing the influence of ideas or concepts over time in order to expose the workings of systems of social control and to open up space for power to be contested and resisted (see Garland, 1997; Rose, 2000). By examining the real-world effects of laws and policies, methodological approaches that fuse legal and penal theory with criminological insights 'have significant potential to limit state power by identifying where punishment's boundaries ought to lie' (Zedner, 2016, 7). In addition, this book draws on insights from psychiatry, psychology, and criminology to question the empirical assumptions that are implicit in the legal and policy framework and to draw out the implications of that framework for individual rights.

On an explanatory level, this book traces the concepts that underpin legal and political attempts to resolve the perceived problem of 'dangerous' offenders and unearths the contradictions and tensions they have produced. The aim is to explain why the present legal and policy framework is the way it is, rather than to present it as it *should* be, and to show the impact of that framework on the rights of individuals. This explanatory stage opens up the possibility for normative debate on whether the current framework has to be the way it is, grounded in a deep understanding of how and why it was constructed and of the assumptions it was built upon. While the evaluation of legal judgments presented in this book demonstrates that the law is to a large extent complicit in the proliferation of preventive measures, human rights law, mental health law, and the criminal law also contain principles that could be used to limit their use.

Chapters 3–5 of this book develop a 'critical reconstruction and reinterpretation' (Loader, 2006, 561) of the origins of the DSPD proposals and the OPD Pathway as well as their implementation and subsequent evolution. This story helps to shed light on the continuing influence of historical compromises between the rights of the individual to liberty and the interests of the collective in security. These chapters further highlight the risks the current legal framework presents for the rights and interests of individuals who are classified as both dangerous and as suffering from personality disorder. In building this account, these chapters draw on contemporary documents and 17 interviews with key informants conducted by the author. The documents include consultation and policy papers, the reports and minutes of evidence of committees of inquiry, parliamentary debates, newspaper articles, and descriptive and outcome studies of the DSPD Programme, the OPD Pathway, and related initiatives. Interviewees include policymakers involved in formulating, promoting, and implementing the DSPD and OPD Pathway proposals and academics or practitioners who gained insider knowledge as independent evaluators or by working within DSPD services. As limited research is available on personality disorder services for women,[12] these chapters focus predominantly on services for men.

Interviewees were identified through searches of contemporary documentary sources and subsequently by using a snowballing approach. The interviews helped to guide the research process, to aid in the interpretation of pertinent events, and to guide the interpretation of documentary sources. Quotations from interviewees are accompanied by a citation denoting the professional group to which the interviewee belonged (Psychiatrist, Psychologist, Academic, Civil Servant, or Politician) and a number (eg Psychiatrist 3). Interviewees were given assurances of anonymity. The categories are accordingly broad so that individuals are not easily identifiable in a small field.

Chapters 6 and 7 adopt a socio-legal methodology to draw out the assumptions and conceptual frameworks that underlie legal responses to

---

[12] While an evaluation of the DSPD Programme for women at HMP Low Newton was completed in 2012, the report was never published. An evaluation of the OPD Pathway for men has been published (Moran et al, 2022). While an evaluation of the OPD Pathway for women was commissioned, its report had not appeared by the time of writing. Efforts to arrange interviews with individuals involved in women's services were unsuccessful.

offenders who are constructed as 'dangerous' and mentally disordered. This approach sees judges not as mouthpieces or discoverers of the law but as socially situated agents who draw, sometimes unknowingly, on extra-legal considerations (beliefs, traditions, values, assumptions) in constructing, interpreting, and applying legal rules and principles (see Annison, 2014 and Rogan, 2018). These chapters examine how domestic courts and the ECtHR interpret concepts with contested or multiple meanings, such as culpability, responsibility, and rehabilitation by examining how judicial accounts of these concepts map on to accounts from philosophy, legal history, law, and criminology. Rather than arguing that these accounts have directly influenced judicial reasoning, I seek to identify what the courts themselves mean when they use certain terms by examining how their reasoning fits with the various possible meanings identified in the literature.

1.7 Structure

Chapter 2 analyses the scientific, ethical, and legal debates surrounding the psychiatric construct of personality disorder. It sets the scene for the examination in subsequent chapters of attempts in England and Wales to address the legal and policy problems posed by 'dangerous' offenders and 'difficult' patients or prisoners. It shows that personality disorder should be regarded as a risk factor for offending rather than a cause, and that current risk assessment technologies cannot yet accurately identify which individuals in a high-risk group will go on to offend. As a result, policies of preventive detention may be expected to result in the overuse of detention. While there is a growing consensus that personality disorder is not necessarily untreatable, there is a continuing lack of robust evidence for the effectiveness of current treatments for antisocial personality disorder and psychopathy. This casts doubt on the idea that access to rehabilitative interventions will limit the use of preventive detention powers. While some jurisdictions have confined the use of mental health law powers to patients with treatable mental illnesses, the UK Government continues to resist calls to introduce stronger safeguards against the long-term detention of people who are unlikely to benefit from treatment. This approach is questionable in light of the principles governing mental health law developed by the ECtHR.

Chapter 3 traces the historical factors and modern concerns that shaped the emergence of the DSPD construct. It demonstrates that the DSPD debate is best understood as the latest instalment in a decades-old battle between the proponents of liberal legal principles and advocates for the preventive detention of potentially dangerous individuals. It shows that the problems that offenders with personality disorder presented for government in the 1980s and 1990s went beyond the headline idea that psychiatrists were refusing to detain 'untreatable' patients. These problems included longstanding concerns about the risks that disturbed and violent prisoners posed to order, safety, and discipline in prisons, and the risks posed to the reputation of secure hospitals by patients who subverted management regimes. The provision of tailored treatments for 'dangerous' offenders presented a means of responding not only to threats to the authority of the state as the guardian of public security but also to its ability to protect the safety of staff and inmates in institutions and to maintain control over them.

Chapter 4 examines what happened when a policy that was devised to strike a 'balance' between the rights of 'dangerous people with severe personality disorder' and those of the public encountered the realities of the prison and secure hospital systems. It investigates whether the pilot DSPD Programme lived up to the high expectations of its originators, and the allied question of whether it could have been expected to do so in view of a long history of unsuccessful attempts to tackle seemingly intractable problems. It demonstrates that the sticky labels of dangerousness and personality disorder can impede movement though systems designed to enable prisoners or patients to engage with rehabilitation as a precondition of release. Requiring them to demonstrate change and regarding their efforts to make progress with suspicion creates a double bind from which it is very difficult to escape. The evidence from the DSPD Programme further shows that participation in treatment could cause harm to individuals. Participation could also generate a risk of disproportionate punishment by increasing the length of a prisoner's detention and imposing greater hard treatment by requiring them to participate in psychological interventions in a coercive environment.

Chapter 5 assesses the reforms undertaken in the name of the Offender Personality Disorder (OPD) Pathway, which came to replace the DSPD Programme in 2011. The OPD Pathway suggests that mental health support follows risk in the criminal justice system, as prisoners who are not considered to pose significant management problems or a high risk of serious reoffending are likely to be left out of services that could benefit them. Conversely, the broad definition of personality disorder under the Pathway risks applying a stigmatizing label to individuals who may not meet the clinical criteria. This chapter further presents an account of a new penal subject constructed by the Pathway: a traumatized subject whose offending and challenging behaviour is a re-enactment of past traumas. This subject has the potential to amplify the clash between therapeutic cultures and cultures of control within prisons. However, the OPD Pathway also suggests a tendency to pathologize disruptive or challenging behaviours and to attribute these behaviours to individual failings rather than to structural failings within the prison system. Treatment under the OPD Pathway further tends to place responsibility on the individual for managing both their risk of reoffending and the symptoms of trauma. This suggests that the radical potential of trauma-informed practice is being compromised in favour of prison culture.

Chapter 6 turns to consider the legal framework. It evaluates the jurisprudence of the ECtHR on two rights that mirror those underlying the DSPD proposals: the offender's 'right to rehabilitation' (van Zyl Smit et al, 2014) and the public's 'right to security' (Lazarus, 2007; 2012a; 2012b; 2015). It demonstrates that the ECtHR deploys two rather different conceptual frameworks for understanding what rehabilitation requires of life-sentenced prisoners: *rehabilitation as risk reduction* and *rehabilitation as redemption*. Both frameworks place the onus on the prisoner to demonstrate that he has achieved rehabilitation and is eligible for release. As a result, the Court's case law does not provide an adequate response to the risk of excessive punishment posed by coercive rehabilitative interventions that are linked to a chance of release from detention. The character-based concept of risk underlying the concept of rehabilitation as redemption poses a particular challenge for offenders who are diagnosed with personality disorders that are associated with unpredictability and untrustworthiness.

Chapter 7 analyses the principles applied by courts when choosing between a sentence with a punitive element and a wholly therapeutic hospital disposal. It demonstrates that the leading sentencing cases decided by the Court of Appeal (Criminal Division) tend to revolve around judgments of culpability, treatability, and risk. Drawing on insights from the history of the criminal law and Cyrus Tata's (2019) concept of 'case-cleansing', this chapter shows that judges borrow doctrines from the trial stage to determine culpability at the sentencing stage. This may be understood as an effort to resist the challenge psychiatric evidence presents to the criminal law's authority to punish responsible offenders. Furthermore, judges have borrowed and reshaped the 'treatability' criterion from the original MHA

1983[13] to prevent patients from being discharged from hospital while they still pose a risk to the public. These sentencing policies do not adequately consider the very real risks imprisonment poses to the fundamental rights of vulnerable offenders. Courts should seek to protect offenders from real risks of death or serious harm in prison and make use of the full range of alternatives to imprisonment that are available to them.

Chapter 8 draws out the implications of the findings of this study for criminological and legal theory and for the rights and interests of individuals. It demonstrates that law and policy seek to shape 'dangerous' individuals into responsible citizens by treating them as responsible for reforming themselves. Given the clear priority accorded to security over individual liberty in the 'balance' struck by human rights law, the offer of rehabilitation may be understood as an effort to render coercive preventive measures taken in the pursuit of security more palatable for liberal governments. Furthermore, reliance on rehabilitative interventions as a means of 'balancing' competing rights in the jurisprudence of the ECtHR is an inadequate safeguard against disproportionate punishment. The chapter sketches out some modest suggestions for addressing these problems. These proposals would ensure more parsimonious use of preventive detention under both the criminal law and mental health law, provide opportunities for rehabilitation on a voluntary basis, and facilitate more realistic tests of recidivism risk. These proposals will have to contend with the symbolic nature of efforts to reassure the public that they are protected from individuals who provoke fear. Creating a productive dialogue between the public, policymakers, experts, people who work within criminal justice or mental health services, and those affected by penal and mental health policies, could be one way forward.

---

[13] See MHA 1983 as enacted, s 37(2)(a)(i). The treatability requirement applied to offenders who met the legal criteria for 'psychopathic disorder' and reserved hospital orders for those individuals for whom treatment in hospital was 'likely to alleviate or prevent a deterioration of his [or her] condition'. The MHA 2007 replaced this requirement with the less stringent requirement that appropriate medical treatment must be available to the patient in hospital.

2
Personality Disorder: A Contested and Evolving Construct

2.1 Introduction

This chapter considers the scientific, ethical, and legal debates surrounding the psychiatric construct of personality disorder. It sets the scene for the examination in Chapters 3–5 of attempts by governments and legislatures in England and Wales to address the dilemmas posed by people who, while not mentally ill, behave in ways that are troubling to society. It further forms the empirical basis for the critical analysis of the legal framework presented in Chapters 6 and 7. It shows that the divisions between mental illness, personality disorder, and offending behaviour are not as clear-cut in practice as in theory. While dimensional approaches to diagnosing personality disorder promise to produce a more nuanced and accurate description of individual personalities, the problem of stigma remains. The high prevalence of personality disorders amongst criminal justice populations further raises the question of whether personality disorder causes, explains, or merely describes offending behaviour.

The evidence presented in this chapter shows that personality disorder should be regarded as a risk factor for offending rather than a cause. While there is better evidence supporting treatments targeting the symptoms of borderline personality disorder (BPD), the evidence for the effectiveness of current treatments for antisocial personality disorder (ASPD) and psychopathy is not robust. This calls into question the assumption that personality disorder and dangerousness are causally linked, and that treatment is necessary to reduce risk. Furthermore, given the weaknesses of current risk assessment tools and the role of intuitive judgements in risk assessment in practice, policies of preventive detention are likely to result in the overuse of detention. While some jurisdictions have confined mental health law powers to patients with treatable mental illnesses, the UK Government has

Law and Personality Disorder. Ailbhe O'Loughlin, Oxford University Press. © Ailbhe O'Loughlin 2024.
DOI: 10.1093/9780191875434.003.0002

resisted calls to introduce stronger safeguards against the long-term detention of people who may not benefit from treatment. This approach is questionable in light of the principles developed by the European Court of Human Rights (ECtHR).

2.2 Defining and Diagnosing Personality Disorder

As Joel Paris (2015, 177) argues, 'it is difficult to separate personality (which we all have) from personality disorder (which only some have)'. This problem reflects the broader challenge of psychiatric diagnosis: how do we distinguish normal variations between people from abnormal variations that amount to mental disorders? A further difficulty is that there is no agreed understanding of the concept of personality itself, even amongst experts in the field (Bergner, 2020). In this sense, the field of personality studies is not much different from other fields in psychiatry and psychology. The phenomena under study are difficult to investigate empirically, and this encourages the development of rival theories that are challenging to prove or disprove.

As a starting point, the American Psychiatric Association (APA) (2023) defines personality as 'the enduring configuration of characteristics and behavior that comprises an individual's unique adjustment to life, including major traits, interests, drives, values, self-concept, abilities, and emotional patterns'. This configuration is 'a complex, dynamic integration or totality shaped by many forces'. While personality theorists disagree on the details, 'all agree that personality helps determine behavior' (APA, 2023). From this general definition, three key ideas emerge. First, the idea that personality is an enduring and innate set of characteristics and behaviour. Second, that personality is inferred from both internal experiences and externally observed behaviours. And, finally, that personality, at least to some extent, determines behaviour.

The construct of 'personality disorder' suggests that some personality variations are normal whereas others are abnormal. In addition, personality disorders are a subset of the broader category of mental disorder. Mental disorders are described in detail by the two leading diagnostic manuals of mental disorders: the APA's (2022) *Diagnostic and Statistical Manual of Mental Disorders* (DSM) and the World Health Organization's (WHO) (2022) International Classification of Diseases (ICD). The latest iterations of these manuals—DSM-5-TR and ICD-11—both describe categories of mental disorders that are organized into groups or families and accompanied by sets of criteria to guide mental health practitioners in making a diagnosis.

According to DSM-5-TR:

> A mental disorder is a syndrome characterized by clinically significant disturbance in an individual's cognition, emotion regulation, or behavior that reflects a dysfunction in the psychological, biological, or developmental processes underlying mental functioning. Mental disorders are usually associated with significant distress or disability in social, occupational, or other important activities. An expectable or culturally approved response to a common stressor or loss, such as the death of a loved one, is not a mental disorder. Socially deviant behavior (e.g., political, religious, or sexual) and conflicts that are primarily between the individual and society are not mental disorders unless the deviance or conflict results from a dysfunction in the individual (APA, 2022, 14).

While some biomarkers have been linked with certain psychiatric disorders, none so far have demonstrated clinical utility (García-Gutiérrez et al, 2020). Rather than undertaking blood tests or brain scans, clinicians infer the presence of a mental disorder from 'signs or symptoms that cause distress or disability' (Paris, 2015, 55). As distress or disability is defined by reference to cultural or social norms, determining whether a person has a disorder is, to a large extent, down to professional judgement. Unsurprisingly, the boundaries between disorder and normality are subject to contestation and disagreement.

Personality disorder is perhaps one of the most controversial constructs within an already contested field. Distinguishing between a personality disorder and merely socially deviant behaviour, as the very definition of mental disorder requires, is fraught with difficulty. Given that personality is considered to be both enduring and, at least to some extent, to determine a person's conduct, the idea that someone's personality is *disordered* implies that they can be expected to behave, long-term, in troublesome ways (see Pilgrim, 2007, 84).

The construct of personality disorder emerged as a means of describing individuals who habitually breached social norms without manifesting delusions or other signs of insanity. Its roots are commonly traced back to the early nineteenth-century construct of *manie sans délire* and the later construct of 'moral insanity' (Saß and Felthous, 2020). The modern personality disorder categories themselves resemble the character disorders or 'psychopathic' personality types described by German psychiatrists in the late nineteenth and early twentieth centuries (Jones, 2016, ch 5; Saß and Felthous, 2020; Tyrer and Mulder, 2022, ch 1).

While 'psychopathic' is currently used to refer to individuals characterized by antisocial, callous, or manipulative behaviour (Hare, 1991), it originally referred to a much broader range of abnormal personality types. Emil Kraepelin first described 'psychopathic personalities' in 1896 and later named specific, mostly dissocial types: the excitable, the unstable, the 'driven' (or impulsive), the eccentrics, the liars and swindlers, and the quarrelsome (Saß and Felthous, 2020, 19). Building on Kraepelin's work, Kurt Schneider described ten 'psychopathic personalities' in 1923, which included both dissocial and non-dissocial types (Saß and Felthous, 2020, 20). In the UK in 1942, David Henderson described three types of psychopath: predominantly aggressive; predominantly passive or inadequate; and predominantly creative (Henderson, 1942, 486). Henderson (1942) conceived of 'psychopathic states' as resulting a combination of a person's constitution and genetics as well as their health and upbringing.

While research on 'normal' personality has pursued the description and measurement of personality traits, research on personality disorders has retained a focus on distinct categories (Tyrer and Mulder, 2022, 7).

Section II of DSM-5-TR defines a personality disorder as:

> an enduring pattern of inner experience and behavior that deviates markedly from the norms and expectations of the individual's culture and is manifested in at least two of the following areas: cognition, affectivity, interpersonal functioning, or impulse control ... This enduring pattern is inflexible and pervasive across a broad range of personal and social situations ... and leads to clinically significant distress or impairment in social, occupational, or other important areas of functioning ... The pattern is stable and of long duration, and its onset can be traced back at least to adolescence or early adulthood ... The pattern is not better explained as a manifestation or consequence of another mental disorder ... and is not attributable to the physiological effects of a substance (e.g., a drug of abuse, a medication, exposure to a toxin) or another medical condition (e.g., head trauma) (APA, 2022, 735).

ICD-11 contains a similar description:

> Personality disorder is characterised by problems in functioning of aspects of the self (e.g., identity, self-worth, accuracy of self-view, self-direction), and/or interpersonal dysfunction (e.g., ability to develop and maintain close and mutually satisfying relationships, ability to understand others' perspectives and to manage conflict in relationships) that have persisted over an extended period of time (e.g., 2 years or more). The disturbance is manifest in patterns of cognition, emotional experience, emotional expression, and behaviour that are maladaptive (e.g., inflexible or poorly regulated) and is manifest across a range of personal and social situations (i.e., is not limited to specific relationships or social roles). The patterns of behaviour characterizing the disturbance are not developmentally appropriate and cannot be explained primarily by social or cultural factors, including socio-political conflict. The disturbance is associated with substantial distress or significant impairment in personal, family, social, educational, occupational or other important areas of functioning (WHO, 2022, sec. 6D10).

While the diagnostic manuals are moving away from describing lists of personality disorder categories, Section II of DSM-5-TR sets out three personality disorder 'clusters' and two catch-all categories: 'other specified personality disorder' and 'unspecified personality disorder'. Cluster A groups together the 'odd or eccentric' types: paranoid, schizoid, and schizotypal. Cluster B describes the 'dramatic, emotional or erratic' types: antisocial, borderline, histrionic, and narcissistic. In Cluster C are the 'anxious and fearful' types: avoidant, dependent, and obsessive-compulsive (APA, 2022, 735). These types can largely be traced back to earlier work on psychopathic personalities discussed above (see Saß and Felthous, 2020). As set out below, research tends to focus on those disorders that are most commonly encountered in mental health practice or amongst forensic populations: borderline or emotionally unstable personality disorder, and antisocial or dissocial personality disorder.

ASPD is 'a pattern of disregard for, and violation of, the rights of others, criminality, impulsivity, and a failure to learn from experience' (APA, 2022, 733). ASPD is similar to the old ICD-10 category of dissocial personality disorder and the ICD-11 trait of dissociality. Diagnostic features include 'failure to conform to social norms with respect to lawful behaviours, as indicated by repeatedly performing acts that are grounds for arrest'; deceitfulness; impulsivity; 'irritability and aggressiveness, as indicated by repeated physical fights or assaults'; 'reckless disregard for safety of self or others'; irresponsibility; and lack of remorse (APA, 2022, 748).

The diagnostic criteria for BPD incorporate some offending behaviours and undesirable social behaviours. BPD is 'a pattern of instability in interpersonal relationships, self-image, and affects, and marked impulsivity' (APA, 2022, 733). BPD resembles the old ICD-10 category of emotionally unstable personality disorder and 'borderline pattern' in ICD-11 is described in very similar terms to BPD. The distinguishing features of BPD according to DSM-5-TR include: 'frantic efforts to avoid real or imagined abandonment'; 'a pattern of unstable and intense interpersonal relationships'; identity disturbance; impulsivity; recurrent suicidal behaviour, self-mutilating threats, gestures or acts; emotional instability; chronic feelings of emptiness; 'inappropriate, intense anger or difficulty controlling anger (eg, frequent displays of temper, constant anger, recurrent physical fights)'; and 'transient, stress-related paranoid ideation or severe dissociative symptoms' (APA, 2022, 752–753).

A key aspect of diagnosis is how to distinguish between a personality disorder and other, similar disorders, such as schizophrenia, major depression, and bipolar disorder. Like the divisions between 'normal' and 'abnormal' personalities, the divisions between personality disorders and mental illnesses are blurred. Broadly, a personality disorder is conceived of as a part of the person themselves, whereas a mental illness is something that befalls a person and that causes them to feel, think, and behave in ways that are not normal for them (Glaser, 1990).

Jill Peay helpfully illustrates this distinction using an analogy proposed by Professor Nigel Eastman: a 'raspberry ripple ice cream with a cherry on the top':

> If one conceived as the cherry being a mental illness, something added on to the person, which might be excised through treatment, then personality disorder was more akin to the ripples; it ran throughout the person and was integral to them, rather than being an optional extra. In this sense, the personality disordered person's current mental state cannot be defined as abnormal in relation to his or her own previous state, but rather only with reference to the population as a whole; and that deviation needs to be perceived as dysfunctional (Peay, 2011a, 23).

Consequently, determining whether a person has a personality disorder involves comparing what is normal for them to what is normal for the general population. The analogy further suggests that, like personality itself, a personality disorder is a core and enduring part of the person.

While both the DSM-5-TR and ICD-11 characterize personality disorders as deviations from cultural or social norms, these norms are left undefined. It is therefore largely up to clinicians, drawing on their training and professional experience, to determine whether someone's thoughts, emotions, behaviours, or abilities deviate from the norm. This judgement is made through history-taking and a clinical interview with the patient, with reference to diagnostic criteria. Empirically validated semi-structured clinical interview guides, self-report questionnaires, and screening tools are available to assist clinicians with diagnosis (Clark et al, 2018).

Given that a personality disorder is indicated by 'distress' *or* 'impairment', and that 'impairment' is judged in relation to normal functioning, a person may receive a diagnosis of personality disorder without feeling much distress about their own situation. They may feel that there is nothing wrong with them, and that any problems are attributable to the failings or demands of other people or of society at large. Or they may feel that clinicians are not interested in what they see as the real source of their problems: often, very troubling and traumatic life experiences (Castillo, 2003).

In practice, it is often difficult to distinguish which feelings, thoughts, and behaviours are integral to the person and which are attributable to a mental illness. The signs of a personality disorder and a mental illness can significantly overlap. For example, the schizoid, schizotypal, and paranoid personality disorders described by DSM-5-TR all have features in common with schizophrenia. This may help to explain why it is very common for a person to be diagnosed with both a personality disorder and a mental illness, or with more than one of each (Grant et al, 2005; 2008; Stinson et al, 2008). In addition, having a personality disorder may predispose a person to developing a mental illness, or having a mental illness may impact upon their personality (Hayward and Moran, 2008; De Fruyt and De Clercq, 2014).

The idea that mental illness can be 'excised' through treatment is not as clear-cut as it may first appear. There are treatment-resistant forms of each of the mental illnesses that fail to respond to medications, and around 30 per cent of people diagnosed with schizophrenia are treatment-resistant (Kane et al, 2019). The idea that personality disorders are long-standing, inflexible, and pervasive patterns of dysfunction has also come under fire from empirical studies. Some personality disorder traits decline with age (Lilienfeld, 2005) and studies of the life course of the disorder shows variation and remission in symptoms (Zanarini et al, 2003; Gutiérrez et al, 2012). These findings, amongst others, have contributed to calls from personality disorder researchers for a move to a dimensional approach to personality disorder diagnosis, considered next.

2.3 Dimensions and Stigma

Originally, the DSM and the ICD described sets of distinct personality disorder categories that differed from each other and from 'normal' personality (Trull and Durrett, 2005). Both manuals have since moved towards a dimensional model of personality disorder. Rather than seeing personality disorders as distinct categories, the dimensional model postulates that they 'represent maladaptive variants of personality traits that merge imperceptibly into normality and into one another' (APA, 2000, 689). These models were developed in response to empirical studies demonstrating that the existing personality disorder categories did not adequately capture clinical presentations (Verheul and Widiger, 2004; Tyrer et al, 2011; 2019). Comorbidity was common, and it was possible for two patients to be diagnosed with the same personality disorder despite sharing no symptoms (First et al, 2002, 128–29; Grant et al, 2005, 2008; Stinson et al, 2008). There is now a consensus that 'normal' personality follows a dimensional model. The five-factor model, which measures the traits of extroversion, agreeableness, neuroticism, openness, and conscientiousness, is most popular (Costa and McCrae, 1992). Studies found that the personalities of people diagnosed with personality disorders closely followed the five-factor model, prompting claims that the DSM personality disorders were on a spectrum with each other and with 'normal' personality (Trull and Durrett, 2005; Widiger and Costa, 2012).

There were also misgivings that the diagnosis was stigmatizing and that clinicians tended to attach it to patients they found difficult and unlikeable (Zachar, 2014, ch 11). The personality disorder construct has been branded as a 'moral judgement masquerading as a clinical diagnosis' (Blackburn, 1988, 511) and as a diagnosis that doctors resort to once treatments for mental illness have been tried and found to be unsuccessful. Some people given the diagnosis see it as 'a label you get when "they" don't know what else to do' or 'a dustbin label given to people who seem difficult' (Castillo,

2003, 69–70). While there is some evidence that professional attitudes towards personality disorder have improved over time (Day et al, 2018), both the personality disorder label and the experience of working with people diagnosed with personality disorder are associated with negative clinical judgements (Lam et al, 2016; Sheehan et al, 2016). Professionals and people with lived experience tend to associate the personality disorder label with a sense of blame, shame, defectiveness, exclusion, and permanence (Lamph et al, 2022).

In one qualitative study conducted by Heather Castillo (2003, 71–75) with UK service users with a personality disorder diagnosis,[1] participants described feeling insulted, angry, anxious, depressed, alienated, bewildered, numb, shocked, or helpless upon receiving their diagnosis. They described personality disorder as a label for mood swings or personality changes; a label for people who are bad; 'being like Jekyll and Hyde'; 'abnormal'; 'untreatable'; and 'bad and evil' (Castillo, 2003, 69–70). In a smaller study of community patients diagnosed with BPD, some participants described the diagnosis more positively as providing a focus for understanding and resolving their problems and as affording a sense of control and hope (Horn, Johnstone and Brooke, 2007). However, such positive attitudes were expressed only where the diagnosis led to support. In the absence of such support, it was experienced as a rejection or as 'the killing of hope' (Horn, Johnstone, and Brooke, 2007, 262). This in turn led some patients to reject mental health services, and may have been the reason they were regarded by practitioners as difficult (Horn, Johnstone, and Brooke, 2007).

Members of the DSM-5 personality disorder work group argued that a dimensional model of personality disorder would help to reduce stigma. This is because such a model would 'recognize and appreciate that the person is more than just the personality disorder and that there are aspects to personality that can be adaptive, even commendable, despite the presence of a personality disorder' (Widiger, Livesley, and Clark, 2009, 246). The architects of the ICD-11 model similarly suggested that it would reduce stigma by counteracting the notion that personality disorder is immutable and untreatable, and by producing a more nuanced, and accurate, description of each person's condition (Tyrer et al, 2011, 248–49). However, as set out below, both the DSM-5 and ICD-10 systems continue to use the term

---

[1] Predominantly borderline/emotionally unstable, antisocial/dissocial, or 'unspecified'.

'personality disorder', which is stigmatizing in itself, and a diagnosis will continue to be based on largely negative moral judgements by clinicians.

DSM-5 (APA, 2013), introduced in 2013, reflects the difficulties encountered by the APA in reaching a consensus that would reflect advances in research on personality disorder whilst meeting the needs of practicing clinicians (Whooley, 2016; Zachar et al, 2016). For the first time in the history of the manual, DSM-5 introduced two models of personality disorder. Section II, intended for clinical use, largely retained the approach of the previous edition, DSM-IV, and describes distinct personality disorder categories. Section III, intended to inspire research, sets out an alternative model that combines personality disorder categories with dimensions. A revised version, DSM-5-TR, was published in 2022 and retains this approach.

While Section II of DSM-5-TR uses the terms 'enduring', 'inflexible', and 'pervasive', Section III describes the impairments and traits associated with personality disorder as '*relatively* inflexible and pervasive across a broad range of personal and social situations' and '*relatively* stable across time' (APA, 2022, 881).[2] Section III describes just six personality disorder categories: antisocial, avoidant, borderline, narcissistic, obsessive-compulsive, and schizotypal (APA, 2022, 883–84). Each category is described using a set of trait domains and trait facets, reflecting the idea that personality disorder traits are on a spectrum. Each trait domain has two opposing poles, and between the poles the trait manifests in differing degrees.[3]

While ICD-10 followed a similar approach to DSM-IV, the architects of ICD-11 took the radical step of abolishing all personality disorder categories (except 'borderline pattern') and introducing an almost fully dimensional model. Under ICD-11, the clinician first assesses the person for the presence of a personality disorder. The disorder is then assigned a severity rating (mild, moderate, or severe) and described using a set of six prominent personality traits: negative affectivity, detachment, dissociality, disinhibition, anankastia,[4] and 'borderline pattern' (Tyrer et al, 2019). The manual contains descriptions and examples of each of the traits to assist clinicians in assessing patients.

---

[2] Emphasis added.
[3] The five trait domains are negative affectivity (versus emotional stability); detachment (versus extraversion); antagonism (versus agreeableness); disinhibition (versus conscientiousness); and psychoticism (versus lucidity) (APA, 2022, 899–901).
[4] Similar to obsessive-compulsive personality disorder in DSM-5.

Compared to DSM-5, the journey of ICD-11 was relatively untroubled. While the architects of ICD-11 intended to abolish all personality disorder categories, criticisms that this would disregard significant advances in treatment for and research on borderline or emotionally unstable personality disorder led to the inclusion of 'borderline pattern' (Herpertz et al, 2017; Tyrer et al, 2019). The creators of ICD-11 argue that the severity-domain model adequately captures BPD and expect that 'borderline pattern' will later be discarded (Tyrer and Mulder, 2018).

The inclusion of 'borderline pattern' shows the endurance of the notion that personality disorders come in distinct types, which can be traced back to the origins of personality disorder discussed above. This endurance suggests a reluctance for psychiatrists to let go of the assumption that psychiatric disorders are medically separate entities with distinctive aetiologies, treatments, and prognoses. It further suggests an attachment to shorthand labels that have a shared understanding amongst clinicians and others in the mental health field.

Both Section III of DSM-5-TR and the ICD-11 use morally loaded judgements and descriptions of socially undesirable behaviours as diagnostic criteria and may therefore not escape the stigma that attaches to the personality disorder label. A diagnosis requires the practitioner to evaluate the attitudes and behaviour of the individual against societal norms. Examples of behaviours associated with 'borderline pattern' in ICD-11 include 'risky sexual behaviour, reckless driving, excessive alcohol or substance use' and 'binge eating' (WHO, 2022, sec. 6D11.5). The DSM-V-TR Section III pathological personality trait of 'hostility', associated with ASPD, is characterized by 'persistent or frequent angry feelings; anger or irritability in response to minor slights and insults; mean, nasty, or vengeful behavior' (APA, 2022, 884). Common manifestations of 'dissociality' in ICD-11 include 'being deceptive, manipulative, and exploitative of others, being mean and physically aggressive, callousness in response to others' suffering, and ruthlessness in obtaining one's goals' (WHO, 2022, sec. 6D11.2).

Consequently, even under dimensional constructs of personality disorder, the argument that a personality disorder diagnosis is tantamount to a declaration of dislike (Lewis and Appleby, 1988; Bowers et al, 2005; 2006) still seems to hold true. Knowledge of what the ICD-11 trait domains indicate amongst the public and practitioners may result in these traits becoming labels that can be attached to individuals in a stigmatizing manner. The attachment of a 'severe' rating to a personality disorder under ICD-11 may draw further associations with dangerousness and intractability.

In sum, personality disorder is a construct beset by difficulties: the borderlines between personality disorder and normal functioning are blurred, and there are concerns that a personality disorder diagnosis is a social judgement rather than an objective clinical diagnosis. Determining the boundaries between a personality disorder and a normal personality is often a case of clinical judgement drawing on social or cultural norms. More recently, there have been calls for a move to a dimensional approach to describing and diagnosing personality disorders in the hope that this can resolve some of the mismatch between the construct and the clinical realities it is supposed to describe or explain. But, given the negative judgements associated with ASPD, BPD, or related traits, these labels are likely to continue to be associated with judgements of untrustworthiness, unpredictability, and a propensity for offending or other objectionable behaviour.

2.4 Personality Disorder and Offending

A diagnosis of ASPD or psychopathy relies to a significant extent on past behaviour and aspects of a person's history that are not amenable to change. Coupled with the idea that personality disorders are enduring and fundamental to the person, it is likely to be difficult for a person to escape from the negative judgements that come with a diagnosis. As set out below, these problems are compounded when it comes to the question of treatment given the limitations of the evidence base.

According to an epidemiological study of mental disorder amongst prisoners in England and Wales conducted by the Office of National Statistics in 1997, 78 per cent of male remand, 64 per cent of male sentenced, and 50 per cent of female prisoners fulfilled the criteria for at least one personality disorder (Singleton et al, 1998, 10).[5] By comparison, 13.7 per cent of adults in the general population of England screened positive for a personality disorder in 2014 (McManus et al, 2016, 175). A more recent but smaller UK study reported that 49.4 per cent of male and 68.7 per cent of female sentenced prisoners screened positive for at least one personality disorder (Tyler et al, 2019, Table 3). International studies similarly show

---

[5] Although this survey is now out of date, no study of similar quality has since been conducted, and it is still frequently cited as a source of information on rates of mental disorder amongst the prison population. The National Audit Office (2017) has called for routine collection of information on the mental health of prisoners in light of the insufficiency of current data.

a high prevalence of personality disorder amongst prisoners (Fazel and Danesh, 2002). Personality disorders are also prevalent amongst people in police custody (Samele et al, 2021), defendants attending court (Brown et al, 2022), and probation samples (Brooker et al, 2012, 259).

The circularity of the ASPD diagnosis may mean that the association with antisocial behaviour is merely trivial or descriptive, as the diagnostic criteria for ASPD include offending behaviour (Howard, 2006). ASPD overlaps to some extent with psychopathy as measured by the *Psychopathy Checklist Revised* (PCL-R), but the relationship is asymmetrical. 'Most offenders with a high PCL-R score meet the criteria for ASPD, but most of those diagnosed with ASPD do not have high PCL-R scores' (Hare, 2020, 81). Psychopathy has also been criticized for its circularity, as 'the psychopath's mental disorder is inferred from his anti-social behaviour while the anti-social behaviour is explained by mental disorder' (Wootton, 1981, 90).

The PCL-R is a dimensional measure of psychopathy that assigns a score based on a checklist rather than a measure that distinguishes clearly between psychopaths and non-psychopaths. Researchers often adopt a threshold or 'cut-off' score for psychopathy, often set at a score of 26 on the PCL-R for European samples (Hare, 2020, 72). People who score 26 or above are often referred to as 'psychopaths'. The PCL-R scale requires clinicians to rate the person against two factors: Factor 1 (interpersonal/affective) and Factor 2 (unstable and antisocial lifestyle). Factor 1 is divided into an interpersonal facet, comprising the traits of glibness/superficial charm, grandiose sense of self-worth, pathological lying, conning, and manipulativeness; and an affective facet, including lack of remorse or guilt, shallow affect, callousness/lack of empathy, and failure to accept responsibility for one's own actions. Factor 2 divides into a lifestyle facet, which includes a need for stimulation/proneness to boredom, parasitic lifestyle, lack of realistic long-term goals, impulsivity, irresponsibility; and an antisocial facet, comprising poor behavioural controls, early behavioural problems, juvenile delinquency, revocation of conditional release, and criminal versatility (Hare, 1991).

Psychopathy is rare amongst the general population. One study of a representative general population sample in England, Wales, and Scotland estimated that only 0.6 per cent had 'possible' psychopathy based on a PCL-R score of 13 or above (Coid et al, 2009a, 67). By contrast, 7.7 per cent of male and 1.9 per cent of female prisoners in a representative sample from England and Wales scored 30 or above on the PCL-R: well above the European cut-off for psychopathy (Coid et al, 2009b, 136).

The prevalence of personality disorder and psychopathy amongst criminal justice populations raises the question of whether these disorders cause, explain, or merely describe socially troublesome behaviours. While there is some association between personality disorder and offending, the picture is complex. In some cases, the presence of a personality disorder may exert a protective effect by reducing a person's opportunities for offending (O'Loughlin and Peay, 2023). Examples include avoidant personality disorder, characterized by social inhibition, and obsessive-compulsive personality disorder, characterized by a preoccupation with rules (APA, 2022, 733).

Rates of violent offending amongst the general population range between 0.6 per cent and 0.9 per cent (Sariaslan et al, 2020) compared to 6–10 per cent amongst those diagnosed with personality disorders and schizophrenia spectrum disorders (Whiting et al, 2021, 150). The association between violence and antisocial personality disorder is more pronounced. A metanalysis of 14 studies found that 14 per cent of individuals diagnosed with ASPD were violent over a median follow-up period of 4.5 years (Yu et al, 2012, 779). Nevertheless, people with ASPD who are violent remain in the minority.

Direct causality between ASPD and violence is difficult to establish due to the multiplicity of confounding factors affecting individuals, including comorbid substance abuse disorders, mental illnesses, and post-traumatic stress disorder (PTSD) (Duggan and Howard, 2009). Based on current evidence, seven individuals diagnosed with ASPD would have to be detained in order to prevent one violent act (Yu et al, 2012, 780). Thus, predictions of violence based on an ASPD diagnosis returns a high rate of false positives: individuals assumed to be violent who would not go on to commit a violent offence.

An early review of the literature found that psychopaths were around four times more likely to violently reoffend than non-psychopaths (Hemphill et al, 1998). The same study found a stronger correlation between PCL-R scores and violent recidivism than between ASPD and violent recidivism. However, a more recent meta-analysis found that the PCL-R was a poorer predictor of violent recidivism than other commonly used risk assessment instruments (Singh et al, 2011). Studies further suggest that only Factor 2 items (unstable and antisocial lifestyle) are associated with offending behaviour, and that Factor 1 items (interpersonal/affective) decrease the overall utility of the PCL-R when it comes to predicting recidivism (Yang et al, 2010). Given that Factor 2 items include evidence of past offending, the association between Factor 2 psychopathy and offending may be circular.

These findings cast doubt on the idea underpinning the DSPD proposals that personality disorder or psychopathy and offending are causally linked. They also cast doubt on the assumption underpinning mental health legislation that we are justified in using mental health law to detain people with mental disorders to protect the public. The rate of violent offending amongst drug and alcohol abusers is similar to that amongst people diagnosed with ASPD (Yu et al, 2012, 784). However, people who are dependent on alcohol or drugs tend to much attract less attention from the media and politicians. Moreover, they cannot be detained under the Mental Health Act (MHA) 1983 unless they suffer from a comorbid mental disorder.[6]

While homicides committed by mental health patients tend to provoke public concern, this group only accounted for 11 per cent of people convicted of homicide in the UK between 2008 and 2019 (National Confidential Inquiry into Suicide and Safety in Mental Health, 2022, 37).[7] Mental health patients are more likely to end their own lives than to kill others: between 2009 and 2019, they accounted for 27 per cent of suicides in the UK (National Confidential Inquiry into Suicide and Safety in Mental Health, 2022, 12).

Personality disorders are also associated with increased risk of suicide. A recent systematic review and meta-analysis of risk factors for suicide found that any personality disorder was associated with a 6.8-fold increase in the odds of suicide (Favril et al, 2022, 151). BPD was associated with a 9-fold increase and ASPD was associated with a 3.4-fold increase (Favril et al 2022, 151). By comparison, depression carried an 11-fold increase and schizophrenia spectrum disorder a 7.8-fold increase (Favril et al, 2022, 151). BPD is also associated with a 9.2-fold increase in the odds of self-harming in prison compared to the general prison population (Favril et al, 2020, 685). This is comparable to major depression, which is associated with a 9.3-fold increase (Favril et al, 2020, 685). While ASPD is strongly associated with self-harm in the community, there is no link between self-harm and ASPD in prison. However, this finding may be due to the high prevalence of ASPD amongst the prison population (Favril et al, 2020, 688).

---

[6] MHA 1983, s 1(3).
[7] The figures for Northern Ireland are from 2009–14.

2.5 Treating Personality Disorder

In the 1990s, many psychiatrists were sceptical about the treatment of personality disorder, seeing it as lengthy, intensive, expensive, of marginal benefit to patients, damaging to staff and services, and disruptive of the treatment of other patients (Cawthra and Gibb, 1998, 8; Kendell, 2002). Improvements in the evidence base for the treatment of personality disorders have contributed to an emerging consensus that they are not necessarily untreatable (Pickersgill, 2013). Nevertheless, treating personality disorder continues to be controversial. What are we trying to treat? The source of the disorder or its symptoms? And how will we know whether treatment is effective? The evidence considered below suggests that current treatments can reduce self-harming behaviour, personal distress, and general reoffending rates. However, the evidence is much less robust when it comes to reducing serious violent or sexual reoffending post-release.

The available treatments are underpinned by different theories of the relationship between personality disorder and problematic behaviours. Some treatments mainly target symptoms while others seek to target possible causes of the disorder. The aetiology of personality disorder is not well understood, but the most widely accepted theory is that personality disorders, like other mental disorders, are caused by a complex combination of biological (or genetic), social, environmental, and psychological factors (Alwin et al, 2006; De Fruyt and De Clercq, 2012). While there is some empirical support for an association between adverse childhood experiences and developing a personality disorder in adulthood, studies have not established that these experiences *cause* personality disorders (Mokros et al, 2020; Winsper, 2018). Not all children who experience abuse subsequently develop personality disorders, and not all individuals with a personality disorder diagnosis report experiencing abuse in childhood (De Fruyt and De Clercq, 2012).

There is insufficient space here to examine the wide range of possible treatments for personality disorder. Instead, the focus will be on those treatments that have been subject to the most extensive evaluation. These include treatments based on cognitive behavioural therapy (CBT), mentalization-based therapies, and trauma-informed interventions. As personality disorders are lifelong disorders, these treatments tend not to aim for a cure but rather to manage the symptoms or manifestations of the disorder, including problematic behaviours.

Much of the existing research on psychological treatments for ASPD focuses on CBT. These treatments are underpinned by the theory that people with personality disorders have a rigid set of beliefs about themselves and others and a limited set of behaviours or coping strategies that are often unhelpful (or 'maladaptive'). According to this theory, such beliefs and behaviours are the result of a combination of pre-existing vulnerabilities and stressors, such as harsh or neglectful parenting (Beck et al, 2016). A related and well-researched treatment for BPD is dialectical behaviour therapy (DBT). DBT combines CBT with mindfulness, distress tolerance, and acceptance techniques derived from Buddhist meditation (Linehan, 1993; Lynch et al, 2007). Generally, both CBT and DBT seek to challenge maladaptive beliefs and to teach participants more effective and socially acceptable coping strategies.

Mentalization-based therapy is underpinned by the theory that disturbances to attachment relationships to caregivers at an early age (particularly through adverse childhood experiences) combine with genetic vulnerabilities to affect a person's capacity to regulate their emotions, control their impulses, and to 'mentalize' (to understand their own mental states and those of others) (Bateman et al, 2016). These deficits are in turn associated with anger and aggression in response to perceived or actual threats, such as threats to self-esteem in ASPD and threats of abandonment in BPD (Bateman et al, 2016; Bateman, 2022). This theory has some support from evidence that people with BPD mentalize 'normally' apart from in close relationships when fear of abandonment arises, and that people with ASPD are less well able to recognize basic emotions and to link mental states to behaviour (Bateman et al, 2016). Mentalization-based therapy focuses on helping participants to improve their mentalization skills in the hope that this will reduce anger and aggression.

Trauma-informed practices range from trauma-specific services, designed to treat the consequences of trauma, to trauma-informed services that are sensitive to the impact of trauma on survivors but do not necessarily attempt treatment (Player, 2017, n.8). An example of a trauma-specific approach is the treatment programme developed at the former DSPD unit for men at HMP Whitemoor. The programme specifically targets trauma and attachment disorders and seeks to modify problematic personality traits as well as to enhance overall functioning and to reduce reoffending risk (Saradjian et al, 2010). The Rampton Hospital DSPD unit implemented a model of trauma-informed care, which was based on the idea that interactions with staff in custodial environments can trigger or reinforce behaviours or thought processes in offenders that are linked with their past trauma. Staff therefore sought to understand the reasons behind rule-breaking behaviour and to prevent the behaviour from escalating (Jones, 2018).[8]

When it comes to determining the effectiveness of treatment, the evidence-based medicine paradigm regards the randomized controlled trial (RCT) as the 'gold standard' (Cairney, 2016, 52). Without a control group and a sufficiently large and representative sample of participants, it is difficult to be sure that any improvements are attributable to a given treatment. However, conducting randomized controlled trials is challenging in criminal justice settings and it can be difficult to disentangle the various components involved in often eclectic interventions (Tyrer et al, 2009). Perhaps reflecting this difficulty, there is a paucity of good quality RCTs of interventions for personality disorder.

Successful treatment for ASPD is often measured in terms of reductions in recidivism or aggression (Gibbon et al, 2020). A recent systematic review of RCTs of psychological treatments for ASPD concluded that 'there is insufficient evidence to support or refute the effectiveness of any psychological intervention' (Gibbon et al, 2020, 41). A review of pharmacological therapies drew the same conclusion (Khalifa et al, 2020, 32). Research on the treatment of psychopathy, as measured by the PCL-R, is even less well-developed. While the findings of an early study (Rice, Harris, and Cormier, 1992) that appeared to show that treatment increased recidivism amongst psychopaths have since been discredited, the idea that psychopaths are untreatable or made 'worse' through treatment has proven difficult to dispel (D'Silva, Duggan, and McCarthy, 2004; Larsen, Javala, and Griffiths, 2020). More recent research has shown that psychopaths do respond to treatment, and that treatment is associated with reductions in sexual and violent recidivism risk (Larsen, Javala, and Griffiths, 2020). However, these findings are not based on RCTs.

Treatments for BPD tend to be evaluated in terms of their impact upon symptoms, including emotional distress and self-harm. A 2010 review of pharmacological treatments for BPD found that some drugs improved some symptoms but concluded that there was no evidence from RCTs demonstrating that any drug reduced overall severity of symptoms (Stoffers et al, 2010, 40). A follow-up review published eleven years later drew similar

---

[8] For more detailed discussion of trauma-informed practices on the DSPD Programme and OPD Pathway, see Chapters 4 and 5.

conclusions (Gartlehner et al, 2021). A review of RCTs of psychological interventions found that psychotherapy was more beneficial than treatment as usual, but the evidence was only of moderate quality and all trials had a high risk of bias (Storebø et al, 2020, 70). DBT and mentalization-based treatment were more effective than treatment as usual in improving some BPD symptoms, but this finding was based on low-quality evidence (Storebø et al, 2020, 70–71).

While trauma-based interventions are a plausible treatment for personality disorder in individuals with a history of trauma, few studies of trauma-based care measure up to the RCT standard. Those studies that do exist are based on women or juvenile participants, and the relevance of their findings to men has yet to be established (McAnallen and McGinnis, 2021). A recent review of the literature identified just one RCT of a trauma-informed violence reduction programme for women convicted of violent offences (McAnallen and McGinnis, 2021). The RCT was based on a sample of 35 women and found a lower rate of re-arrest amongst women who completed the programme (Kubiak et al, 2016). Other studies suggested that trauma-informed practices were associated with reductions in violent behaviour within institutions, greater feelings of safety, and improvements on mental health outcomes, including anger (McAnallen and McGinnis, 2021). More rigorous research is needed to establish whether these findings can replicated in adult male populations and in populations with personality disorder traits.

In the context of a developing evidence base, the National Institute for Health and Care Excellence (NICE) guidelines on the treatment and management of ASPD and BPD are cautiously optimistic. Both guidelines state that people diagnosed with ASPD or BPD should not be excluded from any health or social care service because of their diagnosis. Nor should they be excluded from services based on a history of antisocial or offending behaviour (in the case of ASPD) or because they have self-harmed (in the case of BPD) (National Collaborating Centre for Mental Health, 2009, para 10.1.1.1.; National Collaborating Centre for Mental Health, 2010, para 8.1.1.1). Both guidelines further recommend that clinicians explore treatment options with patients 'in an atmosphere of hope and optimism, explaining that recovery is possible and attainable' (National Collaborating Centre for Mental Health, 2009, para 10.1.4.1.; National Collaborating Centre for Mental Health, 2010, para 8.1.4.1).

For ASPD, the guideline recommends that clinicians 'consider group-based cognitive behavioural interventions, in order to address problems such as impulsivity, interpersonal difficulties and antisocial behaviour' (National Collaborating Centre for Mental Health, 2010, paras 8.4.2.1.–2). For people in community and institutional settings who meet the criteria for psychopathy or DSPD, it recommends adapting these interventions by extending their nature and duration, and 'providing booster sessions, continued follow-up and close monitoring' (National Collaborating Centre for Mental Health, 2010, para 8.5.1.1). For BPD, the guideline recommends that clinicians delivering psychotherapy should do so in a structured setting. It further recommends that clinicians should consider providing dialectical behaviour therapy to women with BPD for whom reducing self-harming behaviour is a priority (National Collaborating Centre for Mental Health, 2009, paras 10.3.4.3–5).

The DSPD Programme was established with the aim of palliating deficiencies in the evidence base for treating personality disorder and led to a proliferation of literature on new treatment models for the DSPD group (Saradjian et al, 2010; 2013; Tennant and Howells, 2010; Tew and Atkinson, 2013). However, there is a paucity of RCTs of the treatment initiatives developed under the DSPD Programme and its successor, the OPD Pathway. A recent independent evaluation of the OPD Pathway that used a matched control sample found that referral to the OPD Pathway resulted in reduced incidents of rule-breaking behaviour in prison. However, referral had no effect on actuarial risk scores, self-harm incidents, recalls to prison, or reoffending (Moran et al, 2022). Consequently, after more than 20 years in operation, it is unclear whether the treatments offered are effective in reducing reoffending and enhancing wellbeing. The evidence emerging from these initiatives are explored in more detail in Chapters 4 and 5.

There is a broader research literature on offending behaviour interventions that may be used with offenders with personality disorders. A recent meta-analysis of prison-based RCTs tested the effectiveness of psychological interventions in reducing recidivism, including CBT-based and psychoeducational programmes. The study noted that smaller trials[9] found a moderate effect on recidivism but larger studies found no significant impact (Beaudry et al, 2021). Consequently, the authors of the study questioned the widespread rollout of CBT-based treatment programmes in prisons (Beaudry et al, 2021, 769). The review found that participation in a therapeutic community that included community-based support was

---

[9] Trials with 50 participants or fewer in each of the intervention and control groups.

associated with decreased rates of recidivism (Beaudry et al, 2021). Prison-based interventions may therefore be more effective if they are linked to community aftercare (Beaudry et al, 2021, 767).

Offending behaviour programmes have been a mainstay of prison-based rehabilitation efforts in the UK since the 1990s, and completing these programmes is a key means for prisoners serving indeterminate sentences to progress towards release (House of Commons Justice Committee, 2022). Impact evaluations of two widely used programmes have produced mixed evidence of their impact on recidivism. Participants in RESOLVE, an anger management programme, were less likely to reoffend, reoffended less frequently, and took longer to reoffend compared to the control group. The impact was small, however: 44.7 per cent of the treated group reoffended within two years compared to 47.4 per cent of the control group. There was no statistically significant effect on violent offending (Robinson et al, 2021, p .3). Participation in Enhanced Thinking Skills, an offence-focused, problem-solving programme, was associated with a reduction of six percentage points in one-year reconviction rates (Sadlier, 2010, i). However, there was no statistically significant impact on severe offending.[10] A recent evaluation of a third programme, Thinking Skills, evaluated the impact of the programme on general proven reoffending rates over a two-year period (Brinn et al, 2023). It found that male participants who completed the programme were less likely to offend, offended less frequently, and took longer to reoffend. While these findings were statistically significant, the effect sizes were very small (Brinn et al, 2023, Summary). The study did not examine the impact on violent or sexual reoffending.

Most concerningly, a well-designed impact evaluation concluded that participation in the prison-based Sex Offender Treatment Programme (SOTP), in use in the UK since 1992, may have *increased* reoffending amongst the treated group (Mews, Di Bella and Purver, 2017). While reoffending rates in both the treated and control groups were low, rates were higher in the treated group. The study found that 10 per cent of those in the treated group committed at least one sexual offence over an average follow-up period of 8.2 years compared to 8 per cent in the untreated group (Mews, Di Bella, and Purver, 2017, 3). The Ministry of Justice has since replaced SOTP with two new accredited programmes: Kaizen (for high-risk groups)

---

[10] Defined by the study as 'violence against the person (eg murder, manslaughter), sexual offences, aggravated vehicle taking, and death by dangerous, drink or drug driving' (Sadlier, 2010, i, n 4).

and Horizon (for moderate risk groups) (McCartan et al, 2018; Henfrey, 2018). HM Prison and Probation Service is rolling out both programmes ahead of a full evaluation of their effectiveness (McCartan et al, 2018). It remains to be seen whether these programmes fare better in eventual evaluations.

While there are reasons to be more optimistic about the evidence base for treating BPD, the effectiveness of treatment in criminal justice settings may be impeded by the fact that offenders and some of those diagnosed with personality disorders tend to have low motivation for treatment (Howells and Day, 2007). While individuals diagnosed with BPD tend to be treatment-seeking and demanding of services, those diagnosed with ASPD tend to resist treatment (National Collaborating Centre for Mental Health, 2009, 36; National Collaborating Centre for Mental Health, 2010, 24–25). As treatments for personality disorder generally require active participation and motivation for change on behalf of the patient, coercive approaches are unlikely to be successful (Peay, 2011b, 240; National Collaborating Centre for Mental Health, 2010, 34). Implicit coercion is likely to be present in the prison environment in which prisoners are expected to comply with rehabilitative programmes in order to progress towards release, and this may jeopardize the effectiveness of treatment.[11]

In conclusion, while there is some evidence that CBT, therapeutic communities, and community-based support can reduce general reoffending, there is a paucity of robust evidence that current treatments reduce serious violent or sexual recidivism. The evidence base therefore casts doubt on the premise that giving prisoners and patients with personality disorder access to treatment will reduce their risk of serious reoffending and allow them to progress towards release. The evidence base for treating BPD is more robust and suggests that treatments including drug therapies, DBT and mentalization therapy may reduce self-harming behaviour and personal distress. However, completing these treatments is unlikely to be sufficient to demonstrate reduced risk to the public. Nevertheless, interventions that can improve institutional behaviour in the short-term may be expected to garner some support from policymakers and practitioners, even if they are not shown to have a robust impact on reoffending. This possibility is explored in Chapters 3–5.

---

[11] See further Chapters 3–5 of this book.

2.6 The Vagaries of Risk Assessment

Mental disorder tends to be associated with dangerousness, violence, and unpredictability in the minds of the public and in the media (Peay, 2011a). When individuals known to the authorities reoffend, calls for governments to respond to public outrage often follow. However, the relationship between mental disorder and offending is complex, and the limits of our abilities to predict recidivism makes it difficult to formulate rational policies in response to such calls. We are far from being able to reliably identify which individuals will actually go on to reoffend, and, in practice, risk assessment is informed by subjective judgements, including gut feelings, impressions, and intuitions about a person's character. Given the negative moral judgements associated with a diagnosis, the combination of personality disorder and high-risk labels may be expected to lead to distrust and risk aversion on behalf of decision-makers. Given the paucity of evidence that current interventions can reduce the serious reoffending, these labels are likely to prove difficult to shift.

There have been four waves in the development of risk assessment methods (Garrington and Boer, 2020). The first wave was unstructured clinical judgement, based on a clinician's professional experience and knowledge of the patient. This was followed by actuarial risk assessment instruments (ARAIs) based on static (or historical) risk factors that are statistically related to offending. The third wave brought ARAIs that seek not only to evaluate risk but to identify offenders' 'criminogenic needs': risk factors for offending that are amenable to change (Andrews and Bonta, 2010, 45–46). Then structured clinical judgement instruments were created to improve the accuracy and objectivity of clinical judgement and to bridge the gap between clinical practice and ARAIs (Singh et al, 2011; Ogloff and Davis, 2020). A fifth generation of risk assessment tools based on 'big data' and machine learning is now emerging (Wormith, 2017; Hannah-Moffat, 2019).

Unstructured professional judgement has poor predictive validity, as the subjective assessments of even experienced clinicians are poor predictors of offending (Ogloff and Davis, 2020, 85). ARAIs are stronger predictors of offending than unstructured clinical judgement (Cooke and Michie, 2011). They use algorithms based on statistical relationships between risk factors and offending established through empirical research to calculate a risk score or assign a given individual to a risk category (eg low, medium, high). Third-wave ARAIs were the product of the influential risk–need–responsivity (RNR) model of rehabilitation (Andrews and Bonta, 2010, 46). This model is underpinned by a cognitive social learning theory of criminal behaviour that assumes a causal relationship between habits of thinking, learned behaviours, and offending (Andrews and Bonta, 2010, 46; Raynor and Robinson, 2005, 105–06). Examples of dynamic risk factors identified by these tools include pro-criminal attitudes and associates, an antisocial personality pattern, a lack of pro-social leisure pursuits, poor family relationships, and poor satisfaction with work and education (Bonta and Andrews, 2007). Some third-wave ARAIs include an assessment of the person's 'strengths' or protective factors against recidivism (Marshall, 2019; Jones, 2020). Fourth-wave structured clinical judgement instruments have similar predictive power to ARAIs (Singh et al, 2011).

While second- and third-generation ARAIs are reasonably good at predicting reoffending at a group level, their accuracy declines when used to make judgements about individuals. This is because they are based on population studies, and their margins of error increase significantly when applied to individuals (Cooke and Michie, 2011). The factors assessed through structured clinical judgement tools are subject to the same weakness. This weakness is compounded when it comes to predicting rare events, like violence, which have a low base rate in the general population and amongst those with mental disorder (Szmukler, 2003; Ogloff and Davis, 2020). The low base rate means that instruments return both false positives (individuals identified as high risk who are not violent) and false negatives (individuals wrongly identified as low risk who are violent) (Szmukler, 2003; Ogloff and Davis, 2020).

The false positive problem can be seen most clearly when predictions are assessed against actual reoffending rates. A meta-analysis of the nine most commonly used ARAIs and structured clinical judgement tools found that 41 per cent of prisoners judged to present a moderate or high risk of violence went on to violently offend over a mean follow-up period of 3 years and 3.4 months (Fazel et al, 2012). Less than a quarter (23 per cent) of those classed as presenting a moderate or high risk of sexual offending went on to sexually offend over a longer mean follow-up period of 6 years and 10.4 months (Fazel et al, 2012). Thus, at current levels of predictive accuracy, two people judged to present a high or moderate risk of violence would have to be detained for over three years to prevent one violent act, and five would have to be detained for almost seven years to prevent one sexual offence (Fazel et al, 2012, 10). The authors concluded that 'even after

30 years of development, the view that violence, sexual, or criminal risk can be predicted in most cases is not evidence based' (Fazel et al, 2012, 5).

While ARAIs are regarded as more objective measures of risk than unstructured clinical judgement, these instruments still require a professional to interpret the criteria and to make judgements about the individual's criminal history, lifestyle, leisure activities, associates, family relationships, attitudes, and finances (Hannah-Moffatt, 2015b). Studies of risk assessment in practice demonstrate that professional judgements also rely on a practitioner's own feelings and intuitions about the person. A study in England and Wales found that judges and lawyers expressed scepticism towards ARAIs, viewing risk assessment in sentencing as an inherently subjective, intuitive, or 'human' process (Jacobson and Hough, 2010, 27). They described dangerousness as something 'overwhelming' that they knew 'instinctively' and risk assessment as 'a gut feeling': a 'purely visceral' and 'very human' reaction to the evidence or to the person (Jacobson and Hough, 2010, 29). Another study found that probation practitioners in England and Wales assessed the risk posed by sexual or violent offenders using a combination of actuarial scores, 'gut feelings', and 'professional experience' (Kemshall and Maguire, 2001, 248). In one Canadian study, seasoned probation professionals considered their own 'experiential knowledge' or 'common sense' to be just as reliable as actuarial scores (Hannah-Moffat et al, 2009, 405).

Consequently, risk assessment in practice is likely to be less accurate and more liable to bias than suggested by carefully controlled validity studies of specific instruments. The role of intuitive judgements further suggests that risk assessments may be coloured by assumptions about a person's character. According to a study of Parole Board decision-making in England and Wales conducted in the 1990s, trust played a role in release decisions and Parole Board members used negative character judgements about offenders convicted of sexual offences when assessing their eligibility for parole (Hood and Shute, 2000). A diagnosis of ASPD or a high PCL-R score that carries a suggestion of enduring characteristics of manipulativeness, callousness, and deceitfulness may be expected to negatively influence these character-based judgements and assessments of trustworthiness. This issue is considered in further depth in Chapters 4 and 5.

Moves towards an 'automated' approach to risk assessment is a source of concern, as the decision-making processes and data sources behind the judgements produced by such tools are hidden from view (Wormith, 2017).

While ARAIs are based on empirical studies of populations conducted by social scientists and psychologists, 'big data' analytics relies upon vast quantities of data pulled from multiple sources that are unlikely to have been collected in accordance with rigorous research methods (Hannah-Moffat, 2019). Automated risk assessment processes may therefore simply replicate the biases and gaps present in police and criminal justice data sets (Wormith, 2017; Hannah-Moffat, 2019). As technologies advance apace, the problems with the reliability and objectivity of risk assessments remain significant.

Given their pitfalls, risk assessments should be treated with caution, particularly when it comes to decision-making that impacts upon a person's liberty. Risk scores may be expected to encourage decision-makers to err on the side of caution given the potentially very serious consequences if a person classed as 'high risk' reoffends (Hebenton and Seddon, 2009). Given the high rates of false positives produced, some people are likely to be detained unnecessarily. While risk assessment technologies have improved over time, the idea that the state can reliably identify 'dangerous' individuals who would go on to offend if given their liberty is not grounded in evidence. The use of subjective and intuitive judgements in risk assessment and the negative connotations of a personality disorder diagnosis further suggests that judgements of high risk are likely to be difficult to escape once they have been applied.

2.7 Legal Controversies

The uncertainties regarding the validity of the personality disorder construct and the efficacy of treatment raise the question of whether individuals diagnosed with personality disorders ought to be detainable under mental health legislation. This question has received different responses from different common law jurisdictions. Some jurisdictions explicitly exclude people with a sole diagnosis of personality disorder from the scope of mental health law. To some extent, these systems respond to psychiatrists' ethical objections to the use of treatments with detained patients that have not been demonstrated to be effective or that are not in their best interests (Mullen, 1999; Buchanan and Leese, 2001; Maden and Tyrer, 2003; Haddock et al, 2001). A full comparative study of the laws applying to dangerous offenders with personality disorders is outside the scope of this book.[12] Some examples are given below to illustrate the diverging paths taken by different jurisdictions.

In England and Wales, the place of individuals with a primary or sole diagnosis of personality disorder within mental health law has been the subject of controversy since at least the 1950s.[13] The definition of 'psychopathic disorder' under the MHA 1959 confined the use of detention and treatment powers to patients who were susceptible to medical treatment.[14] This evolved into the 'treatability' criterion contained in the MHA 1983, which came to be viewed by the New Labour Government in the late 1990s as an impediment to the protection of the public from dangerous people with severe personality disorders.[15] The MHA 2007 was eventually passed, broadening the definition of mental disorder in the MHA 1983 to include 'any disorder or disability of mind' and replacing the treatability criterion with the 'appropriate medical treatment' test. Under the new test, 'appropriate medical treatment' would have to be 'available' to the patient in hospital, and the 'purpose' of such treatment would have to be 'to alleviate, or prevent a worsening of, the disorder or one or more of its symptoms or manifestations'.[16]

Legislatures in other common law jurisdictions have shored up the division between the mental health and criminal justice systems by significantly limiting powers to detain and treat people with a sole diagnosis of personality disorder under mental health law. While similar concerns arose in Scotland regarding the release of dangerous offenders from prisons or hospitals in the 1990s, Scotland opted not to abolish its equivalent of the treatability requirement (Ferguson, 2021). Instead, it introduced the order for lifelong restriction (OLR): an indefinite prison sentence available where a person is convicted in the Scottish High Court of a serious sexual, violent, or life-endangering offence, or is convicted of an offence that, it appears to the court, shows that the person has a propensity to commit a serious sexual, violent, or life-endangering offence.[17] The Court must also be satisfied that

---

[12] Readers will find more detailed discussion of international legislative regimes governing dangerous offenders in McSherry and Keyzer (2011). For discussion of international regimes governing people with personality disorders or psychopathic disorders, see Felthous and Saß (2020).
[13] See Chapter 3.
[14] MHA 1959 s 4(4).
[15] See Chapter 1.
[16] MHA1983, s 145(4).
[17] Criminal Procedure (Scotland) Act 1995, s 210B. For further details of the OLR, see O'Loughlin et al (2022), 46–47.

'there is a likelihood that [the person], if at liberty, will seriously endanger the lives, or physical or psychological well-being, of members of the public at large'.[18] Prisoners subject to an OLR are subject to a risk-monitoring plan for the rest of their lives (Ferguson, 2021).

In Scotland, it is not possible to transfer a sentenced prisoner to hospital unless 'medical treatment which would be likely to – (i) prevent the mental disorder worsening; or (ii) alleviate any of the symptoms, or effects, of the disorder, is available for the offender'.[19] This presents a barrier to the use of psychiatric hospitals for the purposes of post-sentence preventive detention with individuals with personality disorder in Scotland (O'Loughlin et al, 2022, 46).

In Ireland, responsibility for managing 'dangerous' offenders with personality disorders rests with the criminal law and with the prison service (Reidy and Kelly, 2021, 3). Detention in hospital under Irish mental health law is only possible where the person suffers from mental disorder, defined as 'mental illness, severe dementia or significant intellectual disability'.[20] Irish law explicitly excludes involuntary admission based on a personality disorder diagnosis alone.[21]

In New Zealand and in all Australian jurisdictions except South Australia, a person must be suffering from 'mental illness' and require psychiatric treatment before they can be detained under mental health law (Gray et al, 2010; Dawson, 2018). In these jurisdictions, definitions of 'mental illness' are tailored to psychosis, thought disorder, or mood disorders, and people with personality disorders can typically only be detained for short periods during acute mental health crises (Dawson, 2018).

Dawson (2018) traces the Australasian unwillingness to detain people whose treatability is questionable back to the influential psychiatrist, Aubrey Lewis. Lewis was wary of the abuse of psychiatry and argued that:

> psychiatrists have no wish to ... act ... as the agents of organized society in getting 'deviants' to conform. If society asks psychiatrists to do this,

---

[18] Criminal Procedure (Scotland) Act 1995, s 210E.
[19] This requirement forms part of the criteria for making a compulsion order under s 57A(3) of the Criminal Procedure (Scotland) Act 1995. A prisoner cannot be transferred to hospital unless the criteria for making a compulsion order are met (Mental Health (Care and Treatment) (Scotland) Act 2003, s 136). Compulsion orders are equivalent to hospital orders under section 37 of the MHA 1983. See Chapter 7 for further discussion of hospital orders.
[20] Mental Health Act (Ireland) 2001, s 3.
[21] Mental Health Act (Ireland) 2001, s 8(2)(b).

with 'psychopathic disorder' as the thin end of the wedge, it may be predicted that they will refuse (Lewis, 1963, 1553).

In Australia, public concerns raised by cases of reoffending by known offenders led to the passing of legislation to enable the post-sentence preventive detention of people with a history of violent or sexual offending. These arrangements allow courts to extend a prisoner's detention in prison or to extend supervision over them in the community based on psychiatric or psychological evidence that they pose an unacceptable risk of reoffending (Keyzer and McSherry, 2015). Such schemes have been enacted in Queensland, Western Australia, New South Wales, Victoria, and the Northern Territory and have been criticized on human rights grounds (Freckelton and Keyzer, 2010; Keyzer and McSherry, 2015). The legislation in New South Wales extends to high-risk violent offenders as well as to high-risk sex offenders (Keyzer and McSherry, 2015).

In the United States, the Illinois Mental Health Code permits involuntary admission to a state mental facility only in respect of patients with mental illness, which excludes disorders 'manifested only by repeated or otherwise antisocial conduct'.[22] In Kansas, 'character disorder' was originally explicitly included within the definition of mental disorder for the purposes of involuntary admission (Habermeyer et al, 2020, 59). The law in Kansas has since been reformed, and ASPD is now excluded.[23] Kansas has a separate civil commitment statute for 'sexually violent predators'. This statute allows the detention of individuals convicted of or charged with a 'sexually violent offense'. It requires evidence that the person suffers 'from a mental abnormality or personality disorder which makes the person likely to engage in repeat acts of sexual violence and who has serious difficulty in controlling such person's dangerous behavior'.[24]

Such post-sentence civil commitment schemes are not permissible in states that adhere to the European Convention of Human Rights (ECHR). As Article 7 of the ECHR prohibits the retrospective application of criminal penalties that are heavier than those applicable at the time of the offence, detention under criminal law can only be imposed by a sentencing court as a sanction following a criminal conviction under Article 5(1)(a).[25] Given

---

[22] 406 ILCS 5/1-129.
[23] Kan Stat Ann § 59-2946.
[24] Kan Stat Ann § 59-29a02.
[25] *M v Germany* [2009] ECHR 2071; *James, Wells and Lee v UK* [2012] ECHR 1706.

the vagaries of risk assessment considered above, the use of indeterminate prison sentences based on judgements of 'dangerousness' is likely to result in over-inclusion of offenders who would not go on to reoffend. The poor evidence base for interventions that aim to reduce serious reoffending and the difficulties associated with demonstrating that a person who has been labelled as 'dangerous' no longer poses a risk to the public suggests that long-term detention is likely to result.

This has been the experience of England and Wales with the sentence of imprisonment for public protection (IPP). Widely regarded as a failure, the IPP was abolished in 2012. An inquiry by the House of Commons Justice Committee (2022) found that IPP prisoners continue to struggle to obtain access to offending behaviour programmes in prisons and to struggle to demonstrate to the Parole Board that they are safe to release (see also Annison, 2018). The Committee declared that the IPP sentence was 'irredeemably flawed' and recommended that the Government bring forward legislation for the resentencing of IPP prisoners (House of Commons Justice Committee, 2022, 60). For the Committee, this was 'the only way to address the unique injustice caused by the IPP sentence and its subsequent administration, and to restore proportionality to the original sentences that were given' (House of Commons Justice Committee, 2022, 61). This resentencing recommendation has not been taken up.

For detention under Article 5(1)(e), the person must be judged to be suffering from a 'true mental disorder' as established by 'objective medical expertise', and that mental disorder must be 'of a kind or degree warranting compulsory confinement'.[26] In addition, the ECtHR recently confirmed in *Rooman v Belgium*[27] that the administration of suitable therapy is required:

> Any detention of mentally ill persons must have a therapeutic purpose, aimed specifically, and in so far as possible, at curing or alleviating their mental-health condition, including, where appropriate, bringing about a reduction in or control over their dangerousness . . . [I]rrespective of the facility in which those persons are placed, they are entitled to be provided with a suitable medical environment accompanied by real therapeutic measures, with a view to preparing them for their eventual release.[28]

---

[26] Established in *Winterwerp v the Netherlands* [1979] ECHR 4, [39].
[27] [2019] ECHR 109.
[28] ibid, [208].

The 'appropriate medical treatment' test in the MHA 1983 is likely to fall short of the active, discharge-oriented therapeutic approach required by *Rooman*. Under the MHA 1983, it is enough for treatment to merely have the 'purpose' of preventing a deterioration in the person's condition.[29] The Independent Review of the Mental Health Act 1983, chaired by Professor Sir Simon Wessely, recently recommended introducing a new test of therapeutic benefit (Department of Health and Social Care, 2018). This would make detention contingent on the availability of treatment that 'would benefit the patient, and not just serve public protection, which cannot be delivered without detention'. The Review further recommended strengthening the criteria so that a person could not be detained unless 'there is a substantial likelihood of significant harm to the health, safety or welfare of the person, or the safety of any other person without treatment' (Department of Health and Social Care, 2018, 113).

The recent Draft Mental Health Bill 2022 published by the UK Government stops short of these proposals. Its definition of 'appropriate medical treatment' is almost identical to the current definition in the MHA 1983. The only difference is that, under the Draft Bill, a person would have to be discharged if no appropriate medical treatment is available that has 'a *reasonable prospect* of alleviating, or preventing the worsening of, the disorder or one or more of its symptoms or manifestations' (Department of Health and Social Care and Ministry of Justice, 2022, Clause 6).[30] This proposal would seem to require an evaluation of the likelihood of treatment having such an effect. Nevertheless, it falls short of the requirement for a 'therapeutic benefit' proposed by the Wessely Review and the requirements of the ECHR.

2.8 Conclusion

Dimensional models acknowledge that 'disordered' personalities are on a spectrum with 'normal' ones, and that personality disorders are not necessarily permanent and pervasive conditions. However, dimensional models continue to base a diagnosis on socially undesirable traits, attitudes, and behaviours, and to require clinicians to make moral judgements about their patients. Unless accompanied by access to suitable treatment or support, a

---

[29] MHA1983, s 145(4).
[30] Emphasis added.

personality disorder diagnosis is likely to be associated with stigma, rejection, and hopelessness. The current evidence on the association between personality disorder and violence and on the predictive accuracy of risk assessment instruments casts doubt on the idea that society can reliably identify 'dangerous' individuals. High rates of false positives mean that the wrong people may be identified as dangerous and detained, perhaps indefinitely. Given that a diagnosis of ASPD or psychopathy is often associated with impulsivity, deceitfulness, and aggression, it is likely to make it very difficult for individuals to prove their suitability for release.

Much higher quality studies are required to dispel continuing doubts regarding the effectiveness of treatments for ASPD and psychopathy. While the evidence for treating BPD is stronger, it tends to support interventions to reduce self-harm and distress. Current evidence casts doubt on idea that access to rehabilitative interventions and regular reviews of recidivism risk will act as an adequate limit on preventive detention. The effectiveness of treatment may be compromised by the implicit or explicit coercion acting upon prisoners and patients when progress is linked to a chance of release. While some common law jurisdictions have sought to limit the detention of people with personality disorder under mental health law, England and Wales has taken the opposite course. This framework is likely to come under increasing pressure from the ECtHR, which requires mental health detention to be accompanied by real therapeutic measures that prepare patients for returning to the community.

The next chapter demonstrates that debates about whether people with personality disorder ought to be subject to mental health law are longstanding. In Chapters 4 and 5, it will be shown that the DSPD Programme and the OPD Pathway have not fully addressed the problems with the evidence base. Chapters 6 and 7 will demonstrate that the legal framework assumes that the state has a duty to protect the public from 'dangerous' people, and that providing the latter with treatment will sufficiently protect their right to liberty. The empirical realities outlined in this chapter casts doubt on these assumptions.

3
The Origins of the Construct of Dangerous People with Severe Personality Disorder

3.1 Introduction

This chapter critically reconstructs the emergence in the late 1990s of an idea that animated controversial governmental proposals to introduce new powers of preventive detention in England and Wales. The idea was that 'dangerous people with severe personality disorder' were at risk of falling through the cracks between the mental health and criminal justice systems and that radical action was required to contain the risks they posed to public safety. This chapter investigates where the political construct of 'DSPD' came from, why it emerged when it did, and what historical factors and modern concerns shaped it. It demonstrates that the DSPD proposals were the latest in a long line of unsuccessful attempts to deal with a core problem for government. To what extent can liberal principles and the rule of law be compromised in response to calls for greater protection for the public from 'dangerous' people?

By allowing individuals with 'psychopathic disorder' to be detained in psychiatric hospitals, the Mental Health Act 1959 led to further problems. Chief amongst these were patients languishing in hospital and distressed or violent prisoners who were refused entry to psychiatric hospitals on the grounds that they were 'untreatable'. Seeking to break with past failures, policymakers devised a new compromise based on New Labour's 'third way' political programme and its interpretation of human rights. The offer of rehabilitation was framed as way of striking a 'balance' between a claimed right of the public to protection from harm and the offender's more readily recognized right to liberty. It was clear, however, that the need to reassure the public would take priority. Despite the efforts of officials and politicians to present the plans as a win–win, they alienated key stakeholders and provoked vociferous opposition.

3.2 Advent and Uproar

On 26 October 1998, Jack Straw, then Home Secretary of the first New Labour Government, announced that the Home Office and Department of Health were 'urgently considering' changes to the law and practice governing 'serious and dangerous persistent offenders' (HC Deb, 26 October 1998, col. 9W). Straw used this opportunity to launch an attack on psychiatrists and to accuse them of failing to take responsibility for patients with personality disorders:

> Quite extraordinarily for a medical profession, the psychiatric profession has said that it will take on only patients whom it regards as treatable. If that philosophy applied anywhere else in medicine, no progress would be made in medicine. It is time that the psychiatric profession seriously examined its own practices and tried to modernise them in a way that it has so far failed to do (HC Deb, 26 October 1998, col. 9W).

In February 1999, Straw announced more specific plans to introduce new legal powers for 'the indeterminate but reviewable detention' of 'a group of dangerous, severely personality disordered individuals from whom the public at present are not properly protected, and who are restrained effectively neither by the criminal law nor by the provisions of the Mental Health Acts' (HC Deb, 15 February 1999, col. 601–602).

In July 1999, a joint Home Office and Department of Health consultation paper entitled *Managing Dangerous People with Severe Personality Disorder* was published. The paper used the phrase 'dangerous severely personality disordered' or 'DSPD' as a shorthand for a troublesome group of individuals it portrayed as at risk of falling through the gaps between the criminal justice and mental health systems (Home Office and Department of Health, 1999, 12). The paper claimed that, while the vast majority of the DSPD group had committed serious violent or sexual offences, most were serving determinate prison sentences. Once their sentences expired, the authorities would have no choice but to release them despite the risk of 'serious anti-social behaviour resulting from their disorder' (Home Office and Department of Health, 1999, 12).

At the time, prisoners diagnosed with personality disorder could not be transferred to hospital by the Home Secretary under the Mental Health Act (MHA) 1983 unless two doctors certified that they were suffering from 'psychopathic disorder' of a nature or degree which made it appropriate for them to be detained in a hospital for medical treatment, and that treatment was 'likely to alleviate or prevent a deterioration' in their condition.[1] The latter requirement became known as the 'treatability' criterion. Similar requirements applied for the civil detention of patients from the community.[2] 'Psychopathic disorder' was not a clinical diagnosis but a legal category. It described 'a persistent disorder or disability of mind (whether or not including significant impairment of intelligence) which results in abnormally aggressive or seriously irresponsible conduct on the part of the person concerned'.[3] Through this definition and the 'treatability' criterion, the MHA 1983 restricted powers to detain people with personality disorders to a subset of individuals who could be expected to respond to hospital treatment.[4] As personality disorder was considered 'untreatable' by some psychiatrists, the paper portrayed the 'treatability' criterion as a stumbling block to detaining 'dangerous' individuals in hospital to protect the public (Peay, 2011a, 176).

The 1999 consultation paper put forward two options for legal and policy change. Under Option A, it proposed to remove the 'treatability' criterion; to create new powers for the supervision of the DSPD group following their discharge from hospital; and to encourage judges to make greater use of discretionary life sentences.[5] It further proposed creating specialist treatment facilities for the DSPD group within existing prison and hospital services (Home Office and Department of Health, 1999, 20–21). Option B was more radical. It proposed the creation of a 'third service' for the DSPD group, entirely separate from the existing prison and secure hospital systems (Fallon et al, 1999a, para 7.12.1). Individuals identified as 'DSPD' were to be

---

[1] See MHA 1983 (as enacted), s 47.
[2] See MHA 1983 (as enacted), s 3.
[3] MHA 1983 (as enacted), s 1(2).
[4] See Chapter 2 for definitions and discussion of antisocial personality disorder and psychopathy.
[5] These are sentences of life imprisonment passed by judges in respect of offences that carry a maximum penalty of life imprisonment. In England and Wales, discretionary life sentences are to be distinguished from other life sentences applying to adults: mandatory life sentences for murder (Murder (Abolition of Death Penalty) Act 1965, s 1), life imprisonment for dangerous offenders (Sentencing Act 2020, s 285), and life imprisonment for a second serious offence (Sentencing Act 2020, s 273). See Ashworth and Kelly (2022), ch 9.8.

detained and treated in the new service under a 'DSPD direction': an order that could be attached by a sentencing court to a prison sentence or made by a court ruling in civil proceedings (Home Office and Department of Health, 1999, 24–25). Controversially, a civil DSPD direction would be available even without a criminal conviction. Instead, those subject to the order would be held under the state's power to detain persons of unsound mind under Article 5(1)(e) of the European Convention on Human Rights (ECHR).

Opposition to the proposals was vociferous and widespread, uniting lawyers, mental health practitioners, service user groups, and civil liberties and mental health organizations (Peay, 1999, 23). Ronald Blackburn, a Professor of Clinical and Forensic Psychology, criticized the DSPD construct as 'inherently circular'. He argued that 'the idea of a clearly demarcated category of "dangerous psychopaths" or "severe personality disorders" represents a disease entity approach which is at best a gross oversimplification and at worst a demonic stereotype' (Blackburn, 2000, 2). Paul Mullen, a psychiatrist, opposed the plans to abolish the treatability requirement on the grounds that they conflicted with medical ethics and were an effort by the Government to co-opt psychiatrists into 'the role of judges and jailers charged with maintaining public order' (Mullen, 1999, 1146). In a similar vein, the Royal College of Psychiatrists (2000) was critical of what it saw as an attempt to use mental health legislation 'to get around any absence of preventative detention in English Law'.[6] An influential paper published in the *Lancet* showed that, in order to prevent one violent act, six individuals in the DSPD category would have to be detained (Buchanan and Leese, 2001). For the Law Society (2000), it was difficult to see how people classed as DSPD 'will ever be able to show they no longer pose a threat to public safety, particularly as they will be unable to rely on any clinical intervention to bring about an improvement in their condition'.

Given the level of opposition, it seemed unlikely that anything as ambitious as Option B would make it off the drawing board. In 2000, a Department of Health White Paper entitled *Reforming the Mental Health Act* stated that any decision between policy options was to be delayed pending the outcome of a pilot assessment and treatment programme for the DSPD group. A 2001 Progress Report confirmed that there would be 'no separate powers or provisions for those who are DSPD' and that more general new legal powers would be created through the reform of the MHA

---

[6] See also Eastman (1999).

1983 (Department of Health, Home Office and HM Prison Service, 2001, 1). Subsequent legal changes and the evolution of the pilot DSPD Programme are explored in Chapter 4.

3.3 Explaining the Emergence of the DSPD Proposals

For criminologists, the advent of the DSPD proposals presents a puzzle. Policymakers seemed to advocate the exclusion of dangerous offenders from society by detaining them indefinitely whilst advocating the development of tailored treatments that could return them to society. The DSPD group were thus presented as dangerous and uncontrollable through normal legal means, yet also as distressed, vulnerable, and capable of learning to conform to the criminal law. Another key aspect of the plans has received limited attention from scholars: the proposition that they would strike a better balance between the rights of the public and those of 'dangerous' individuals.

Mike Boyle, then head of the Mental Health Unit at the Home Office, used the language of human rights when explaining the DSPD proposals to the House of Commons Select Committee on Health in May 2000:

> where you have damaged, disordered individuals who are not receiving adequate services either from the Prison Service or from the NHS, who are distressed themselves, cause distress to their families and communities around them, and we are saying in effect there is no response to that, that seems to me to be an infringement not only of their human rights but of the human rights of the rest of society.[7]

This seeming commitment to human rights seemed to conflict with the core commitment of the policy: to facilitate the detention of individuals who were thought to be a danger to the public but for whom little or no effective treatment was available to enable them to eventually be discharged from hospital.

Criminologists sought to explain the DSPD initiative in light of wider 'volatile and contradictory' (O'Malley, 1999) penal policy trends. In an

---

[7] Evidence of Mike Boyle, Head of the Mental Health Unit of the Home Office, to the Select Committee on Health (2000), para 635.

influential commentary, Toby Seddon (2008, 309) portrayed the DSPD initiative as a 'hybrid' development that signified a 'coupling together of a novel focus on risk with a more archaic concern about dangerous subjects' (Seddon, 2008, 301; 309). He further saw it as a reflection of New Labour's political programme, in which a 'self-conscious "toughness" ... sat alongside a more conventionally progressive faith in the transformative potential of interventions with offenders' (Seddon, 2008, 301). Although Seddon's account acknowledged the progressive elements of the DSPD strategy, his analysis saw the exclusionary aspects of the policy as taking priority. He argued that, as personality disorder 'is essentially an unchanging characteristic', the DSPD group were marked out as ' "monsters" requiring an exclusionary response' (Seddon, 2008, 309).

Andrew Rutherford (2006) similarly characterized the DSPD proposals primarily as an exclusionary risk management response to dangerous 'others'. He portrayed the proposals as an example of Nikolas Rose's (2000) 'risk thinking' in which measures are taken to neutralize those who for whom social inclusion is deemed impossible, including measures of preventive detention that may require waiving the rule of law (Rutherford, 2006, 82). In the same vein, drawing on Richard Ericson's (2007) work, Bill Hebenton and Toby Seddon (2009) saw the DSPD initiative as an example of 'counter-law' deployed to circumvent traditional legal safeguards that were perceived by the Government to present barriers to the pre-emption of harms.

These explanatory accounts seem to fit well with criminological theories that locate measures taken against the dangerous within broader social trends: a popular and political loss of faith in experts, the demise of the post-war rehabilitative ideal, and the ascendance of populist punitive policies (Simon, 1998; Garland, 2001; Hutton, 2005; Loader, 2006; Pratt, 2007; Lacey, 2012). For David Garland, strategies of crime control in the 1990s were marked by a repudiation of 'the once-dominant welfarist criminology which depicted the offender as disadvantaged or poorly socialized and made it the state's responsibility—in social as well as penal policy—to take positive steps of a remedial kind' (Garland, 1996, 462). According to Garland, policies of rehabilitation retained a place not due to their welfarist claims, but through the claim that rehabilitating offenders would protect future victims from harm (Garland, 2001; see also Maurutto and Hannah-Moffat, 2006; Robinson, 2008). The revival of legal measures to preventively detain sexual and violent offenders in the 1980s and 1990s have also been characterized as reflecting an 'eliminative ideal' that 'strives to solve present and emerging problems by getting rid of troublesome and disagreeable people with methods that are lawful and widely supported' (Rutherford, 1997, 117).

Yet, the DSPD proposals do not fully mesh with these explanatory theories. In the proposals, personality disorder and dangerousness were conceived of as potentially mutable qualities and the search for effective treatments for personality disorder was central to the scheme. This casts doubt on characterizations of the DSPD initiative as a policy that sought to indefinitely exclude 'dangerous' offenders from society and to express popular punitive sentiments towards 'monsters'. Rather than a form of 'counter-law', the legal changes proposed by the DSPD proposals were based on existing legal frameworks. Sentencing law already permitted discretionary life sentences, which were used by judges from the 1950s onwards 'as a measure of preventive detention for mentally unstable and dangerous offenders' (Cullen and Newell, 1999, 109). The old 'treatability' criterion had already been significantly watered down through case law.[8] The focus of the DSPD proposals on enhancing wellbeing further contrasts with accounts that describe contemporary policies and practices of rehabilitation as aimed solely at reducing recidivism and protecting potential victims from harm.

These features of the DSPD proposals suggest that there is a need to look beyond accounts of the decline of penal welfarism or the emergence of populist punitive policies. Little attention has been paid to the influence that a much longer history of unsuccessful attempts to tackle a difficult problem for government had on the DSPD proposals. In addition, little attention has been paid to how the language of human rights was used to frame detention and treatment as advancing individual rights to better health as well as a collective right to safety and security. The remainder of this chapter develops a historical re-construction of the development of the DSPD proposals to more fully illuminate the contextual factors that contributed to their emergence.

3.4 Tracing the Origins of the DSPD Proposals

At first glance, the DSPD proposals seemed to reflect the 'outrage dynamic', in which a social 'evil' is exposed to the public by the media, sparking calls

---

[8] *Hutchison Reid v Secretary of State for Scotland* [1999] 2 AC 512.

for 'something to be done' and a swift, but not always prudent, government reaction (Pettit, 2002). In line with this analysis, the proposals have been characterized by some commentators as a populist 'law and order' (Mullen, 2007) response to 'public fears about predatory paedophiles and serial killers' (Pickersgill, 2013, 35). Several accounts trace the origins of the DSPD proposals back to the case of Michael Stone, who was convicted on 23 October 1998 of the murders of Lin and Megan Russell and the attempted murder of Josie Russell (Howells et al, 2007; Seddon, 2007, 2008; Peay, 2011a; McRae, 2015; McBride, 2017). However, Tony Maden argues that the 'true motivation' for the DSPD proposals 'was not a single case but longstanding frustration within government at the refusal of psychiatrists to address the problem of high-risk offenders with personality disorder' (Maden, 2007, s 8). Rutherford (2006) also points to earlier roots: the formation of a small joint working group of officials from the Department of Health and Home Office sometime between the May 1997 General Election that brought New Labour into power and the arrest of Stone two months later.

The links drawn in the literature between the Stone case and the DSPD proposals are not surprising given that Jack Straw's announcement of plans to tackle the problem of dangerous offenders came in response to a Parliamentary question about Stone (HC Deb, 26 October 1998, col. 9W). However, the Government denied that the DSPD proposals were a response to Stone (Francis et al, 2006). The findings of a subsequent independent inquiry suggest that Stone was an unlikely target for the Government's plans. While Stone was presented in the media as a violent 'psychopath' whom psychiatrists had refused to detain because he was 'untreatable' or 'too dangerous' (Francis et al, 2006, Table 14.1), the inquiry exposed these and other sensationalist claims to be glaringly inaccurate (Francis et al, 2006, para 1.8). Although he posed problems of diagnosis and there had been some failings in his care, the inquiry stated that he was 'emphatically not a case of a man with a dangerous personality disorder being generally ignored by agencies or left at large without supervision' (Francis et al, 2006, 5). The inquiry concluded that if Stone had committed the crimes of which he had been convicted,[9] it 'found no evidence that they would have been prevented

---

[9] Stone maintains his innocence. According to a website campaigning for Stone's release, there was no forensic evidence tying him to the scene of the crime and he was convicted principally on the grounds of a confession made to a fellow prisoner, and that this confession contained information than could have been gleaned from newspaper reports available at the time (see http://www.michaelstone.co.uk). Stone's application to the Criminal Cases Review Commission (CCRC) was rejected and, in 2011, the High Court rejected Stone's application

if failings in provision of treatment, care, supervision or other services to Mr Stone had not occurred' (Francis et al, 2006, 4). Despite these findings, the myth that Stone was an 'untreatable' psychopath who was left free to kill in legal limbo and the associations drawn between Stone and the DSPD initiative have proven persistent (see, for example, Lloyd and Bell, 2015, 2).

For Rutherford (2006, 80), the Stone case was a convenient 'presentational' tool that provided 'a narrative into which embryonic proposals might be located alongside the rationale and justification to carry them forward into the political arena'. Former members of the joint Home Office and Department of Health working group that produced the DSPD proposals interviewed for the purpose of this book gave credence to Rutherford's account. One former member conceded in interview that, while the DSPD proposals were not a direct response, the Stone case contributed to an 'atmosphere of needing to demonstrate that the Government was doing something' about an issue of public concern (Civil Servant 1). Another former civil servant disclosed that the joint working group had come together informally four months before the 1997 election (Civil Servant 3). According to both interviewees, this small group of civil servants saw themselves as continuing the work of the Reed Review (1994), which had been established in 1990 to conduct a review of health and social services for offenders with mental disorder.

A review of the history of 'severe personality disorder and the law' presented by the 1999 consultation paper demonstrates that civil servants were aware of a much longer history of attempts to grapple with the difficulties presented by 'moral defectives', 'socially dangerous' people and, later, 'psychopaths' (Home Office and Department of Health, 1999, 36–37). As set out below, political awareness of these problems can be traced back to the 1957 report of the Royal Commission on the Law Relating to Mental Illness and Mental Deficiency, chaired by Baron Percy of Newcastle. The more

---

for judicial review of the decision on the grounds that it was one the CCRC was entitled to reach (*R. (Michael Stone) v CCRC* [2011] EWHC 3995). In April 2023, Sky News reported that Levi Bellfield had confessed to the murders of Lin and Megan Russell (Lynch, 2023). In July 2023, the Criminal Cases Review Commission (CCRC) concluded that there was 'no real possibility' that the Court of Appeal would overturn Stone's convictions and there were therefore no grounds to refer his case to the Court (Criminal Cases Review Commission, 2023a). On 3 October 2023, the CCRC agreed to undertake a fresh review of Stone's murder convictions following a request from his representatives. However, it specified that this new review would not affect the conclusions of its previous reviews that there was 'no credible evidence or argument that raised a real possibility of the convictions being quashed' (Criminal Cases Review Commission, 2023b).

immediate influences on the DSPD proposals will be returned to later in this chapter. First, the role played by the ultimately unsuccessful attempts of elite expert groups between the 1950s and the 1970s to contain the problems presented by 'psychopaths' and, later, people with personality disorder, will be drawn out.

Expert compromises and intractable problems

Interrogating the longer history of the problems targeted by the DSPD proposals can help us to understand why civil servants and politicians felt in 1999 that a radical new approach was needed. As set out below, the DSPD debate was the latest instalment in a decades-old battle between proponents of liberal legal principles and advocates for the preventive detention of 'dangerous' individuals. What could be done with individuals who seemed to have a proclivity for violent or sexual offending but who were not deterred by the experience of punishment and who were not straightforwardly susceptible to psychiatric treatment? How could these individuals fit into a mental health system predicated on minimizing compulsion, maximizing liberty, and providing treatment for the benefit of the patient? And how could they be dealt with under a desert-based system of criminal law that militated against retroactive punishments? The historical compromises devised by government-appointed expert groups in response to these problems were not sufficient to suppress public demands for better protection from dangerous individuals and gave rise to further problems for prisons and secure hospitals.

The remit of the Percy Commission, appointed in 1954, was to streamline a complex system of mental health legislation and to devise better safeguards for liberty. In terms not dissimilar to the New Labour Government's later claims about the DSPD group, witnesses voiced concerns to the Percy Commission about 'aggressive psychopaths who are known to be homicidal and yet are not considered certifiable' (Percy Commission, 1957, para 347). Some recalled 'cases in which patients who had been admitted to hospital after committing crimes of violence or sexual offences again committed crimes of this nature after leaving hospital' (Percy Commission, 1957, para 347).

At the time of the Percy Commission, 'psychopath' was a catch-all term for people whose personalities were 'either predominantly inadequate or predominantly aggressive' and whose emotions were 'warped or blunted, over-inhibited or uncontrolled' (Percy Commission, 1957, paras 167–68). The Percy Commission's understanding of the term was likely influenced by the work of David Henderson (1942), who was then a leading expert on psychopathic personalities (Jones, 2016, ch 7).[10] According to the Percy Commission, while most 'psychopaths' were merely socially inadequate, workshy, or impulsive petty offenders, some were liable to commit sexual and violent offences or even homicide with little obvious motivation (Percy Commission, 1957, para 169). While some were certifiable under the Mental Deficiency Act 1919 as 'moral defectives'[11] these powers were applied inconsistently in practice (Percy Commission, 1957, para 177).

The Percy Commission had many of the hallmarks of liberal elitism that characterized crime control policy in the mid-twentieth century and assigned paramount importance to 'the rule of law, the maintenance of public order, and the goal of an efficient and humane penal system' (Loader, 2006, 569). The Percy Commission was wary of the suggestion that psychopaths should be subjected to detention on the grounds of their behaviour rather than any 'loss of reason or serious lack of intelligence' as this would be 'almost equivalent to the creation of a special quasi-criminal code for them alone' (Percy Commission, 1957, para 30). It was further concerned at the prospect that, if the law were changed, some psychopaths might 'be kept in hospital when their detention can no longer be justified by the prospects of benefit from further treatment' (Percy Commission, 1957, para 364). This would have gone against the Commission's desire to minimize the use of detention and its principle 'that no patient should be compelled to enter hospital unless the hospital can provide care, training or treatment suited to his needs' (Percy Commission, 1957, para 352).

Even at the time of the Percy Commission, a range of treatments was available for those it termed 'psychopaths'. This included 'training'[12] in mental deficiency hospitals, and physical treatment,[13] psychotherapy, and

---

[10] Henderson's psychopathic states were precursors of the later personality disorder categories. For further details on the history of psychopathy or personality disorder, see Chapter 2.

[11] Moral defectives were defined in legislation as 'persons in whose case there exists mental defectiveness coupled with strongly vicious or criminal propensities and who require care, supervision and control for the protection of others' (Mental Deficiency Act 1919, s 1(1)(d)).

[12] 'Training' was 'designed to promote the mental or physical development of severely subnormal and psychopathic patients' and intended to 'make the patient fit to live in the general community' (Percy Commission, 1957, para 47) or to 'develop their characters and teach them how to live and work with other people' (Percy Commission, 1957, para 87).

[13] Physical treatment included electroconvulsive therapy, drug therapy, and surgery (Percy Commission, 1957, para 103).

group therapy in mental or neurosis hospitals (Percy Commission, 1957, para 344). Belmont Hospital in Surrey had begun treating patients in 1947 in an experimental therapeutic community (Jones, 1952). By 1957, this had become a specialized social rehabilitation unit for 'psychopathic' patients (Percy Commission, 1957, para 344). However, after reviewing the evidence, the Percy Commission concluded that treatment was not effective for all psychopaths.

Nevertheless, the Commission recognized a need to 'balance the possible benefits of treatment or training, the protection of the patient and the protection of other persons, on the one hand, against the patient's loss of liberty on the other' (Percy Commission, 1957, para 314(v)). To strike such a compromise, it proposed the creation of clearer legal powers for the detention of aggressive psychopaths in secure hospitals. Given the possibility that treatment would benefit some psychopathic patients, its recommendations would allow adult 'psychopaths' to be detained in hospital where their behaviour was serious enough to constitute a criminal offence and where treatment was more appropriate than punishment (Percy Commission, 1957, paras 356–57).

The Percy Commission was opposed to including a formal definition of 'psychopathic disorder' in legislation. The following definition was formulated by the Government: 'a persistent disorder of personality (whether or not including subnormality of intelligence) which results in abnormally aggressive or seriously irresponsible conduct on the part of the patient, and *requires or is susceptible to medical treatment*'[14] (Gibbens and Jennings, 1960, 414). This definition was eventually incorporated into s 4(4) of the Mental Health Act (MHA) 1959. The MHA 1959 created powers to detain and treat patients with mental disorder, including psychopathic patients, in hospital under both civil and criminal powers. The definition of psychopathic disorder would serve to exclude individuals who merely presented a social nuisance from the scope of these powers. Later, these provisions would evolve into the treatability criterion and definition of psychopathic disorder in the MHA 1983.

The proposal to create a clearer statutory basis for the detention of 'psychopaths' was not uncontroversial. Objections in Parliament were made in terms not dissimilar to the literature on negative clinical attitudes towards personality disorder patients in the 1990s.[15] Dr A.D.D. Broughton, then a

---

[14] MHA 1959 s 4(4). Emphasis added.
[15] See Chapter 2.

Labour Party MP, remarked in a debate on the MHA 1959 that 'psychopaths' in mental hospitals 'can be a very disturbing influence, tiresome to the staff and harmful to other patients' (HC Deb, 26 January 1959, col. 756). Dr Reginald Bennett, then a Conservative MP, went further, stating that 'the psychopath is almost entirely unsuitable for hospital treatment':

> No hospital can stand more than one or two psychopaths in the whole hospital, let alone in one ward. The place becomes a bear garden. They put the other chaps up to tricks and they are frightfully clever in finding out bright ideas for perhaps the duller members of the community or the more disturbed ones (HC Deb, 26 January 1959, col. 783–84).

For Bennett, the only treatment available for psychopaths was 'simply ageing in custody' (HC Deb, 26 January 1959, col. 783). These comments appear prescient in light of the scandal that was to unfold at Ashworth Hospital in the 1990s, discussed below (Fallon et al, 1999a). Despite these reservations, the MHA 1959 was passed, and the problem of psychopathic patients was temporarily contained at a time of liberal elitism in which criminal justice policy was relatively well-insulated from the demands of public opinion and governments tended to follow the recommendations of expert commissions.

This history contradicts more recent claims that, before the DSPD Programme, there was 'no place' in psychiatric hospitals 'for anyone showing signs of personality disturbance' and that mental health services were 'almost exclusively for those deemed mentally ill' (Benefield et al, 2015, 4). It further contradicts the Home Office's assertion that the MHA 1983 'marked a fundamental shift away from the previously-held view that the management and, where possible, treatment of people with psychopathic disorder . . . was a legitimate function of the health service' (Home Office, 2000, para 6). Rather, the treatability criterion itself was a compromise. It was introduced alongside new powers to detain psychopathic patients in hospital to ensure that such patients would only be detained if they could benefit from treatment.

There were already signs by the early 1960s that this compromise was fragile. Psychiatrists hoped that the new statute would shield them from the demands of a large section of the public who would have been 'willing to see sex deviants and others segregated semi-permanently' (Gibbens and Jennings, 1960, 416). From another perspective, the 1961 Ministry of Health Working Party on the Special Hospitals was nervous of the assumption implicit in the MHA 1959 that psychopathic disorder *could* be treated, and worried that the health service would be forced to take on large numbers of new patients for whom care and treatment were problematic (Fallon et al, 1999a, paras 6.1.24–28). These concerns later proved prophetic.

The compromise in the MHA 1959 did not prevent public pressures from resurfacing a decade later following serious reoffending by two patients given conditional discharge from Broadmoor Special Hospital (Butler, 1975, para 4.1). In 1972, the Government responded by appointing another expert committee: the Committee on Mentally Disordered Offenders chaired by Lord Butler, a former Home Office minister. 'What to do about the psychopath' was one of the most perplexing questions the Committee faced (Butler, 1975, para 5.1). A joint memorandum of evidence submitted by the Home Office and the Department of Health and Social Services to the Committee drew attention to a problem created by a combination of the criminal law and the treatability requirement: 'the legal obligation to release, at the end of determinate prison sentences, a small number of men who are probably dangerous but who are not acceptable for treatment in hospital' (Butler, 1975, para 4.34). This was the same problem that would later be targeted by the DSPD proposals. Its appearance in the Butler Committee report demonstrates that joint working between Health and Home Office officials on the problem of 'dangerous' offenders dates back to the 1970s.

The Butler Committee report demonstrates that psychiatrists have long held a variety of views on the potential for 'psychopaths' to respond to treatment. This history contradicts Jack Straw's claim in 1998 that the refusal by some psychiatrists to take on 'untreatable' patients marked a recent change in practice (HC Deb, 26 October 1998, col. 9W). In the early 1970s, 'psychopathic' patients were being treated by psychologists in the Special Hospitals and a therapeutic community at Grendon Prison claimed successes with selected patients. Nevertheless, the Committee concluded that 'the great weight of evidence' confirmed 'that psychopaths are not, in general, treatable, at least in medical terms' (Butler, 1975, para 5.34). The Butler Committee highlighted another problem that would later be targeted by the DSPD proposals: a group of aggressive prisoners who were difficult to control and who had little prospect of a therapeutic regime catering to their needs. These prisoners were excluded from psychiatric hospitals by a treatability requirement that effectively allowed doctors to choose their patients (Butler, 1975, para 5.38).

The Committee recommended establishing prison 'training units' for these prisoners that would allow suitable volunteers to take advantage of a structured regime and vocational training opportunities intended to encourage the natural process of maturation and lead to their eventual release (Butler, 1975, paras 5.38–39 and 5.49). The Committee hoped that the units would also spearhead advances in the treatment of 'dangerous psychopaths' (Butler, 1975, para 5.38).

Like the Percy Commission, the Butler Committee resisted using retrospective criminal legislation or mental health law to address the perceived problem of dangerous 'psychopaths'. It was wary of giving courts the power to re-sentence prisoners who were already serving determinate sentences and it would only support the use of hospital orders[16] at sentencing for 'psychopathic' individuals where treatment was expected to benefit them (Butler, 1975, para 437). The Committee instead proposed a future-facing solution that would have pushed the problem of 'psychopaths' into the prison system: a discretionary, reviewable sentence for newly convicted offenders who had 'a propensity to cause serious physical injury or lasting psychological harm' to others (Butler, 1975, paras 4.39; 4.10). This sentence would not be 'punitive in intent but designed to enable the offender to be detained only until his progress under treatment…[would] allow him to be released under supervision without serious risk to the public' (Butler, 1975, para 4.39).

Like the reviewable sentence, Butler's training units were never established. After 1975, therefore, the problems posed by 'psychopathic' prisoners remained. The DSPD proposals were a slight reformulation of these unresolved problems. Psychopathy became 'personality disorder' and prisoners who were difficult to manage were combined with prisoners serving determinate sentences who were thought to be highly likely to seriously offend after their release. Together, this group became 'dangerous people with severe personality disorder'. They were 'dangerous' both within and outside prisons, and 'severely disordered' both in terms of having a proclivity for offending and exhibiting troublesome institutional behaviour.

3.5 Immediate Influences

Jack Straw's attack on psychiatrists in October 1998 seemed to reflect a popular loss of faith in the capacity of experts to 'do something' about

---

[16] These orders could be made by a sentencing court under s 60 MHA 1959 to send convicted offenders to hospital for treatment. They are currently available under s 37 of the MHA 1983. For further discussion of this power, see Chapter 7.

crime. In such a climate, Loader and Walker (2007, 198) have argued that politicians, 'faced with what they hold to be a febrile, emotionalized climate of fear—have sought to speak for and give voice to the claims of "ordinary people" against those of remote, liberal-minded professional expertise'. However, a closer look at the immediate influences on the DSPD proposals suggests that policymakers did not lose faith in experts. Rather, they sought to harness those experts who would support a more optimistic stance on treatment: a stance that they saw as central to resolving long-standing problems. Straw emphasized that society 'should not write anybody off' and that 'somebody may be deemed untreatable by a particular group of psychiatrists, but be susceptible to treatment by clinical psychologists, psychoanalysts or psychotherapists, or just within a therapeutic community' (HC Deb, 15 February 1999, col. 605). Furthermore, the DSPD proposals were influenced by three contemporary expert committees: the Reed Review, the Fallon Inquiry, and the Richardson Committee. Ultimately, however, the joint working group decided to go its own way, at least in part because the proposals of the expert committees did not go far enough to address the public concerns raised by high profile cases of 'dangerous' offenders.

Harnessing expertise

The Reed Review was commissioned in 1990 by John Major's Conservative Government, New Labour's predecessors. For the Review's chair, Dr John Reed, it was 'extraordinarily difficult . . . to produce very positive conclusions' on the subject of 'psychopathic disorder' (Fallon et al, 1999a, para 6.1.75). Similarly to the Butler Committee in 1975, Reed concluded that 'we do not know what [the disorder] is caused by, we do not know how to measure it, we do not know what interventions are effective and we do not know very well how to measure the consequences of intervention' (Fallon et al, 1999a, para 6.1.75). Perhaps unsurprisingly, the Reed Review recommended instigating 'a comprehensive programme of research' on treatment (Home Office and Department of Health 1999, 38; Reed, 1994).

In 1997, the same Government appointed Peter Fallon QC to investigate allegations made by a former patient of the personality disorder unit (PDU) at Ashworth Hospital. The allegations included 'possible paedophile activity on one of the wards of the PDU, the availability of pornography, drugs and alcohol, and financial irregularities' (Fallon et al, 1999a, para 1.1.1). The Inquiry was encouraged by ministers to consider the broader 'controversies surrounding the diagnosis, treatment and treatability of personality disorder' and services for those 'at the severe end of the spectrum' (Fallon et al, 1999a, paras 1.2.6 and 1.2.8).

At the time of the Inquiry, there was no blanket assumption that personality disorder was 'untreatable'. Around 10 per cent of forensic psychiatrists 'were totally dismissive of psychopaths and their treatability' while another 10 per cent 'stated equally vehemently that psychiatrists had a duty to treat this group of patients who caused suffering to themselves and society' (Fallon et al, 1999a, para 6.6.4). The rest were 'somewhere in between' (Fallon et al, 1999a, para 6.6.4). The Fallon Inquiry heard evidence from enthusiasts, including psychiatrists and psychologists, who 'deem[ed] it right never to give up, and never to stop trying' (Fallon et al, 1999a, para 6.6.5). However, the optimists were often unable to supply more than anecdotal evidence of their successes.[17] Nevertheless, while few studies met the stringent methodological requirements of medical research, there was insufficient evidence to support the contention that 'nothing works' in the treatment of personality disordered offenders (Fallon et al, 1999b, 5–7).

The Fallon Inquiry and other sources provide a detailed explanation of why mere containment would not have been an adequate response to the problems presented by 'dangerous psychopaths' in the 1990s. While there was no consensus that personality disorder was intrinsically untreatable, inquiries and studies in the 1980s had exposed a culture of containment in the Special Hospitals and a sense that psychiatrists did not know what treatment to give such patients (Boynton, 1980; Dell and Robertson, 1988). Some patients were considered by hospital authorities to be 'undischargeable' due to the seriousness of their offences (Dell and Robertson, 1988, 78). At Broadmoor, the practice of transferring prisoners to hospital late in their sentences, known colloquially as 'ghosting' (Taylor 2011, 294), resulted in a group of 'hostile, bitter and uncooperative' patients (Dell and Robertson 1988, 67).

By 1993, patients diagnosed with personality disorder uncomplicated by psychosis made up 26 per cent of all patients in the Special Hospitals (Taylor et al, 1998, 218). The Fallon Inquiry found that 'the functions of hospitals and prisons . . . [were] dreadfully confused' and that secure hospitals were being 'used as surrogate prisons' (Fallon et al, 1999a, para

---

[17] See, for example, the evidence of Dr Bob Johnson, a consultant psychiatrist who led a special unit for disruptive prisoners at HMP Parkhurst from 1991 to 1996 (Fallon et al, 1999b, 339–68).

1.43.7). The nine patients interviewed by the Fallon Inquiry 'gave a sense of time passing with precious little progress' and 'an atmosphere of inertia ... in which poor practice, apathy and corruption [could] flourish' (Fallon et al, 1999a, para 1.25.34). Expanding the remit of the MHA 1983 to detain even greater numbers of potentially untreatable patients risked exacerbating these problems.

A majority of forensic psychiatrists felt that hospital orders and preventive detention in hospital on the grounds of 'psychopathic disorder' should be outlawed and that special treatment units should be established in prisons (Cope, 1993, 226–27). However, prisons were also struggling to manage violent or distressed prisoners who showed signs of personality disorder. Some prisoners were being shunted between prisons and hospitals due to their difficult behaviour, and hospitals sometimes refused to admit them on the grounds that they were untreatable, or because they were too dangerous or too disruptive (Coid, 1992, 80). Prisons did not have the luxury of refusing to take individuals who still had time left to run on their sentence and often bore the brunt of containing violent individuals who were rejected by hospitals (Coid, 1992, 91). The vast majority were 'dealt with on general location, with no specific provision to meet their needs' (Fallon et al, 1999a, para 1.35.6). The most disruptive were 'transferred from segregation unit to segregation unit, often every six weeks' receiving 'little or nothing in the way of constructive activity or opportunity to address their behaviour' (Fallon et al, 1999a, para 1.35.8). This practice, nicknamed the 'merry-go-round', was repeatedly condemned by prison inspectors and, when the worst happened, by coroners (HM Inspectorate of Prisons, 2006, 5).

Psychiatrists also felt the burden of being responsible for making decisions regarding the admission, treatment, and discharge of patients under the MHA 1983.[18] Blame was often stridently attributed to psychiatrists by the media in the aftermath of terrible crimes committed by current or former mental health patients. Consequently, some psychiatrists used the legal category of 'psychopathic disorder' in the MHA 1983 as a way of 'devolving responsibility' for offender-patients when something went wrong (Evidence of Professor Pamela Taylor, Fallon et al, 1999b, 505).

---

[18] Prior to the MHA 2007, psychiatrists were responsible for these decisions as responsible medical officers (RMOs). Note that the RMO did not have the power to discharge restricted patients. This role is now the 'responsible clinician' (RC) and is open to mental health professionals without medical qualifications.

Like the Government, the Fallon Inquiry felt that 'doing nothing' was not an acceptable policy (Fallon et al, 1999a, para 7.4.4). The Fallon Inquiry had early access to the plans for a 'third service' for the DSPD group but it ultimately rejected those proposals. Like the Percy Commission and Butler Committee, the Inquiry asserted that 'only those who are willing and able to benefit should be transferred to and remain in hospitals' (Fallon et al, 1999a, para 7.2.1). The Inquiry suggested that hospital orders should no longer be an option for offenders with personality disorders (Fallon et al, 1999, para 7.6.8). Instead, following the example of the Butler Committee, it recommended introducing a reviewable prison sentence. The Fallon Inquiry's proposals would not, however, have addressed the more immediate problem posed by offenders serving determinate sentences, and its reviewable sentence proposal was not taken up.

The report of the Fallon Inquiry came out in the same year as the proposals for a new Mental Health Act developed by an expert committee chaired by Professor Genevra Richardson. The Richardson Committee presented a vision of a new Mental Health Act based on the principles of patient autonomy, reciprocity, and non-discrimination (Department of Health, 1999). Under its scheme, compulsory powers would only apply to patients who were suffering from a mental disorder that was sufficiently serious to require hospitalization and where the person lacked capacity to consent to their care and treatment. The Committee acknowledged that most personality disorder patients would fall outside a capacity-based test (Department of Health, 1999, para 4.15). Consequently, the Committee proposed that the autonomy of patients with capacity could be overridden only where there was 'a *substantial* risk of *serious harm* to the health or safety of the patient or to the safety of other persons' and 'positive clinical measures' were 'likely to prevent deterioration or to secure an improvement in the patient's mental condition' (Department of Health, 1999, para 5.95). These proposals were therefore even more stringent than the MHA 1983 detention criteria.

In sum, the recommendations of the Fallon Inquiry and Richardson Committee did not provide the response the Government desired to the problem of 'dangerous' offenders. As a result, the joint working group decided to go its own way. However, the concerns raised by expert groups were not entirely ignored. Rather, as set out below, the joint working group sought to formulate a solution that would respond not only to the problem of premature release but also to the problems presented by violent prisoners for prison management and by 'psychopathic disorder' patients for hospital regimes. The Fallon Inquiry report further demonstrates that 'treatability' was a nuanced issue. While there was a lack of clear evidence from clinical trials that current treatments were successful, enthusiasts in both prisons and secure hospitals were providing treatment to small numbers. Although there was no consensus that personality disorder was untreatable, the treatability test allowed hospitals to reject difficult, dangerous, and unrewarding patients. These problems were, at least in part, generated by the Percy Commission's compromise between those who pressed for powers to detain 'dangerous' individuals and those who opposed their detention in hospital.

Compromise, rights, and penal welfarism

The solutions devised by the joint working group sought to reach a new compromise between competing views and values that drew on the postwar ideals of penal welfarism but was couched in the more modern language of human rights. The New Labour Government's rejection of the recommendations of expert committees can be understood in light of a political context in which deference to expertise was in decline but in which there were important continuities with the rehabilitative ideal and penal welfarism. The proposals were further shaped by New Labour's aim to invest in '*human capital*' and to generate productive citizens who would, in the long-term, cost less to govern (Giddens, 1998, 117).

This compromise was not immediately apparent from early statements by Jack Straw in Parliament. Six months prior to the publication of the proposals, the promise of treatment had the appearance of an afterthought:

> We need a third approach, under which those who are suffering from severe personality disorders and who pose a grave risk to the public can be kept in securer conditions as long as they continue to pose that risk. There they may have treatment, if such treatment can be identified (HC Deb, 18 January 1999, col. 551W).

Closer to the publication of the plans, the tone changed and references to the health needs and social reintegration of the DSPD group gained prominence. In February 1999, Jack Straw asserted that 'the key aim must be to protect the public while meeting the health needs' of the DSPD group and giving them 'the best possible chance of becoming safe so as to be returned to the community' (HC Deb, 15 February 1999, col. 602).

After the proposals were published, the Home Office was careful to highlight their intended health benefits. The Home Office stressed that:

> [The] detention of dangerous severely personality-disordered people for the purpose of protecting the public is only one—albeit a very important one—of the Government's objectives in this area. Effecting a significant improvement in the way in which these people are treated, and the level of threat they present reduced, is a parallel priority (Home Office, 2000, para 2).

This combination of welfarist and public protection justifications was, at least to some extent, attributable to collaboration between officials in the Home Office and Department of Health. According to one civil servant, the motivation of the Home Office 'was entirely public protection' while that of the Department of Health 'was wellbeing'. The narrative that developed was born of a 'need to marry these two objectives together' (Civil Servant 2). As the longer history set out earlier demonstrates, there were also important convergences between the priorities of the mental health and criminal justice agencies. Both the prison service and mental health services and their staff were frequently on the receiving end of blame and anger when discharged patients or released prisoners reoffended.

While Michael Stone had not in fact been rejected by services because he was 'untreatable', media reports nevertheless drew attention to a 'perennial' problem: the obligation to release still 'dangerous' offenders from prison at the end of a determinate prison sentence (Annison, 2015, 31). As one psychiatrist with experience of working in secure hospitals summarized in interview:

> I mean everyone's focused on Michael Stone, but I think the concern had been around for a long time before that. I can remember civil servants saying that approximately once a month the Home Secretary had a case coming across his desk of someone who'd got to the end of a determinate sentence and was considered dangerous, and the psychiatrist wouldn't take him because he had a personality disorder and they didn't think it was treatable or there was no way to treat it (Psychiatrist 1).

Then Minister Paul Boateng offered anecdotal evidence of this problem to the Home Affairs Committee. Boateng described a visit to HMP Durham where prison officers told him about a man who was shortly to be released from a special unit. Prison officers described him as 'highly dangerous' and 'were absolutely convinced' he would reoffend. Although he had spent a long time in prison, his 'condition remained as it was and [he] presented a risk to the public' (Home Affairs Committee, 2000, para 4).

In addition to managing the risk that certain patients and prisoners were believed to pose to the public, the New Labour Government was concerned to manage risks to the reputation of the state and state agents as guardians of the safety and security of its citizens, both inside and outside institutions. These concerns were put into sharp relief by the Fallon Inquiry. The patients and prisoners who made up the DSPD group:

> were a difficult group to manage, they were a difficult group to control, and they presented a huge risk, reputationally and actually, to the reputation of the medical profession, to the reputation of the criminal justice fraternity, the law enforcement fraternity, and to the public because they were dangerous (Politician 1).

The DSPD proposals were also an attempt to respond to the problems that violent and distressed individuals posed for prisons:

> The proposition that Michael Stone was knocking on the door of a hospital only to be turned away perhaps is a bit apocryphal. But I've come across enough examples where the health service did not want an offender because they were too difficult or too dangerous and the custodial system was incapable of managing them properly or humanely because there was not an adequate component of health or psychiatric involvement to make sure that that person's needs were properly managed (Civil Servant 2).

Given past experiences, the solution to 'dangerous' individuals could not be 'just about locking them up and throwing away the key in the prison service' nor 'about some sort of therapeutic ideal' in the health service (Civil Servant 3). While simply detaining those labelled as DSPD indefinitely may have appealed to some sections of the public and the media, doing so without a complementary treatment programme would not have resolved, and risked exacerbating, the long-standing and increasingly pressing problems offenders diagnosed with personality disorders posed for security and safety within prisons and secure hospitals.

Jack Straw's successor in the Home Office, David Blunkett, sought to address the problem presented by 'dangerous' offenders through sentencing reforms in the Criminal Justice Act 2003 (Annison, 2015, ch 2). These measures included the creation of the sentence of imprisonment for public protection (IPP).[19] One minister interviewed by Harry Annison in his study of the IPP sentence saw it as a response to a similar question to that addressed by the DSPD proposals:

> how do you ensure effective protection of the public, minimize the risk of re-offending, help people to reintegrate, get them off drugs and alcohol problems and those kinds of things (Minister, quoted in Annison, 2015, 41).

The policymakers involved in formulating the DSPD proposals were not in favour of the IPP sentence. For one, it was 'only reasonable to deprive people of their liberty for a clear purpose, and only if you're able to combine depriving of their liberty with taking other steps to ensure that you can restore their liberty' (Civil Servant 3). By allocating significant funding to research into tailored treatments, the DSPD proposals aimed to strike a 'balance' 'between the human rights of individuals [in the DSPD group] and the right of the public to be protected from these very dangerous people' (Boateng and Sharland, 1999, 7). The IPP risked 'pandering to the Daily Mail approach to the punitive end of things' (Civil Servant 3). Another interviewee felt that the IPP was 'too blunt an instrument' as it would 'capture too many other people who clearly ought not to be detained' (Politician 1). The DSPD proposals were more progressive in appearance than the IPP sentence, and this is likely attributable to the involvement of the Department of Health alongside the Home Office.

The evidence heard by the Fallon Inquiry left the door open for a more optimistic stance on treatment for personality disorder. Policymakers sought to break with the perceived scepticism and therapeutic nihilism of some psychiatrists, and to present treatment as a humanitarian duty and a win–win for offenders and the public. They argued that 'there's nothing we can do for [the DSPD group] now based on our present knowledge, and we need to just keep banging away until we find what that is' (Civil Servant 3). This solution was based on a similar premise to the rehabilitative ideal, which assumed that treatment could change the offender 'in the interests

---

[19] See Chapter 1.

of his own happiness, health and satisfactions and in the interest of social defense' (Allen, 1959, 226).[20] Enhanced wellbeing was thus presented as a benefit that could be given to the offender in exchange for his or her liberty:

> Society has both a right and a need to protect itself from the actions of this small group of people who because of their disordered personality, pose an unacceptable level of risk of causing serious harm to others. But in return for taking action to protect itself by detaining these people, possibly indefinitely, society incurs an obligation to provide effective services to these people. Services designed to help them make the changes they need to so that they can return to the community safely (Boateng and Sharland, 1999, 7).

The idea that detention gave those in the DSPD group a right to treatment has more than an echo of the Richardson Committee's principle of reciprocity.

Previous commentators have paid little attention to how the discourse of human rights has offered criminal justice policymakers a new way of reframing an old debate between the proponents of civil liberties and social defence. The claim that society has a 'right' to protection from dangerous offenders is a species of the 'right to security' often claimed by governments on behalf of a nebulous 'public' (Lazarus, 2007; 2012a; 2012b; 2015). This right was understood by New Labour not only as a right to 'objective' security—the state of being protected from real or actual threats to safety—but also a right to subjective security—'the positive condition of feeling safe, and freedom from anxiety or apprehension' (Zedner, 2003, 155; see Ramsay, 2012b, chs 3 and 7). This was epitomized in Straw's slogan that 'everyone should enjoy that most basic of human rights: the right to live life free from fear and free from crime' (HC Deb, 8 April 1998, col. 370).

Gwen Robinson (2008, 433) has argued that contemporary rehabilitative approaches with offenders are 'a far cry from the rights-based model of offender rehabilitation, which many would wish to revive'. At first, this claim appears to conflict with the central justification for the DSPD proposals put forward by policymakers. However, while the DSPD proposals were couched in the language of human rights, there were key differences between the vision of human rights underpinning the DSPD proposals

---

[20] For further discussion of the rehabilitative ideal, see Chapter 1.

and the rights-based model of rehabilitation promoted by Egardo Rotman (1986; 1990). This model articulates a right to rehabilitative interventions on behalf of prisoners and a reciprocal duty on the authorities to provide them. By contrast to the DSPD model, the rights-based model requires a penal system based on proportionate punishment, in which the authorities should abstain from forcing unwilling prisoners to participate (Rotman, 1986; 1990). It was clear from the DSPD proposals, however, that the 'rights' of the public would take precedence over those of the offender. This pattern can be seen in two other controversial penal innovations introduced by New Labour: the IPP sentence and the antisocial behaviour order (Ramsay, 2012a; 2012b, chs 3, 4).

New Labour presented a vision of human rights law that prioritized 'the needs and rights of victims and law-abiding citizens' (McLaughlin et al, 2001, 304). Rehabilitation was thus presented by New Labour as a pragmatic choice that would promote civil liberties while maintaining a sense of individual responsibility and humanizing a 'monstrous prison regime' (Blair, 1993). The proposals therefore gave priority to another right: the right of the public to be protected from harm. A generous reading of the state's positive duty to protect the right to life established in *Osman v UK*[21] gave Mike Boyle, then head of the Mental Health Unit at the Home Office, grounds to assert that the ECHR 'impose[d] upon states an obligation to protect the public from predictable dangers that individuals may cause' (Select Committee on Health 2000, para 636).

Case law on 'treatability' also left the door open for a departure from the compromise introduced by the Percy Commission. The decision of the House of Lords in *Hutchison Reid v Secretary of State for Scotland*[22] gave a very broad interpretation of the concept of 'treatability' in domestic law. The House of Lords held that even though the patient was not receiving treatment for his personality disorder, his detention in a secure hospital 'was preventing a deterioration of his condition because his abnormally aggressive or seriously irresponsible behaviour was being controlled or at least being modified'.[23] The definition of 'medical treatment' was 'wide enough to include treatment which alleviates or prevents a deterioration of the symptoms of the mental disorder, not the disorder itself which gives

---

[21] [1998] ECHR 101; (2000) 29 EHRR 245. For further discussion of the 'right to security' in human rights law, see Chapter 6.
[22] n 8.
[23] *Hutchison Reid* (n 8), 531.

rise to them'. The fact that the patient's anger management showed improvement in hospital was enough to satisfy this test.[24]

This position was approved by the ECtHR in the subsequent case of *Hutchison Reid v UK*,[25] which confirmed that there was no equivalent to the 'treatability' criterion in the ECHR. Under Article 5(1)(e) of the ECHR, the New Labour Government could have dropped the emphasis on treatment almost entirely, so long as there was objective medical evidence that the patient was suffering from a 'true mental disorder . . . of a kind or degree warranting compulsory confinement'[26] and detention was effected in 'a hospital, clinic or other appropriate institution'.[27]

Exposure to efforts in other countries further permitted policymakers to envisage a separate service for the DSPD group. On the one hand, the architects of the DSPD proposals saw the American sexually violent predator laws as too 'focused on the issue of management and control [and] much too relaxed about keeping people incarcerated for long, long periods' (Politician 1). On the other hand, they perceived the Dutch *terbeschikkingstelling* (TBS) system to be 'much more driven by therapy' (Politician 1). Thus, the DSPD proposals 'sought to chart a middle course' (Politician 1). The radical idea of a 'third service' for offenders with personality disorders, free from the past failures of both the prison and secure hospital systems, seemed the perfect solution. The emphasis would not only be on treating the aspects of the person that led them to be a risk, as in the American model, but also on more holistic interventions to improve the offender's wellbeing and to provide them with a more therapeutic environment. As will be seen in Chapter 4, the focus of the DSPD proposals on facilitating preventive detention undermined the Government's efforts to present the plans in a progressive light and to appeal to a broad range of stakeholders.

3.6 Conclusion

The origin story of the DSPD proposals yields key insights into the mechanisms that condition the emergence of seemingly radical responses to penal problems. The initiative was shaped by past efforts to respond to offenders

---

[24] *Hutchison Reid* (n 8), 531.
[25] [2003] ECHR 94. For further discussion of the concept of treatability in the context of criminal law and mental health law, see Chapter 7.
[26] *Winterwerp v the Netherlands* [1979] ECHR 4, [39].
[27] *Aerts v Belgium* [1998] ECHR 64, [46].

who did not suffer from mental illness but who nevertheless seemed to have a predisposition for serious offending and who were unmoved by punishment. These efforts had resulted in an unstable compromise between liberal rule of law principles and pressures to pre-empt crimes. Under that compromise, 'psychopaths', later conceptualized as people with personality disorders, could only be detained in secure hospitals if their disorders were amenable to treatment and the problem of premature release from determinate prison sentences could only be resolved prospectively by creating new sentencing powers. Nevertheless, mental health law was used to preventively detain offenders with personality disorder, and this practice led to significant numbers of patients languishing in secure hospitals and the deterioration of regimes to manage them. Violent or distressed prisoners also caused management problems in prisons, and the options to treat them in hospital were limited because of a reluctance amongst doctors to take the responsibility (and blame) for dangerous or disruptive patients.

The DSPD proposals, and particularly the idea of creating a separate service, were an attempt to break with this history. Therapeutic optimism generated the idea that treatment could provide a means of reconciling the competing 'rights' of individual liberty and collective security, and protect the Government's reputation as the guarantor of the security of the public and of those detained in institutions. However, the Government misjudged its ability to bring together conflicting ideals, and the proposals were overwhelmingly viewed negatively. The DSPD Programme itself, discussed in the next chapter, illustrates the detrimental effects of arguably misplaced optimism and unrealistic expectations on the implementation of policy.

The origins of the DSPD initiative further highlights the flexibility of human rights discourse. This can be used not only to justify the protection of individuals from state coercion, but also to justify such coercion in the name of collective security (see further Lazarus, 2012a; 2012b; 2020; and Mavronicola and Lavrysen, 2020). Chapter 6 delves deeper into the claim that the offer of treatments is sufficient to 'balance' competing rights.

4
The Pilot DSPD Programme

4.1 Introduction

This chapter considers what happened when the compromise devised by the authors of the dangerous and severe personality disorder (DSPD) proposals encountered the realities of the prison and secure hospital systems. It investigates whether the pilot DSPD Programme lived up to the high expectations of its originators and whether it could have been expected to do so in view of the history explored in Chapter 3. This chapter further critically evaluates the impact of selection for the DSPD Programme on the welfare of prisoners and patients and on their ability to progress towards release from detention. Finally, it presents reflections on the contested legacy of the DSPD Programme.

While some commentators have accused the DSPD Programme of intentionally 'warehousing' individuals the authorities were too afraid to release (Tyrer et al, 2010, 97), this chapter paints a more complex picture. While its therapeutic ambitions were clear, the priority given by policymakers to reassuring the public and to using secure hospitals as venues for preventive detention resulted in the DSPD Programme replicating several of the mistakes of the past. The characteristics of the DSPD cohort and the strains they placed on staff meant that an intensive, and relatively brief, therapeutic programme was an unrealistic expectation. Tensions between the aims of security and therapy further constrained the extent to which the units could pursue their therapeutic models. Consequently, while warehousing was not the intention behind the Programme, progress through the units was slow, and some patients were merely being contained in the hospital units.

The evidence from the DSPD Programme demonstrates that treatment programmes are valued not only for the promise that they will protect future victims but for their potential to transform difficult and disruptive prisoners into self-regulating prisoners (O'Loughlin, 2019). However, it also complicates the narrative that the offer of treatment can help to reconcile the human rights of 'dangerous' offenders with those of the public.

The tensions between the construction of the DSPD offender as dangerous and manipulative but potentially treatable resulted in a double bind that could impede the progress of patients and prisoners towards release. As a result, selection for a treatment programme for personality disorder generates a risk of disproportionate punishment that must be taken seriously. In addition, participation in treatment can cause harm to prisoners (de Motte et al, 2017). This evidence raises concerns that the state did not meet its duty of care towards vulnerable individuals in state custody under the DSPD Programme.

4.2 The Pilot DSPD Programme and the Problem of 'Warehousing'

As set out in Chapter 3, New Labour's plans to create special powers to detain the DSPD group sparked widespread and vociferous opposition. The plans were eventually shelved alongside the proposal to create a separate service for the DSPD group. While awaiting new mental health legislation, the Government commissioned a pilot assessment and treatment programme to operate within existing legal and institutional structures. The aims of the pilot DSPD Programme were to improve public protection, to develop new treatment services to improve mental health outcomes and reduce risk, and to improve understanding of 'what works' in the treatment and management of those who met the DSPD criteria (DSPD Programme et al, 2008, 6).

In September 2000, the first pilot assessment centre for men opened at HMP Whitemoor, a high security men's prison in Cambridgeshire. This was followed by a high security unit for men at HMP Frankland in County Durham, and two high secure hospital units for men at Rampton Hospital in Nottinghamshire and Broadmoor Hospital in Berkshire. A medium secure hospital unit for men opened in Newcastle in December 2004 and was followed by two further medium secure hospital units and three hostels for men in London (Moran et al, 2008, 14; 5–6). The only pilot DSPD service for women was a 12-bed unit at HMP Low Newton, a closed women's prison in County Durham, which opened in December 2006 (Department of Health, 2011, 4).

While the pilot was underway, the Government continued its efforts to reform mental health law, which were coloured by its determination to remove barriers to detaining 'dangerous' people (Daw, 2007). While the process of introducing the Mental Health Act (MHA) 1983 was characterized by consultation, negotiation, and consensus with interest groups, New Labour sought to introduce a new Mental Health Act through a top-down and combative approach that prioritized public safety over patients' rights (Cairney, 2009, 676–77).

In the face of continuing opposition both within and outside Parliament, the Government scaled down its ambitions and devised the Mental Health Bill 2006—a piece of legislation that would amend the MHA 1983 rather than replacing it (Daw, 2007). The eventual MHA 2007 broadened the definition of mental disorder in the MHA 1983 to include 'any disorder or disability of mind' and replaced the treatability criterion with the much less stringent 'appropriate medical treatment' test.[1] The DSPD Programme began several years before the MHA 2007 was introduced, demonstrating that the MHA 1983 as originally enacted was sufficiently flexible to permit the detention of people with personality disorder in psychiatric hospitals.

In a context in which both the Government and professionals were concerned to avoid blame, Michael Cavadino argued that the prospect for the DSPD group looked 'less likely to be a wonderful cure effected by treatments developed in the shiny new facilities followed by rehabilitation and timely release, and more likely to be old-fashioned long-term warehousing because no one knows how to treat them, but we are too scared to let them out' (Cavadino, 2002, 188). This commentary foreshadowed the accusations that would later be launched by the IMPALOX group[2] tasked with evaluating the pilot DSPD assessment programme for men (Tyrer et al, 2010, 97).

IMPALOX found that prisoners undergoing assessment spent less than 10 per cent of their time in therapeutic activities (Tyrer et al, 2010, 97; Barrett et al, 2009). This prompted some members of the team to conclude that the Government was 'warehousing' offenders in a programme that would allow them to 'be "parked" for long periods thereby preventing them from being released from custody and re-offending in society' (Tyrer et al, 2010, 97). While this accusation was strongly refuted by practitioners and researchers associated with the DSPD Programme (Howells et al, 2011), subsequent evaluations of the treatment programme for men in high secure settings lent credence to the allegation of 'warehousing' (O'Loughlin, 2014).

---

[1] See Chapter 2.
[2] IMPALOX was a group of researchers from Imperial College, Arnold Lodge, and the University of Oxford (Tyrer et al, 2007; 2009).

The IDEA group[3] found that formal therapy took up an average of less than two hours per week in each of the four high secure pilot units for men (Burns et al, 2011, 237).[4] At the HMP Whitemoor unit, which had been in operation for six years, weekly prisoner timetables showed an average of just 3.4 hours of scheduled therapeutic activity and 0.2 hours of 'milieu therapy' (Burns et al, 2011, 140).[5] Prisoners at HMP Whitemoor spent the majority of their time between 9am and 9pm on lockdown (24.7 hours per week), in their cells (13.2 hours), or in recreation (11.9 hours) (Burns et al, 2011, 140).

Stays on the DSPD Programme were longer than expected and progress onwards from the units was slow (Trebilcock and Weaver, 2010b, 33). Between 2006 and 2009, very few prisoners in the DSPD units had progressed onwards from the programme, and even fewer saw a reduction in their security category (Trebilcock and Weaver, 2010b). Between 2005 and 2015, just 9 per cent[6] of men referred successfully completed the treatment programme at HMP Frankland (de Motte et al, 2017, 296). Together, these findings suggested a greater focus on containment than would be expected from a supposedly intensive therapeutic initiative.

The IDEA study found little difference between the prison and hospital units in terms of treatment outcomes. There were weak but statistically significant reductions in Violence Risk Scale (VRS) scores[7] in both prisoners and high secure hospital patients, suggesting that treatment may have reduced the risk of reoffending in the short term (Ministry of Justice, 2011, 7).

---

[3] IDEA stands for 'Inclusion for DSPD: Evaluating Assessment and Treatment'. The IDEA evaluation was led by the University of Oxford.

[4] The Multi-method Evaluation of the Management, Organisation and Staffing (MEMOS) in high security treatment services for people with DSPD was conducted by a separate team at Imperial College and King's College London at the same time as the IDEA study. The MEMOS study reported that patients spent slightly more time in therapy, at less than 2.7 hours on average per week (Trebilcock and Weaver, 2010b, 53). Keyworker sessions at the hospital units added another 69 minutes of 'milieu therapy' (Trebilcock and Weaver, 2010b, 54). Burns et al (2011, xiv) noted an additional 2.7 hours of 'milieu therapy' in the hospital units.

[5] While 'milieu therapy' was not given a specific definition in the IDEA report, in the MEMOS report it referred to 'community meetings, ad-hoc counselling and individual support sessions that were not part of the formal treatment programme' (Trebilcock and Weaver, 2010a, 14). More broadly, 'milieu therapy' refers to providing a supportive therapeutic environment in which patients can benefit from interactions with staff and other patients (Jones, 2015).

[6] This represents 26 men out of 286 referred to the unit.

[7] The VRS is a standardized, third-wave risk assessment instrument that measures six historical or static risk factors, including the individual's age at first conviction, and 20 dynamic risk factors, including criminal attitudes, emotional control, and insight into violence to give an indication of the likelihood that the person will be violent in future (Burns et al, 2011, 45–46). For discussion of risk assessment instruments, see Chapter 2.

Due to the lack of a control group, it was not possible for the researchers to say for certain these changes were the result of treatment or other factors affecting the participants (Ministry of Justice, 2011, 7). There was some evidence that the management of inmates in prisons may have been more effective than in hospitals, as fewer violent incidents were reported in prison units than in hospital units. However, hospitals may have had a lower threshold for recording such incidents than prisons (Burns et al, 2011, 73 and 177). Nevertheless, 'despite the dangerousness of the sample and the very negative and hostile emotions expressed, relatively few security incidents occurred' (Burns et al, 2011, xvii). The researchers attributed this to 'relational and procedural security, including the high staff ratio based in relatively small units' (Burns et al, 2011, xvii).

Given the independent evaluations were not able to demonstrate a robust impact on reoffending rates, their findings raise the question of why the DSPD Programme has survived in the guise of the Offender Personality Disorder (OPD) Pathway. Its survival suggests that there is a need to look beyond the rhetoric of reducing reoffending that infuses official policies on rehabilitation.

4.3 Explaining the Outcomes of the DSPD Programme

The accusation that the DSPD programme was engaging in the mere 'warehousing' of offenders the Government was too afraid to release would seem to fit with the contention that the aim of late-modern penality is to control and contain rather than to change offenders (Garland, 2001; Rutherford, 1997; Simon, 1998). However, the centrality of treatment to the compromise underlying the DSPD proposals discussed in Chapter 3 suggests that 'warehousing' was not the intention. The outcomes of the DSPD initiative therefore present a puzzle: why were patients and prisoners spending so little time in therapy or in constructive activities? And why was progress through the Programme so slow?

As set out below, policymakers overlooked key lessons from the past in their haste to reassure the public that something was being done about 'dangerous' offenders. In the DSPD units themselves, the characteristics of a difficult patient group, coupled with tensions between the therapeutic models of the units and the wider security practices of their host prisons, impeded progress in therapy. While the DSPD Programme achieved some successes in safely managing prisoners, the evidence it generated did not meet the high standards of evidence-based medicine. A review published in 2012 concluded that 'the key question—what treatments are effective for high-risk personality disordered offenders—remains unanswered' (Völlm and Konappa, 2012, 165).

Unrealistic expectations and the need 'to be seen to be doing something'

Given the difficulties encountered in treating 'psychopathic' patients and prisoners in the past,[8] it may seem that policymakers involved in the DSPD Programme were naïvely optimistic about what it could achieve. It would, however, be more accurate to say that civil servants were aware of some of the difficulties involved but pressed ahead, and that the political priorities of ministers took precedence when it came to implementing the plans. Jack Straw and Tony Blair had long been preoccupied with the problem of 'dangerous' and 'prolific' offenders (Annison, 2015, 31–32). Ministers focused on responding to perceived public concerns amplified by media campaigns: a dynamic that characterized other criminal justice initiatives of the Blair era (Kemshall and Weaver, 2012; Annison, 2015, ch 2).

The DSPD Programme was based on the idea that there was a causal link between the risk of reoffending and personality disorder (Duggan and Howard, 2009). Like the DSPD proposals, the 'underpinning philosophy' of the Programme was 'that public protection [would] be best served by addressing the mental health needs of a previously neglected group' (DSPD Programme et al, 2008, 6). This can be seen from the entry criteria for men's high secure services:

> An individual will be considered to meet the criteria . . . if he is assessed as being more likely than not to reoffend, resulting in serious physical or psychological harm from which the victim would find it difficult or impossible to recover. The risk of reoffending must also be linked to the presence of a severe personality disorder (DSPD Programme et al, 2008, 2).[9]

---

[8] See Chapter 3.
[9] Similar criteria were in place for women (DSPD Programme et al, 2006, 8). For more detailed discussion of the DSPD criteria, see O'Loughlin (2014) and O'Loughlin (2019).

However, although there is an association between personality disorder and violence, it is unclear whether the relationship is causal (Howard, R., 2015, 1; see Chapter 2). Even if the causal link were stronger, there was a paucity of good quality evidence for the effectiveness of existing treatments at the time the DSPD Programme began. A review of the evidence commissioned by the Home Office found a near-total lack of clinical literature on either 'severe' or 'dangerous' personality disorder and concluded that, overall, there was 'no evidence that "DSPD" can or cannot be treated' (Warren et al, 2003, 120). While some studies reported successes in treating offenders with personality disorder, several were methodologically flawed and it was unclear if their findings could be generalized to high-security prisoners (Warren et al, 2003). The most promising intervention was participation in a therapeutic community and there was some evidence to support the use of dialectical behaviour therapy (DBT) with women with borderline personality disorder (BPD) (Warren et al, 2003).

A civil servant involved with the pilot programme nevertheless envisaged an intervention 'in the pharmacological sense' (Civil Servant 2) in which patients and prisoners would receive two or three years of intensive treatment and then move on. The scant evidence-base for existing treatments suggests that this was an unrealistic expectation. Another problem with this expectation was expressed by a different policymaker:

> given the nature of the sorts of patients who had been cared for in those [DSPD] units ... and the complexity and the lack of understanding [of their disorders], the fact that it was a developmental service, almost made it inevitable that you weren't going to see results for ten or twenty years (Civil Servant 1).

Another interviewee expressed this more bluntly: 'Nobody in their right mind could believe in a million years that personality disorder can be treated within a three-year period. It goes against all the science' (Academic 1). There was, however, pressure on the Programme to demonstrate results very speedily. A decade or two was 'a very long time for policy, because governments turn over so quickly' (Civil Servant 1).

Policymakers involved with the DSPD Programme recognized some of the problems with its premises. One described the idea of a demonstrable link as 'a bit of a fudge' because 'how would you know whether something was causative or co-occurring?' (Civil Servant 2). Nevertheless, they were clearly willing to forge ahead. Part of the explanation can be found in how they viewed their role:

> if there's a policy imperative from ministers and they wish to see something happen, then the job of the civil service is to find a way of enabling the policy to be put into effect (Civil Servant 1).

From the point of view of ministers, the DSPD Programme offered a means of alleviating political pressure. The pilots would provide 'a vehicle for putting difficult things in a box and saying "yes, we're doing something about it, but we'll need to wait to see what the results are" ' (Civil Servant 2). Then, by the time the pilots had gotten off the ground, 'to some extent the imperatives, the immediacy around being seen to be doing something had gone, because you *were* doing something' (Civil Servant 2).

The plans for the DSPD group clearly helped ministers to respond to high profile cases of released offenders that garnered media attention. This not only included the Michael Stone case[10] but also the impending release of notorious convicted sex offenders such as Robert Oliver (HC Deb, 15 February 1999, col. 601). In response to questions in Parliament, Minister Paul Boateng specified that 'violent, predatory paedophiles' would be targeted by the DSPD initiative (HC Deb, 25 February 1999, col. 394W).

Ministerial priorities meant that reassuring the public took precedence over working out the finer details of the DSPD Programme. While the high secure units were intended to fit into a 'whole service' approach that would encourage progression (Department of Health, Home Office and HM Prison Service, 2001, 1), the 75 places planned in NHS medium secure units and hostels for men were dwarfed by the 300 places planned for high secure services (DSPD Programme et al, 2008, 6–7). No pilots were established in lower security category prisons for men and only 12 dedicated prison places were created for women (DSPD Programme et al, 2006).

The reason for the focus on high secure services was explained by one policymaker:

> We would never have got the money from the Treasury to set up the whole end-to-end service as a single entity from the start from scratch. Never, ever, ever. What you had to do was to start focusing on the people

---

[10] See Chapter 3.

who were of the greatest public concern, and they're the people in the high security services, and so you try doing something about them and then spread out from that (Civil Servant 3).[11]

As a result, options for onward progression were limited and uncertainties regarding pathways out of the units had a detrimental effect on prisoner and patient engagement with therapy (Trebilcock and Weaver, 2010b; 2010a; Burns et al, 2011).

The DSPD units not only received individuals who were thought to be dangerous to the public but also individuals who presented management challenges (Kirkpatrick et al, 2010, 278).[12] This not only included individuals with high psychopathy ratings but also those whose behaviour was 'characterised by high levels of emotional instability or repeated incidents of self-harm indicative of [borderline personality disorder]' (Kirkpatrick et al, 2010, 278). Many prisoners in the HMP Whitemoor DSPD unit had spent time in segregation and tightly controlled close supervision centres (CSCs) due to violent or self-harming behaviour, substance abuse, or inappropriate relationships with staff (Saradjian et al, 2013, 435).

Concentrating large numbers of such individuals in small units would make the DSPD units challenging places to work for any staff who were enthusiastic enough not to be put off by the barrage of criticism the DSPD initiative attracted from professional groups (Royal College of Nursing, 2000a; 2000b; Royal College of Psychiatrists, 2000; Haddock et al, 2001, 294). While policymakers recognized this difficulty, high staff turnover, burnout, staff shortages, and young and inexperienced staff were recurring themes in the high secure units (Trebilcock and Weaver, 2010a). The medium secure units also experienced problems with staff recruitment, retention, and stress due to an extremely challenging patient group (Moran et al, 2008).

To some extent, these difficulties could have been foreseen. In the early 2000s, inspections of close supervision centres (CSCs), much smaller than the DSPD prison units, highlighted the strains on staff health and morale associated with concentrating the most disruptive prisoners in small units. Little meaningful activity was being provided for prisoners in the most restrictive CSCs, lockdown was common, staff were under considerable stress

---

[11] The Treasury was also a source of resistance to the IPP sentence on cost grounds. See Annison (2015), 71–72.
[12] The OPD Pathway, the successor of the DSPD Programme, also targets disruptive prisoners. See Chapter 5 for further discussion.

with high levels of sickness absence, and there was poor progression for prisoners (HM Chief Inspector of Prisons, 2000; Clare and Bottomley, 2001). Given that the DSPD prison units encountered many of the same problems, it seems that lessons were not fully learned.

A further difficulty was the challenge of motivating inmates to engage with treatment. The prospects for treating a population who were viewed as 'untreatable' by some psychiatrists and who had little incentive to co-operate with a programme that seemed to have begun with the object of detaining them indefinitely were poor (Peay, 1999). Psychological treatments required participants, at the very least, to engage with their therapists, and success required motivation for change and perseverance. While the plans for the DSPD Programme recognized this, 'considerations of need and public safety' took priority in admission decisions (DSPD Programme et al, 2008, 12) and transfer to a DSPD unit for assessment could take place without the candidate's consent (DSPD Programme et al, 2006; 2008).

While the Fallon Inquiry had advised ending the use of hospitals 'as surrogate prisons' (Fallon et al, 1999a, para 1.43.7), political determination to use hospitals for preventive detention meant that the problems associated with transferring prisoners to hospital late in their sentences resurfaced under the DSPD Programme. Up to 90 per cent of patients admitted to high secure DSPD hospital units had been transferred there from prison, and most (65 per cent) had been serving determinate sentences (Trebilcock and Weaver, 2012b). Most were admitted close to their expected release date, with 20 per cent of determinate sentenced prisoners transferred to hospital less than two weeks before they had expected to be released (Trebilcock and Weaver, 2012b).[13] This resulted in a significant minority of patients who were refusing to engage with treatment, as described by a psychiatrist who worked in a hospital DSPD unit:

> there were these cohorts of people coming in at the absolute end of their sentence, and quite literally thinking "I'm going to be a free man tomorrow but hey, here I am in [a high secure hospital] with the prospect of another lengthy stay". So there were very disaffected, disgruntled, disillusioned people coming in as a result. And obviously since they were not happy, they expressed their anger and frustration in behavioural ways (Psychiatrist 2).

---

[13] This figure has been calculated by the author from Trebilcock and Weaver (2012b).

Patients in medium secure units similarly expressed frustrations with being 'arrested' at the prison gate and taken to hospital (Moran et al, 2008, 161). The presence of patients in the high secure hospital units refusing to engage with treatment was seen by other patients as having a negative influence on their own motivation (Burns et al, 2011, 217–19).

While prisoners were not subject to compulsory treatment powers under the MHA 1983, some prisoners undergoing assessment for the DSPD Programme felt they had been coerced into agreeing to it. This was either because the Parole Board demanded they complete assessment or because they were threatened with losing their enhanced status on the Incentives and Earned Privileges scheme (Tyrer et al, 2007, 52). These prisoners were more recalcitrant than the 'treatment-seeking' early volunteers (Tyrer et al, 2007, 51).

With the benefit of hindsight, the aims of the DSPD Programme in respect of treatment were unrealistically optimistic. Despite recognizing some of the problems with the premises of the pilot programme, policymakers pressed forward with the plans due to political pressures 'to be seen to be doing something' about public concerns. The premise that personality disorder and offending were causally related was questionable, and the evidence-base for successful treatments was thin. Both the prison and hospital units housed disruptive or distressed individuals for whom therapy was likely to be a slow process and who put strain on staff. While experience cautioned against using hospitals for the purposes of preventive detention, the hospital units were left with a disgruntled group of patients who resisted treatment. Any impact on recidivism would take many years to come to light, and the tightly controlled environments of the DSPD units made testing out progress in treatment difficult. As a result, the extent to which the DSPD units could provide the intensive therapeutic interventions envisaged by policymakers was compromised.

Security and therapy

Specialist therapeutic units are vulnerable within the prison setting, and conflicts between therapeutic aims and the aims of the prison tend to be resolved in favour of the prison (Genders and Player, 1995; 2010; 2022; Sparks, 2002). Importantly, the aims of the prison go beyond a concern with reducing reoffending and include maintaining external security, upholding order and control, and providing a safe and 'decent' environment for prisoners (Crewe, 2009, 26). The empirical evidence from the DSPD Programme shows that the survival of experimental therapeutic units hinges on the extent to which such units serve the interests of the prison. Secure hospitals have similar concerns in respect of forensic patients, albeit with a greater emphasis on providing a therapeutic environment, improving patients' mental health, and enhancing their quality of life (Bartlett and Kesteven, 2010). The decision to decommission the DSPD hospital units may be attributable to the difficulties the hospitals experienced in managing a difficult patient group, coupled with a realization of the costliness of hospital places. By contrast, the DSPD units produced benefits for the wider prison system, particularly for the management of difficult prisoners, and contributed to a growing sense that personality disorder can be treated.

The same civil servant who envisaged the DSPD Programme as a 'pharmacological' intervention attributed the failure of this model to the cultures of the secure hospital and prison estates:

> The prison service model and the health model to a degree colluded . . . to put the programme in the space of therapeutic environment. So you spend as long as you need to before you get the benefit, as opposed to it's a relatively short period of active intervention, you get intensive support, intensive challenge, you review, you say yes it's worked or it hasn't worked (Civil Servant 2).

Both prisoners and patients interviewed by the IDEA team commented that security procedures interfered with the therapeutic aims of the high secure DSPD units (Burns et al, 2011, 215–17). In addition, the security policies of the host institutions restricted the extent to which the DSPD units could operate in line with their clinical models (Trebilcock and Weaver, 2010b; see also Taylor, 2011).

There is, however, evidence that the prison DSPD units made progress in successfully negotiating the tensions between security and therapy. At the time the DSPD Programme began, prisons were focusing on security. High profile prison escapes in the mid-1990s ushered in 'a new era of "security first" and risk management' and a move from '"fostering choice and responsibility" towards secure containment' (Liebling, 2016, 490). At HMP Whitemoor, by 2010 'a broad and dominant security orientation . . . squeezed out relationships, humanity, trust, and in the eyes of prisoners, legitimacy' (Liebling, 2013, 216). One of the many drivers of this process was a political climate that was resistant to 'pampering' prisoners (Liebling,

2013, 215). Nevertheless, Alison Liebling and her team described good relationships between staff and prisoners in the HMP Whitemoor DSPD unit (Liebling et al, 2011, 163). The prison's 'strength seemed to lie in the careful and close management of extremely difficult individual prisoners, in small or special locations, where partnership working (eg with mental health staff and external services) was exceptional' (Liebling et al, 2011, 164).

Tensions between wider prison culture at first generated resistance to therapeutic measures amongst prison officers working in the HMP Whitemoor DSPD unit. Officers were wary of the therapeutic model as they felt it threatened the smooth management of prisoners and generated risks to the safety and security of staff (Fox, 2010). Prison officers who embraced their therapeutic role were treated with suspicion by colleagues both within and beyond the DSPD unit who disapproved of 'caring' for prisoners (Fox, 2010). These tensions were eventually resolved as officers came to see that the programme was working towards reductions in risks to the public in the long-term and became more tolerant of the short-term risks to safety and good order provoked by treatment (Fox, 2010).

Practitioners in the former DSPD prison units revealed in interview that tensions with their host prisons required ongoing negotiation. One psychologist practicing in a DSPD unit commented that the unit was 'walking on a tightrope between security and therapy', and that while 'security always comes first', there was room for some negotiation (Psychologist 1). While the DSPD prison units came to be accepted by their wider prisons as places that could manage the most difficult prisoners, the apparent current consensus on rehabilitation as an aim of prisons relied on therapy serving the interests of the prison.

Similar tensions between therapy and security played out in high secure DSPD hospital units. In the 1980s and 1990s, high secure hospitals in England and Wales were criticized for having a prison-like culture (Bartlett, 2016, 24). But the 1999 Fallon Inquiry revealed lapses in security that were exploited by patients in the personality disorder unit of Ashworth hospital. In the wake of the Ashworth scandal and the DSPD initiative, mental health services were again 'told to focus on risk, not treatment' (Bartlett, 2016, 306). The frustrations experienced by patients on the DSPD Programme with low levels of therapeutic activity suggest that this culture persisted into the 2000s.

As one psychiatrist who worked within a DSPD unit commented, 'the whole ethos of high security hospitals in relation to personality disorder was not so much treating them but just kind of waiting them out and custodial'

(Psychiatrist 1). This suggests that secure hospitals in the DSPD era continued to rely upon the notion that the natural process of aging would reduce patients' risk of reoffending. In the 1980s, maturation was often cited by psychiatrists in Broadmoor as a reason for discharging 'psychopathic' patients (Dell and Robertson, 1988, ch 8). Broadmoor doctors assumed that aging in older men would diminish their physical strength and sexual drive, and that young men would 'calm down as they [got] older' (Dell and Robertson, 1988, 121 and 100). This idea is supported to some extent by research showing that antisocial behaviour peaks in adolescence and decreases markedly with age (Moffitt, 1993) and that most antisocial and psychopathic personalities go into remission when patients reach their 30s and 40s (Martens, 2000). However, this approach is likely to lead to frustration, particularly amongst patients who see treatment as a route towards release (see McRae 2013; 2015).

While the DSPD Programme did not seem to live up to the expectation that it would provide intensive therapeutic interventions, one of its neglected successes is that it managed to engage with a challenging population who had previously been regarded as untreatable (Howells et al, 2011, 130). Prisoners reported subjective benefits from the assessment process for the DSPD Programme, including greater insights into their own problems and new ways of thinking they believed would help them to move forward (Tyrer et al, 2007). None of the prisoners had previously been offered such an opportunity, although some reported having participated in the Sex Offender Treatment Programme (SOTP) (Tyrer et al, 2007). This reflects the paucity of treatment provision in prisons for personality disorder prior to the establishment of the DSPD programme. While the IDEA study found that patients and prisoners were frustrated with time spent 'waiting' for therapy, some participants felt they had benefitted from therapeutic input, work and creative or recreational activities (Burns et al, 2011, 209–12).

Investment in the DSPD Programme also led to the development of national personality disorder services and research programmes that could be expected to benefit people beyond the DSPD category (Tyrer et al, 2010; see also Howells et al, 2011). The provision of specialist personality disorder training by the Department of Health and the formulation of clinical guidelines on BPD and antisocial personality disorder (ASPD) would not have taken place without the DSPD initiative (Duggan, 2011). More concretely, the purpose-built DSPD units provided the additional treatment capacity needed to accommodate patients with personality disorder within the hospital system, and, as set out above, the prison DSPD units managed difficult and disruptive prisoners at a much lower cost than in other parts of the prison system. A combination of the introduction of the DSPD Programme and the promotion of the idea that personality disorder should 'no longer [be] a diagnosis of exclusion' (National Institute for Mental Health in England, 2003) has contributed to an emerging consensus that personality disorder is treatable (Pickersgill, 2013). It is likely that the achievements of these ongoing processes were cemented and legitimized by eventual legislative changes rather than prompted by them.

It was also clear that the DSPD Programme achieved some successes in managing violent and self-harming prisoners at a lower cost than in other parts of the prison estate (O'Loughlin, 2014; 2019). The Department of Health (2011, 6) found that if DSPD Programme were to close, the use of CSCs was likely to significantly increase, costing £60,000 more per prisoner per year. Managing these prisoners without therapeutic interventions was also likely to put additional pressure on prison segregation units and to lead to greater use of transfers to costly secure hospitals (Department of Health, 2011, 6). The Ministry of Justice later acknowledged the problems experienced by the hospital DSPD units and advised that transfers should take place as early in sentence as possible (Ministry of Justice and NOMS, 2010). Late transfers nevertheless remain a legal possibility so long as the legal criteria are 'scrupulously satisfied'.[14]

Despite these positive achievements, participation in the DSPD Programme could cause harm to individuals. Concerningly, an independent evaluation of the Chromis Programme at HMP Frankland found that treatment was associated with an increase in self-harm incidents and rule-breaking behaviour (de Motte et al, 2017). The authors of the study suggested that this was due to the emotional demands that treatment placed on prisoners and the absence of dedicated support for self-harming prisoners (de Motte et al, 2017, 296). The risks that participation in therapeutic programmes in coercive settings pose to prisoners are returned to below.

It is also clear that the DSPD Programme has a tainted legacy. In 2018, Professor Sir Simon Wessely, chair of the Independent Review of the MHA 1983, characterized the decisions made by the Government in the lead-up to the MHA 2007 as an overreaction to the failings in risk management revealed by the cases of Michael Stone and Christopher Clunis (Department of Health and Social Care, 2018, 7). For Wessely, the initial optimism

---

[14] *R (SP) v Secretary of State for Justice* [2010] EWCA Civ 1590; [2009] EWHC 2168 (Admin).

sparked by the DSPD initiative had 'largely given way to disappointment as it became clear that most were just being detained for the protection of the public' (Department of Health and Social Care, 2018, 7).

When I spoke to them more than 10 years after its demise, the idea of a separate service for the DSPD group was generally still regarded by the policymakers who developed the DSPD proposals as the best solution to the problems identified. One policymaker expressed regret that it had never come to pass and attributed this failure to the inability of the policy team 'to be completely crystal clear about describing this group in a way that would resonate with politicians generally and with other opinion formers and with the public' (Civil Servant 3). Another agreed that the third service was still the best way of doing things, and that it had not been 'given a sufficient enough try' (Politician 1). A third was perhaps more realistic, commenting in relation to the third service that 'you could say, "well it was always rose-tinted spectacles that would have said that you can develop the whole thing"' (Civil Servant 1).

How do we measure success?

The challenges to conducting robust empirical research in secure settings further impeded the extent to which the DSPD Programme was able to demonstrate success in the short term. While policymakers hoped that the pilots would develop a 'what works' evidence-base' for the management of the DSPD group (Department of Health, 2000, para 6.23), they became a battleground for competing views on what could be taken as evidence of success or failure. Researchers encountered barriers to conducting high-quality outcome research, and the DSPD Programme did not live up to the expectation that it would produce appreciable results quickly. As a result, doubts as to the effectiveness of treatments for personality disorder persist.

As Williams and Glasby argue, the call for evidence-based policy 'is essentially a statement of a dilemma rather than a positive blueprint for the way forward' (Williams and Glasby, 2010, 95). The argument that policy should be evidence-based raises more questions than it answers: 'what constitutes valid evidence? Who decides? Are some forms of evidence granted more weight than others? What happens when the evidence is partial, fragmented or even contradictory?' (Williams and Glasby, 2010, 95). Different groups involved in the DSPD Programme took rather different perspectives on what is meant by evidence-based policy or practice. The Programme's evaluators followed the evidence-based medicine paradigm, which views the randomized controlled trial (RCT) as the 'gold standard' (Cairney, 2016, 52). By contrast, DSPD Programme practitioners and researchers favoured the 'practice-based evidence gathering' and 'improvement science' approach described by Paul Cairney (2016, 72–74).

These rather different perspectives emerged in series of articles in which authors affiliated with the DSPD Programme clashed with Professor Peter Tyrer, the leader of the IMPALOX evaluation, and colleagues on his research team. Kevin Howells and colleagues (2011) affiliated with the University of Nottingham and the DSPD unit at Rampton hospital wrote a response to Tyrer et al's (2010) accusation that the DSPD Programme was 'warehousing' prisoners. Howells and colleagues contended that 'a scientific rather than a scientistic approach' was required for the future evaluation of the Programme (Howells et al, 2011, 132). The former 'would involve systematically and organically building up knowledge about the population, their characteristics and needs, the service itself and the therapies offered and their outcomes' while 'the latter would jump prematurely and exclusively to methods wearing the badge of scientific respectability' (Howells et al, 2011, 132). They cited the RCT as an example of such a method, which they contended had 'an important, but not exclusive, role to play in the longer term' (Howells et al, 2011, 132). These comments contrasted with the evidence-based medicine approach endorsed by the Department of Health (2000), which commissioned the IMPALOX team to carry out an RCT of the assessment process for prisoners.

Another area of contention was whether the treatments delivered by the DSPD Programme could be described as 'evidence-based'. This appeared to be a misleading term when applied to the DSPD Programme given that a Home Office-commissioned review concluded that there was 'no evidence that "DSPD" can or cannot be treated' (Warren et al, 2003, 120). The programmes developed by the individual DSPD units did, however, draw on treatments that were supported by some evidence from studies with other populations, including DBT for self-harm in women with BPD (Linehan et al, 1991; 1993; Linehan, 1993) and cognitive behavioural therapy (CBT) for patients with ASPD (Davidson and Tyrer, 1996).

The use of such treatments can be understood through the lens of 'improvement science' (Cairney, 2016, 74). DSPD practitioners drew on the available evidence to develop experimental treatment programmes, conducted their own studies of the DSPD cohort, and published literature describing their treatment models (Saradjian et al, 2010; 2013; Tennant and

Howells, 2010; Tew and Atkinson, 2013). This approach was, however, unlikely to produce the type of evidence required by the evidence-based medicine paradigm (see Tyrer et al, 2015).

The nature of DSPD services presented further barriers to the production of robust evidence. Conducting RCTs is challenging in secure settings as the needs of the experiment often conflict with the established security protocols and institutional practices that tend to take priority in the day-to-day running of services (Tyrer et al, 2009, 142). Consequently, the research produced by independent evaluations fell short of the 'gold standard'. While Tyrer and colleagues did attempt to conduct an RCT of the DSPD assessment process, the results of the experiment were compromised as the staff responsible for selecting prisoners for assessment did not always follow the randomization protocol (Tyrer et al, 2015). The IDEA and MEMOS studies did not include control groups. Instead, outcomes for the same inmates were compared over time and descriptive data of the services and treatment groups were gathered alongside qualitative data from interviews with staff and inmates. As set out in Chapter 2, there continues to be insufficient evidence to conclude whether current treatments for ASPD are effective, particularly when it comes to reducing serious recidivism. The picture is more positive for BPD, but the evidence demonstrates reductions in distress and self-harm rather than in violence.

4.4 Competing Constructions of 'Dangerous' People with Severe Personality Disorders

Despite the difficulties encountered in generating robust evidence for the effectiveness of the DSPD Programme, completing the intervention became a key means for prisoners and patients to progress towards release. I have argued in earlier work that the DSPD Programme presented a means for disruptive or difficult prisoners to move from exclusionary practices of risk management predicated on long-term segregation into mainstream practices that promised a more humane and cost-effective means of governing them (O'Loughlin, 2019). Building on this analysis, the discussion below demonstrates that competing constructions of the DSPD group in practice tended to undermine this ambition and to create a double bind. Offenders were required to engage with the DSPD Programme to have any chance of release, but complying with it was not a clear path to release. Participation could even slow down their progress through two mechanisms: longer stays in prison on indeterminate sentences and extensions to detention through transfers to hospital.

On the one hand, treatment programmes constructed the DSPD group as rational subjects with the capacity to learn self-control and to regulate their own behaviour. On the other hand, the DSPD label suggested that participants in the programme were unpredictable, aggressive, manipulative, and dangerous. Personality disorder is a 'very sticky label' (National Institute for Mental Health in England, 2003, para 40) and the same has been said about psychopathy (Hare, 1998). Sticky labels tend to follow a person through life, and the stigma and negative attitudes associated with them can adversely affect how the person is treated by the criminal justice and health systems.[15] Similarly, judgements of dangerousness or high risk are often based on past behaviour, such as offending or institutional disciplinary infractions, and such labels are therefore difficult to shed and can become self-fulfilling (Ashworth and Zedner, 2014, 123). In the case of DSPD, these sticky labels interacted with the risk aversion and therapeutic scepticism of decision-makers charged with determining progressive moves towards release.

Where a prisoner's risk of reoffending is considered by the prison authorities to be linked to a personality disorder, prisoners who refuse to engage with treatment are unlikely to progress down through prison security categories and towards parole. This can be seen from case law. As the first DSPD units were in Category A prisons, the Parole Board was unlikely to recommend prisoners serving indeterminate sentences for transfer to open conditions or to direct their release from prison.[16] Category A Review Teams (CART) are responsible for considering applications for downgrading a Category A prisoner's security category. The CART makes recommendations to the Deputy Director of Custody (High Security) in HM Prison and Probation Service, who is ultimately responsible for categorization decisions (NOMS, 2013).[17]

In *S*, the Deputy Director of Custody High Security decided not to downgrade a prisoner to Category B on the grounds, inter alia, that he was 'not satisfied that he [could] make the judgment on risk which he is required to make without the whole six years of the Fens Unit [DSPD] programme

---

[15] For further discussion of personality disorder and stigma, see Chapter 2.
[16] These are the only options open to the Parole Board in respect of such prisoners (Beard, 2023, 9).
[17] HM Prison & Probation Service was formerly part of the National Offender Management Service (NOMS).

being completed'.[18] This decision was upheld by the High Court on judicial review. In *Falconer*,[19] a CART refused to recommend that the claimant's security category be downgraded because, although his behaviour in prison had been good and he had participated in some programmes, he had not addressed his violent offending. The High Court held that it was 'in the prisoner's own interests that he undertakes the work required by the DSPD programme, onerous as it is, so as to establish the grounds for a finding that the risk he presents is substantially reduced'.[20] In the absence of participation in the programme he was unlikely to make further progress towards release.

Discharge directly into the community from a secure hospital is rare and patients, like prisoners, are expected 'to undertake a journey through the different levels of security' (Trebilcock and Weaver, 2010b, 65). Prisoners serving determinate sentences who are transferred to secure hospitals will not be discharged from detention until their sentence expires and the First Tier Tribunal (Mental Health) in England or the Mental Health Tribunal for Wales is *not* satisfied:

> (i) that [the patient] is then suffering from mental disorder or from mental disorder of a nature or degree which makes it appropriate for him to be liable to be detained in a hospital for medical treatment; or (ii) that it is necessary for the health and safety of the patient or for the protection of other persons that he should receive such treatment; or (iia) that appropriate medical treatment is available for him.[21]

Given these criteria, engaging with treatment is a key means for secure hospital patients to progress towards discharge from hospital.

The empirical evidence makes clear that engaging with the DSPD Programme was not a straightforward route towards release for patients and prisoners given the DSPD label, and that selection for the programme could impede their progress. In a study of decision-making by members of the Parole Board and Mental Health Review Tribunal (MHRT),[22] both groups expressed scepticism regarding the effectiveness of treatment on the

---

[18] *R (S) v Secretary of State for Justice* [2009] EWHC 2168 (Admin), [65].
[19] *R (Falconer) v Secretary of State for Justice* [2009] EWHC 2341 (Admin).
[20] ibid, [29].
[21] MHA 1983, s 72(1)(b). Emphasis added.
[22] The MHRT has since been renamed the First Tier Tribunal (Mental Health) in England. In Wales, the relevant tribunal is the Mental Health Tribunal for Wales.

DSPD Programme (Trebilcock and Weaver, 2012b; 2012a). Despite these reservations, some MHRT members 'suggested that until patients had engaged with and completed treatment, they were unlikely to be considered by the MHRT for a progressive move' (Trebilcock and Weaver, 2010b, 76). MHRT members were also likely to err on the side of caution when it came to making decisions about patients who were detained in DSPD units in order to avoid blame. They reported that Tribunals and other key decision-makers in the mental health system had become increasingly risk-averse. MHRT members 'were concerned not only about the risks of DSPD patients to themselves or others, but also sensitive of the risks to the credibility of MHRT decision-making' (Trebilcock and Weaver, 2010b, 70).

Similarly, selection for the DSPD Programme could have the effect of delaying a prisoner's progress. Parole Board members were concerned that the lengthy assessment and treatment process associated with the DSPD Programme could delay prisoners' progress into lower security settings. The DSPD Programme was perceived as a disruption to prisoners' expected journeys through the prison system as it 'introduced unknown, unaccredited and individualised treatment interventions into a highly structured system' (Trebilcock and Weaver, 2012a, 148).

Both MHRT and Parole Board members were concerned that the high security, surveillance, and staffing levels of the DSPD units meant that participants' progress in treatment was not being adequately tested, and that improvements in their behaviour could be attributed to the tightly controlled environment (Trebilcock and Weaver, 2012a; 2012b). Paradoxically, therefore, the need to demonstrate reduced risk requires institutions to take the risk of an adverse incident occurring, but the need to avoid adverse incidents precludes risk-taking.

The views of MHRT members in respect of the DSPD group suggest a more fundamental scepticism regarding the capacity for patients diagnosed with personality disorders to change for the better. While Parole Board members attached more weight to the high security categorisation of prisoners on the DSPD Programme than to the label 'DSPD', MHRT members saw DSPD patients and other 'psychopathic disorder'[23] patients as 'fundamentally different to other patients' (Trebilcock and Weaver, 2010b, 66). While MHRT members saw mental illness as 'episodic, amenable to medical intervention and a condition that patients had potential to

---

[23] This category has since been abolished by the MHA 2007.

"recover" from', they saw personality disorder 'as an enduring, or even fixed characteristic of the patient requiring long term management' (Trebilcock and Weaver, 2012b, 250). MHRT members viewed DSPD patients as 'particularly manipulative and skilled at convincing professionals that they are ready for discharge' (Trebilcock and Weaver, 2010b, 70) and seemed 'to regard the likelihood of reoffending by DSPD patients to be high, almost inevitable' (Trebilcock and Weaver, 2010b, 67).

Similar scepticism regarding the capacity of prisoners with personality disorder to change can be seen in the recent case of *Clarke*,[24] in which a prisoner challenged the refusal by a CART to recommend him for Category B. Even though the applicant had completed several offending behaviour courses, psychologists were concerned that he was engaging in 'impression management' to secure recategorization and that this was a manifestation of his personality disorder. The CART concluded that the claimant's personality traits influenced his behaviour and that '[his] progress through interventions may be unreliable as an indicator of significant change'.[25] This case suggests that engaging with treatment can be interpreted by prison authorities as an attempt at manipulation and a confirmation of personality disorder traits.

A similar dynamic can be seen in Dany Lacombe's (2008) ethnography of a sex offender treatment programme in prison and in Leon McRae's (2013; 2015) study of prisoners who sought transfer to a specialist personality disorder ward in a medium secure hospital. In order to show progress, prisoners in Lacombe's study had to internalize the teachings of the programme and confess to having deviant sexual fantasies. This led some to invent such fantasies. If they complied too well with the programme's teachings, however, they were subject to accusations of manipulation and psychopathy. In McRae's (2015, 331) study, the strategy of prisoners seeking treatment in a medium secure unit in order to expedite release:

> was generally taken as evidence of the very behaviour justifying the diagnosis of [severe personality disorder], rather than a form of amoral currency spent to avoid the threat of preventive detention.

The clinical literature that emerged from the DSPD Programme leaves little room for considering whether prisoners had rational reasons for

---

[24] *R (on the application of Clarke) v Secretary of State for Justice* [2022] EWHC 2577 (Admin).
[25] ibid, [39].

participating or refusing to participate in treatment. In the pilot assessment scheme, cooperative behaviour on behalf of prisoners could be interpreted by psychologists as 'manipulation' (Tyrer et al, 2010, 98). At HMP Whitemoor, refusal to engage in treatment and excessive recourse to complaints procedures, lawyers, and litigation were labelled 'treatment interfering behaviours' and explicitly understood as manifestations of personality disorder (Murphy and McVey, 2010, 136).

Taken together, this evidence suggests that DSPD patients and prisoners could find themselves in a double bind. Those who were referred to the Programme who refused to engage with treatment would have very little change of progressing towards release. But engaging with the Programme could slow down their progress towards release, and seeming to engage too well could be taken as confirmation of manipulative personality disorder traits. This double bind casts doubt on the alluring idea that the offer of innovative treatments in exchange for preventive detention would help to 'balance' the rights of 'dangerous' offenders to liberty against the right of the public to protection.

This double bind is likely to operate beyond the DSPD Programme where prisoners are identified as posing a risk to the public that is linked to a personality disorder. Prisoners who are approaching the end of a determinate prison sentence may find themselves transferred to a secure hospital, where they are expected to engage with treatment in order to work towards discharge. Or a prisoner who is serving an indeterminate prison sentence may find that they cannot make progress towards lower security settings and release without completing treatment in prison. However, scepticism on behalf of key decision-makers as to the effectiveness of treatments for personality disorder and the genuineness of participation suggests that completing treatment may not be enough to progress. High secure settings also make real-world assessments of risk more difficult, and risk averse decision-makers may be expected to err on the side of caution when deciding whether to recommend a progressive move for individuals who are thought to be dangerous. Dispelling the continuing doubts surrounding the effectiveness of the treatments offered by the DSPD Programme could go some way towards counteracting this double bind. However, it is likely to persist given the continuing paucity of evidence to support the effectiveness of interventions in reducing serious reoffending amongst those diagnosed with personality disorder.

To counteract this double bind, more robust studies are required. The gold standard would be a randomized controlled study with community follow-up on an agreed set of outcome measures, including measures of reoffending post-release. Such a study should be designed as far as possible to separate out the benefits of treatment from other effects, including maturation effects. If an RCT is not possible, a follow-up study comparing those who completed treatment under the DSPD Programme or the OPD Pathway with a retrospectively identified, well-matched control group of prisoners who were eligible for the programme could address some of the gaps in the evidence.

Better evidence will not be enough on its own. It is also necessary to address the culture of risk aversion amongst key decision-makers and the stereotyping of people diagnosed with personality disorders. Greater awareness of the research evidence on personality disorder and risk discussed in Chapter 2 amongst decision-makers, politicians, and the public could go some way towards addressing these problems. Drawing attention to the fact that personality disorders are a risk factor for offending on a par with drug and alcohol abuse could help to counteract the judgements of dangerousness that tend to attach to people who are given the label. Similarly, greater awareness of the life course of personality disorders and the capacity for people given the diagnosis to change could help to counteract stigma. Drawing attention to the limits of our current abilities to predict serious reoffending could perhaps help to counteract the blame culture that leads to risk aversion amongst decision-makers. But, fundamentally, greater tolerance of the risk that a person known to the authorities might go on to reoffend is needed to enable patients and prisoners to test out their progress in treatment and to have a realistic chance of being released.

The personality disorder double bind further raises the prospect that participants on the DSPD Programme were subjected to greater punishment than they would have been without the DSPD Programme. This possibility is considered next.

4.5 Risks of Harm and Disproportionate Punishment

The finding that treatment on the Chromis Programme was associated with increases in self-harm amongst men in a high secure DSPD unit (de Motte et al, 2017) raises the concern that prisoners were not adequately protected. Under Article 2 of the European Convention on Human Rights (ECHR), prison authorities have a duty to protect the lives of prisoners, and to do all they reasonably can to protect them from 'real and immediate' risks of suicide, including unintentional suicide through self-harming behaviour.[26] They also have a positive duty to protect prisoners from inhuman and degrading treatment and punishment or torture under Article 3 of the ECHR.[27] This includes a duty to provide mentally ill prisoners at risk of self-harm and suicide with adequate medical monitoring and treatment.[28] Providing prisoners with a rehabilitative intervention that increases their risk of self-harm without providing an adequate component of aftercare or self-harm prevention raises concerns under both Article 2 and Article 3.

It has further been shown that the judgement that a person's risk of re-offending is associated with a personality disorder can delay their release from prison or discharge from hospital into the community. This raises the possibility that patients and prisoners on the DSPD Programme were subjected to punishment beyond that deserved for their offence. This prospect ought to be taken seriously. As Lucia Zedner comments, the 'privileging of purpose' in distinguishing between penal and ostensibly non-penal forms of state power, such as preventive detention, 'does not mitigate the pains imposed by coercive measures' (Zedner, 2016, 4).

While a prisoner serving an indeterminate sentence who has surpassed their punitive tariff is not intentionally punished, the prisoner may experience their continued detention as additional punishment. This prospect is enhanced by the environments in which prisoners and patients are detained. In England and Wales, the preventive and punitive portions of indeterminate and extended determinate sentences are often served in the same prison environment and under similar conditions (Annison and O'Loughlin, 2019). Thus, the distinction drawn at sentencing between the punitive and preventive elements of an indeterminate sentence makes little difference to the prisoner's experience. The longer the prisoner is detained on preventive grounds, the greater the punishment they experience for their offence.

Similarly, while the purpose of hospital detention is not punishment, a prisoner who is transferred to hospital late in sentence for the purposes of

---

[26] *Keenan v UK* (2001) 33 EHRR 38; *Renolde v France* (2009) EHRR 42. For further discussion of duty of care, see Genders and Player, 2014.

[27] Inhuman treatment was defined by the ECtHR in *Pretty v United Kingdom* (2346/02) [2002] 2 FLR 45; [2002] 2 FCR 97; (2002) 35 EHRR 1, [52], as ' "ill-treatment" that attains a minimum level of severity and involves actual bodily injury or intense physical or mental suffering'. For more detailed discussion of the state's duties, see Genders and Player (2014) and O'Loughlin (2021b).

[28] *Keenan* and *Renolde* (n 26).

protecting the public may experience this detention as an additional punishment. As John Stanton-Ife (2012) recognizes, detention in hospital involves some of the same material deprivations that characterize imprisonment. These include limitations on freedom of movement, impaired comfort and amenity, isolation from friends, family, and the community, reduced autonomy, and loss of privacy. What seem to be missing are the 'symbolic' aspects of punishment, which include the communication of censure and blame and the intention to punish (Stanton-Ife, 2012). While Stanton-Ife acknowledges that detention under the MHA 1983 may be psychologically stigmatizing for the individual, he argues that, unlike a criminal conviction, it is not intended to be so. Nevertheless, a detainee who is insensitive to these symbolic features 'may see little or no difference between civil detention and imprisonment' (Stanton-Ife, 2012, 153). Furthermore, the types of treatments developed for offenders detained in hospitals do not differ much from those deployed in prisons (see Burns et al, 2011). In light of this, the argument that detention in hospital post-sentence is not punitive appears less convincing.

The inevitable hard treatment that comes with imprisonment may also be exacerbated by the requirement to engage with treatments that are geared towards protecting the public. Dawn Moore and Kelly Hannah-Moffat (2005) contend that rehabilitative programmes in the prison context are essentially punitive. This is because the prisoner is often forced to face traumatic past experiences and their own problems or inadequacies in a context in which they are separated from family and friends and have no freedom to choose their therapist (Moore and Hannah-Moffat, 2005). As set out in the next chapter, these risks persist continue under the successor to the DSPD Programme—the OPD Pathway.

4.6 Conclusion

Policy implementation should be regarded as a process of negotiation and compromise as policies encounter the priorities, realities, and cultures of the institutions in which policymakers are seeking to effect change. While cultures of control and containment within mental health and criminal justice institutions can impede the extent to which therapeutic programmes can achieve their aims, therapy can also be co-opted to fit with the aims of criminal justice and forensic mental health institutions. These aims are much broader than public protection, and include maintaining internal order and external security, providing a safe and humane environment to prisoners and patients, protecting staff from harm and burnout, and managing reputational risks from adverse incidents.

It is clear that the sticky labels of dangerousness and personality disorder can impede movement though systems that require prisoners or patients to engage with treatment as a prerequisite to release. Applying such labels to a person and regarding their efforts to make progress with suspicion creates a double bind from which it is very difficult to escape. This casts doubt on the idea that the state is justified in preventively detaining 'dangerous' individuals and that providing treatment can help to 'balance' their rights against those of the public. While a more robust programme of research has the potential to confirm whether rehabilitative programmes are achieving their goals, coercive treatment strategies are unlikely to succeed with offenders, and may subject them to further harm or punishment beyond what they deserve for their offences.

After the DSPD Programme, a further dilemma remains: where do serious offenders with personality disorders belong? The next chapter shows that the OPD Pathway and subsequent legal changes are funnelling people with personality disorders towards management in the prison system rather than in the mental health system. As Chapter 7 demonstrates, however, the normative debate about where these individuals belong has not yet concluded.

5
The Offender Personality Disorder Pathway

5.1 Introduction

The Offender Personality Disorder (OPD) Pathway came to replace the DSPD Programme in 2011. Under the OPD Pathway, rehabilitative interventions and trauma-informed 'custodial care' play an increasingly prominent role in managing prison safety and order. The entry criteria for the Pathway suggest that 'personality disorder' has become a shorthand for difficult and disruptive prisoners who are judged to be at a high risk of serious reoffending. While there is evidence that participants are benefitting from it, the OPD Pathway for men has not yet been able to demonstrate an impact on proven sexual or violent recidivism (Moran et al, 2022, 17–24, 27, 28). This leaves the initiative vulnerable to cuts in a policy context that focuses on rehabilitation as a means of reducing crime rates.

The OPD Pathway promotes an understanding of offenders as traumatized subjects whose challenging behaviour is a re-enactment of their past adverse experiences. While therapeutic values dictate that such behaviours require an empathetic response, the dominant cultures of the prison and probation systems continue to construct offenders as responsible and rational subjects who must be punished for breaking rules. In this context, trauma-informed care can best be characterized as a sticking plaster on a criminal justice system that places the onus on 'dangerous' offenders to demonstrate their safety to release while constructing ever-higher barriers to their reintegration into society. Like the DSPD Programme, the OPD Pathway presents a risk of causing harm to participants and of increasing the punishment they experience. While a truly rights-based framework of rehabilitation offers a potential response to these risks, efforts to rebalance the system are likely to trigger demands for 'something to be done' in response to public fears of 'dangerous' people.

5.2 The Advent of the Offender Personality Disorder Pathway

In 2011, the Conservative–Liberal Democrat Coalition Government that succeeded Labour in 2010 promised to expand the DSPD programme in prisons and in the community while dismantling the hospital units under the new, less stigmatizing title of the OPD Pathway (Department of Health and Ministry of Justice, 2011; Department of Health and NOMS, 2011a; 2011b). These reforms formed part of a broader governmental strategy of reviving rehabilitation as an aim of the criminal justice system (Ministry of Justice, 2010). The strategy also aimed to respond to Lord Bradley's (2009) Review of People with Mental Health Problems or Learning Disabilities in the Criminal Justice System, which had called for an interdepartmental response to the needs of prisoners with personality disorder beyond the DSPD group. The Department of Health and Ministry of Justice decided to absorb the original high secure DSPD prison units into the new OPD Pathway and to decommission the DSPD hospital units, which were taken over by NHS England. The resources recouped were funnelled into new treatment and progression units in lower security category prisons and in the community. The overall aim was to provide interventions for a greater number of offenders using the same resources as the DSPD Programme (Department of Health, 2011; Department of Health and NOMS, 2011a). By 2023, the budget for OPD Pathway services was £72 million, comprised of £58 million from NHS England and £14 million from HM Prison and Probation Service (HM Prison and Probation Service and NHS, 2023, 13). The focus of this chapter will be on the OPD Pathway in prisons and secure hospitals, drawing on evidence from probation services where appropriate.

Over a decade later, the OPD Pathway now incorporates a wide range of treatment, progression, and psychologically informed case management initiatives within prisons and probation, as well as specialist personality disorder services in psychiatric hospitals (NOMS and NHS England, 2015; Moran et al, 2022). While the 'main objective' of the Pathway is 'to improve public protection' it is also expected to contribute to 'reducing reoffending, improving psychological health and well-being and tackling health inequality' (Department of Health and NOMS, 2011a, para 36). Services for women on the Pathway aim more explicitly at enhancing wellbeing than those for men. Thus, the aim of the high secure Primrose Service at HMP Low Newton is to 'reduce risk to self and others, and to provide women with pro-social life skills which enhance their physical, emotional, spiritual and mental wellbeing' (d'Cruz, 2015, 51).

Initial plans for the Pathway, which ostensibly built on learning from the DSPD Programme, assumed that personality disorder and offending were linked, and that better treatment and management of the disorder would reduce recidivism (Department of Health and NOMS, 2011a, para 36). However, the OPD Pathway emphasizes identifying, monitoring, and managing the risks posed by prisoners over delivering treatments to the few that engage. The promise of the OPD Pathway, according to one interviewee involved in its development, was that it 'could make things more effective in terms of output, although not necessarily in terms of outcome' (Civil Servant 4). This distinction is important, as it shows that aspirations have narrowed. Indeed, as the same interviewee said, 'treatment is the smallest part of our programme' (Civil Servant 4).

The OPD Pathway is much larger in scale than the pilot DSPD Programme. While the New Labour Government estimated in 1999 that only 2,000 very seriously disordered and high-risk people would fall within the DSPD category, 20,000 men were expected to be eligible for the OPD Pathway in 2015 (Boateng and Sharland, 1999; Benefield et al, 2015, 4). The expansion in the number of women thought to be eligible is even more striking. Up to 1,500 women were expected to be eligible for the Pathway in 2015, compared to just 50 under the DSPD Programme (DSPD Programme et al, 2006, 8; d'Cruz, 2015, 48). In practice, the numbers entering the Pathway are even higher: by December 2017, 31,090 men and 1,996 women were on the OPD Pathway (Skett and Lewis 2019, 168). In 2023, HM Prison and Probation Service and the NHS (2023, 10) estimated that 35,000 adults in custody and the community are eligible for the OPD Pathway at any one time: 32,000 men and 3,000 women. Of these, only 3,000 are expected to access at least one intervention at one time (HM Prison and Probation Service and the NHS, 2023, 10).

This vast expansion in numbers results from significantly broader entry criteria, which have attracted little scrutiny from scholars. Men are eligible for the OPD Pathway if they are 'at any point during their current sentence, assessed as high or very high risk of serious harm to others, and serving a sentence for a violent or sexual index offence' (HM Prison and Probation Service and NHS, 2023, 9). This suggests that prisoners who have progressed down through security categories are eligible. The criteria for women are much broader than the original DSPD criteria and include women whose index offences fall below the threshold of 'serious harm' set by the OPD Pathway criteria for men (d'Cruz, 2015; Skett et al, 2017, 214).

While entrants onto the DSPD Programme were required to meet a diagnostic threshold and undergo a period of clinical assessment before admission,[1] male participants in the OPD Pathway need only be 'likely to satisfy the criteria for "personality disorder", to a level that has significant and severe consequences for themselves and others' (HM Prison and Probation Service and NHS, 2023, 9; see also Benefield et al, 2015, 6).[2] While a 'clinically justifiable link' with a high or very high risk of serious harm to others is required (HM Prison and Probation Service and NHS, 2023, 9; Skett et al, 2017, 214), it is unclear how this link is to be determined where the person lacks a formal diagnosis.

The OPD Pathway, like the DSPD Programme, deploys therapeutic interventions and therapeutic environments to manage the risks that distressed, self-harming, and violent individuals pose to the prison and probation systems as well as risks to the public. The developers of the OPD Pathway have chosen to adopt 'a rather loose definition of severe personality disorder' in order to target resources 'at those individuals who are causing the most concern, and the most risk, across the system' (Skett et al, 2017, 215). The features of a 'severe' personality disorder under the Pathway do not map precisely on to any distinct personality disorder category. Rather, the Pathway targets individuals in custody or under probation supervision who are 'troubled, difficult to manage and a threat to both themselves and others' (Skett et al, 2017, 216). Indicators of personality disorder under the Pathway include 'childhood difficulties, history of mental health problems, current risk to staff, and current disruptive behaviour' (Skett and Lewis, 2019, 169). The OPD Pathway aims more explicitly than the DSPD Programme to target disruptive individuals whose behaviour presents problems for the 'smooth running' of prisons or probation services (HM Prison and Probation Service and NHS, 2023, 9).

Those who are identified through OASyS screening as potentially eligible for the Pathway are referred for case consultation, formulation, and the development of a Pathway plan. A Pathway plan may include referral to treatment services, but interventions are reserved only for a minority of those eligible for the OPD Pathway (Skett and Lewis, 2019). For the majority, participation in the Pathway will involve psychologically-informed

---

[1] See Chapter 4.
[2] Emphasis added.

case formulation and case management by offender managers,[3] supported by psychologists (Moran et al, 2022, 6).

Under-inclusive and over-inclusive criteria

There is a tension at the heart of the OPD Pathway: while its architects recognize that the personality disorder label is stigmatizing and can lead to exclusion or blame, the Pathway retains the term 'personality disorder' in its title (Skett and Lewis, 2019). The generality of the entry criteria raises the question of what exactly distinguishes individuals with personality disorders from other prisoners who pose management problems. As set out in Chapter 2, while offending behaviour is part of the diagnostic criteria for some personality disorders, such behaviour alone is not sufficient for a diagnosis. The person should also exhibit relatively stable traits, attitudes, and ways of thinking and feeling that are characteristic of a personality disorder. The focus of the Pathway criteria on challenging behaviours, including self-harm and aggression, suggests that 'personality disorder' has become a shorthand for people who are difficult for prisons to manage.

While the removal of the stigmatizing 'dangerous and severe' label is a positive step, the Pathway entry criteria present three significant problems. First, the removal of the requirement for a personality disorder diagnosis may result in individuals who do not meet the criteria for a personality disorder being given a stigmatizing label and drawn into a Pathway that will not meet their needs. Second, the label of 'high risk, high harm' has similar implications to dangerousness and is likely to prove difficult for participants to remove. Third, the focus of the Pathway on high-risk groups will limit its ability to meet the aims of enhancing wellbeing and reducing health inequalities amongst prisoners with personality disorder.

The first and second problems suggest that the OPD Pathway criteria are over-inclusive and are likely to draw in prisoners who do not have a personality disorder or who do not present a high risk of serious reoffending. Rather than focusing on prisoners who have the highest mental health needs, the Pathway targets those who have disrupted or undermined prison

---

[3] Offender managers are also known as probation officers. Offender managers are responsible for developing risk assessments and sentence plans for prisoners and people released on licence in the community.

security, safety, and discipline, or who have questioned penal authority. Features likely to lead to referral to the OPD Pathway include:

> frequent adjudications;[4] spending significant amounts of time in segregation; continuing to offend whilst in prison; engaging in self-harm; having a history of 'sabotaging' their progress on a sentence plan; being querulous and involved in litigation against the prison system; having committed assaults on staff; having had inappropriate relationships with staff; and frequently failing to complete courses (Moran et al, 2022, 14).

Thus, the loose definition of 'personality disorder' deployed under the Pathway is a means of targeting resources at individuals who are visibly disruptive or challenging to manage, whether or not they actually meet the clinical criteria for a personality disorder. In this way, the OPD Pathway tends to pathologize disruptive or challenging behaviours and to attribute these behaviours to individual failings rather than to structural failings within the prison system. This process leaves little space for considering the detrimental impact of imprisonment on individuals, which include separation from family, friends, and social networks, loss of employment and housing, threats to physical safety, and risks to physical and mental health (Liebling and Maruna, 2005, ch 1).

Through this process, the OPD Pathway further risks attaching a stigmatizing label to people who would not necessarily meet the diagnostic criteria for a personality disorder. The paucity of robust evidence for the effectiveness of current treatments in reducing serious reoffending, set out in Chapter 2, is likely to make it difficult to remove this label once it has been applied. Even for those prisoners who do meet the criteria for a personality disorder, being drawn into a Pathway for 'high-risk' offenders may be a retrograde step in their progress out into the community.

The looseness of the entry criteria poses the further risk that individuals who have a different mental health or developmental condition may enter a Pathway that is not appropriate to their needs. Worryingly, a recent evaluation of the OPD Pathway for men found that only some of those in custodial or secure NHS services were aware they were on the OPD Pathway, and most of those in community services were unaware of this fact (Moran

---

[4] Adjudications are disciplinary hearings carried out when a prisoner is alleged to have broken prison rules.

et al, 2022, 17). This lack of awareness gives offenders little scope to challenge their referral to Pathway services, which comes with the problematic labels of high risk, high harm, and personality disorder. These labels are likely to impact upon the prisoner's subsequent journey through the criminal justice system, even if they are unaware they have been applied to them.

There is evidence that OPD Pathway services are drawing in prisoners with a range of mental health needs. Prisoners on the OPD Pathway report histories of trauma, difficulties in dealing with their emotions and relating to others, frequent conflict with others, and self-harm and suicide attempts (Moran et al, 2022, 17). Self-reported rates of mental illness are high, with half of one sample of OPD Pathway participants reporting that they had experienced a psychotic illness (Moran et al, 2022, 17). This suggests that the OPD Pathway is filtering in individuals whose mental health challenges are not confined to personality disorder. This may be problematic if participants do not receive care that is appropriate to their needs.

The broad approach taken to identifying personality disorder under the OPD Pathway further suggests that people with mental health problems may be identified at the screening stage but then rejected when they are found not to meet the entry criteria for a particular treatment or progression service. It is unclear what happens to individuals who are found not to meet the OPD Pathway criteria after the initial screening (Trebilcock et al, 2019). Given the significant gaps in mental health screening and mental health care in prisons (Criminal Justice Joint Inspection, 2021a), individuals who are identified as having mental health needs but then rejected by the Pathway may lose out on appropriate care.

The third problem suggests that the OPD Pathway is under-inclusive, as the focus of the Pathway on disruptive individuals and those who pose a high risk of serious reoffending may exclude less visible individuals who may benefit from treatment. Given that the evidence base for treating borderline personality disorder (BPD) suggests that treatment can reduce distress and self-harm, the Pathway may exclude lower risk or less visibly disruptive individuals who could benefit from treatment. While the OPD Pathway strategy for women claims to pursue the 'woman-centred', holistic approach advocated by the Corston Report (2007), the strategy nevertheless focuses on women assessed as presenting a high risk of relatively serious reoffending.

Empirical evidence from the London Pathway Project suggests that a large proportion of individuals identified as having problems suggestive of a personality disorder do not receive further services. Based on a sample of 3,414 offenders who were screened as eligible for the Pathway, the study found that 1,607 had a Pathway Plan in place. While almost all offenders who had a Pathway plan also received service recommendations, less than half were referred to a service, and less than half of those who were referred actually commenced a service (Jolliffe et al, 2017b, 226). Of the total sample, just 11 per cent started a treatment or progression service (Jolliffe et al, 2017b). The reasons for this are unclear. The Pathway may be identifying large numbers of individuals who are not suitable for the interventions it provides, or it may not have sufficient capacity to meet the needs identified.

The entry criteria further suggest that the goals of managing risks of reoffending and risks to the management of prisons takes priority over enhancing prisoner wellbeing. High security prison units are reserved for those prisoners displaying antisocial personality traits or behaviours who pose the highest risks to the public, and who are unlikely to be motivated for treatment (Department of Health and NOMS, 2011a, para 49). Entry to these units does not require the consent of the prisoner and an element of coercion is therefore likely to be present (O'Loughlin, 2019; 2020). As was the case under the DSPD Programme, this may jeopardize the effectiveness of psychological treatments. Concentrating treatment-resistant prisoners in high secure units means that they are likely to be particularly difficult to manage, and the units are likely to struggle with staff retention and motivation.

Under the OPD Pathway, health services continue to be co-opted to delay the release of serious offenders serving determinate sentences. Secure hospitals are expected to take on the more challenging and complex cases that cannot be dealt with by the prison service, and to continue to preventively detain individuals at the end of determinate prison sentences (NOMS and NHS England, 2015, 17). Given the disruption caused to the work of the DSPD hospital units by patients who were resisting treatment explored in Chapter 4, the extent to which the Pathway builds on learning from the DSPD Programme is questionable.

In sum, rather than focusing on the most distressed individuals or those who could derive the most benefit from therapeutic input, the OPD Pathway prioritizes the needs of prison management. Mental health resources follow risk rather than need, including both risk of reoffending and risks to prison authority and control. Under the OPD Pathway, 'personality disorder' seems to have become a shorthand for people who are difficult to manage as well as those who pose a high risk to the public. If interventions under the OPD Pathway do not convince Parole Boards that an individual's risk of reoffending is reduced, this may result in people becoming stuck in the system. Conversely, some individuals who could benefit from treatments that aim to reduce their distress and self-harming behaviour may be left out.

Evaluations of the OPD Pathway

While the Pathway emphasizes psychologically informed case management and de-emphasizes treatment, evaluations of the Pathway for men focus on the impact the initiative is having on measures of risk, reoffending rates, and wellbeing. The findings of empirical research on these outcomes are mixed. While there is some evidence to suggest that the OPD Pathway has had a positive impact on relationships between staff and prisoners, there is insufficient evidence to show that it reduces reoffending. More robust evidence is also needed to confirm whether the OPD Pathway is having an effect on measurable outcomes of psychological wellbeing.

Media reports purportedly based on leaked results of NEON,[5] a large-scale evaluation of the OPD Pathway led by Professor Paul Moran at the University of Bristol, suggested that offenders who completed the Pathway were more likely to reoffend than those who did not (Rose, 2021). While NEON was completed in Autumn 2020, publication of the report was delayed until Autumn 2022. This led the House of Commons Justice Committee (2022, paras. 80–81) to raise concerns about the lack of transparency from the Ministry of Justice regarding the outcomes of programme evaluations, and to call on the Government to publish the NEON report.

While NEON does not provide evidence for the claim that treatment *increased* reoffending amongst participants on the OPD Pathway, neither did it establish that it reduced proven reoffending rates. The report's conclusions are replete with caveats:

> Although a beneficial effect on proven offending behaviour was not observed statistically, this may not be indicative of Programme failure and it is too soon to definitively conclude whether the OPD Pathway is achieving its intended outcomes. It is important to note that, given the

---

[5] National Evaluation of Offender Personality Disorder Pathway. While a team led by Moran conducted an evaluation of the Pathway for women, only the report of the evaluation of the Pathway for men has been published.

limitations to the quantitative evaluation, findings should be regarded as indicative and treated with caution. (Moran et al, 2022, 2–3).

While the report is very cautious, the design of the NEON study was more robust than the evaluations of the DSPD Programme and compared outcomes for a treatment group with a comparator group. The treatment group had received complex case formulations or had been referred to an OPD intervention service while the comparator group had been referred to the OPD Pathway but did not progress to other OPD services or only received a basic case formulation. The average follow-up period was short, at around one year (Moran et al, 2022, 16). As acknowledged in the NEON report, this period would not allow enough time for offenders to pass through the Pathway, and any significant gains in terms of risk or psychological well-being are likely to occur over a longer period (Moran et al, 2022, 16).

The NEON study suggests that complex case formulation or treatment on the OPD Pathway did not have a discernible impact on most of the OPD Pathway's key outcomes, except for adjudications. Both the treatment and comparator group showed similar reductions in actuarial risk scores, self-harm incidents, and recalls after referral to the OPD Pathway. Complex case formulation or treatment therefore had no effect on these measures. Both the comparator and treatment groups showed increased rates of non-violent offending after referral to the Pathway and a similar pattern was discerned in respect of sexual offending and violent offending (Moran et al, 2022, 27). Progression through the Pathway therefore had no effect on reoffending (Moran et al, 2022, 27–28). The study did, however, find a statistically significant reduction in the rate of adjudications amongst the sub-group referred for interventions compared to the comparator group (Moran et al, 2022, 26).

While the DSPD Programme evaluations found that the prison DSPD units were associated with cost savings,[6] the NEON evaluation concluded that the cost savings associated with a reduction in adjudications did not offset the cost of case formulation and treatment. Case formulation alone was, however, associated with lower costs compared to the comparator (Moran et al, 2022, 16).

The difficulties involved in evaluating the OPD Pathway must be borne in mind when assessing these results. The NEON study relied upon confirmed

[6] See Chapter 4.

reoffending rates: an imperfect measure of reoffending that relies upon offences being identified and processed by the criminal justice system. In addition, the power to refer offenders for recall is a discretionary power, and different offender managers or services may apply different thresholds. A follow-up study over a longer period would be required to provide more robust conclusions regarding the impact of the Pathway on its key outcome measures.

Worryingly, the NEON study team could not evaluate the impact of referral to the OPD Pathway on psychological wellbeing because the Pathway did not routinely collect any data on this outcome (Moran et al, 2022, 16). Instead, routine data was gathered on self-harm incidents and adjudications: measures that rely upon staff recording incidents and assessing their severity. This again suggests that the Pathway primarily aims to facilitate the management of offenders in the system. Without regular measures of psychological wellbeing on the Pathway it will be difficult to assess its impact on mental health.

Similar findings to the NEON study were produced by an evaluation of the London Pathways Project that compared a group of offenders who accessed the Pathway with a matched group that did not (Jolliffe et al, 2017a). Participation in the Pathway was linked with a reduction in criminogenic risk factors and general offending risk amongst those who accessed it. However, there was no impact on violent offending risk (Jolliffe et al, 2017a). In addition, case consultation had no effect on outcomes and greater inputs on the Pathway (eg case consultation or service recommendations) were not associated with greater reductions in risk (Jolliffe et al, 2017a).

The qualitative data gathered by NEON paints a more optimistic picture of the Pathway than the quantitative results and suggests that participants in the OPD Pathway gained more subjective benefits than from the DSPD Programme.[7] Participants were largely positive about the impact of case formulation, citing improved relationships with their offender managers, recognition of the impact of adverse childhood experiences, and a focus on their strengths (Moran et al, 2022, 17–19). Experiences of treatment were variable, but some participants reported that they felt more hopeful and optimistic, and that their abilities to control their temper and to relate to others had improved (Moran et al, 2022, 19–20). Some reported that their

[7] See Chapter 4.

self-harming behaviour had reduced or stopped completely since referral to the Pathway (Moran et al, 2022, 20).

Some of the most positive findings related to relationships between participants and staff. Research in prisons by Alison Liebling and colleagues has identified that there is a strong relationship between prisoner wellbeing and their treatment by staff, and that prisoner distress levels are linked to perceptions of safety, respect, and fairness (Liebling, 2011). In turn, levels of distress are linked with institutional suicide rates (Liebling, 2011). Participants on the OPD Pathway described receiving a high level of support from staff, feeling understood rather than judged, feeling respected, and feeling safe (Moran et al, 2022, 18–20). Staff similarly reported that their relationships with participants in the Pathway had improved, and that participants were 'more compliant, less aggressive and less argumentative' (Moran et al, 2022, 22). Smaller studies present a similarly positive picture of improved relationships and a perception amongst prisoners that the Pathway allowed them to develop greater insights into their behaviour (Cooke et al, 2017; McMurran and Delight, 2017; Shaw et al, 2017). This evidence suggests that the OPD Pathway is helping to create safer and more constructive prison environments. However, as the OPD Pathway did not track psychological wellbeing using standardized measures, these qualitative findings could not be confirmed by the quantitative data gathered by the NEON team.

Staff expressed doubts to the NEON team as to whether observed changes in offenders' behaviour and risk would continue into the community, and whether it would be possible to establish a causal relationship between reoffending rates and the Pathway (Moran et al, 2022, 23). Challenges identified by participants in the Pathway and staff suggest that some of the problems experienced by the DSPD Programme continue under the OPD Pathway. These include included staffing shortages and gaps in services and the admission of offenders from outside the Pathway into OPD intervention services. Staff further identified a 'pervasive stigma surrounding mental health among both prisoners and prison staff' (Moran et al, 2022, 23).

In sum, the evidence suggests that participants in the OPD Pathway feel that their relationships with staff, their wellbeing, and their behaviour have improved. However, it continues to be challenging to produce robust evidence of the impact the OPD Pathway is having on its target outcomes: reducing reoffending and enhancing psychological wellbeing. Given the centrality of these outcomes to the justifications for the OPD Pathway, the positive gains indicated by qualitative studies of the Pathway are precarious. As set out below, there is evidence that the more fundamental conflict between security, discipline, and therapy seen under the DSPD Programme is continuing under the OPD Pathway.

5.3 The Traumatized Subject

While trauma is a risk factor for developing a personality disorder rather than a direct cause,[8] the OPD Pathway takes a trauma-informed approach to managing and treating participants. The treatment programme at HMP Whitemoor, which was originally established under the DSPD Programme, continues to deliver interventions on the OPD Pathway that explicitly target trauma through group and individual therapies (Blagden et al, 2023). This suggests a movement towards interpreting offending and troublesome behaviour as a manifestation of victimization. Genders and Player (2022, 17) argue that holistic, trauma-informed rehabilitative programmes in prisons are susceptible to 'erosion and dilution' in a prison context in which custodial rather than therapeutic aims take priority. They argue that the vulnerability of therapeutic initiatives in prisons is attributable not only to the prison's fundamental role as a custodial institution, but also to deeply entrenched support for retributive and deterrent punishment in criminal justice politics and a commitment to the principle of less eligibility. The principle of less eligibility holds that offenders, who have broken the social contract between the state and its citizens, 'are undeserving recipients of public resources that would be better spent on their victims or other "innocent" parties' (Genders and Player, 2022, 19). Genders and Player (2022) contend that the argument that rehabilitation will reduce reoffending is a better fit with this politics than the argument that it can advance the wellbeing of the individual. As set out below, the evidence from the OPD Pathway both reinforces and complicates this account.

The OPD Pathway tends to construct participants in services as traumatized subjects, setting up a clash between the rational, self-managing subject of the criminal justice system and the vulnerable, victimized subject of OPD services. This trauma-informed approach is vulnerable to erosion and dilution to the extent that it conflicts with the priorities of security, control, and discipline within prisons. However, therapeutic initiatives like the

---

[8] See Chapter 2.

OPD Pathway can also be co-opted to serve the broader aims of the prison. These not only include reducing reoffending but also maintaining external security, upholding order and control, providing a safe environment for prisoners, and maintaining a capable workforce (see Crewe, 2009, and Chapter 4). The contribution of trauma-informed, holistic programmes to these priorities may help them to survive despite criminal justice policies that emphasize the principle of less eligibility. In turn, however, by adapting to the prison's priorities, therapeutic initiatives in prison can subject prisoners to a risk of harm and disproportionate punishment.

Trauma-informed care should be distinguished from trauma-specific services or interventions. While trauma-specific services are designed to treat the symptoms of trauma, trauma-informed services do not necessarily attempt treatment. Rather, they 'are informed about, and sensitive to, trauma-related issues present in survivors' (Player 2017, fn 8). The idea of trauma-informed care is not new, and it has become mainstream in relation to women in custody (Ministry of Justice 2018b, para 117). However, until the advent of the OPD Pathway, trauma-informed care was not the dominant model for working with men with personality disorder. The treatment programme at the pilot DSPD unit at HMP Whitemoor was trauma-based, and the unit continues to deliver both individual and group therapies that focus on 'resolving childhood histories of trauma' under the OPD Pathway (Blagden et al, 2023, 1037). This trauma-based approach was not, however, originally adopted at the other three high secure DSPD units for men (Burns et al, 2011). The OPD Pathway therefore represents an expansion of trauma-informed practices within men's prison and probation services and a further entrenchment of trauma-informed services for women.

As set out in Chapter 4, the DSPD Programme constructed its participants as rational yet dangerous and manipulative subjects. The subject of the OPD Pathway, by contrast, is a traumatized subject whose troublesome behaviour is attributed to histories of abuse and neglect but who, with the help of psychologically informed practices and supportive staff, can achieve empowerment, desistance, and self-actualization (see Jeffcote, Gerko, and Nicklin, 2018; Jones, 2018; Lewis, 2018). On the OPD Pathway, offender managers undertaking case formulation seek explicitly 'to understand how the offender's childhood (which usually involves trauma, neglect and other types of abuse) influenced their emotional and social development' (Ramsden et al, 2016, 4). This approach differs from conventional offending-behaviour programmes, which tend to frame problematic behaviours as linked to errors and distortions in thinking and poor problem-solving and interpersonal skills.

At first, this trauma-informed approach appears to have revolutionary potential. Conventional offending-behaviour programmes based on risk–need–responsivity (RNR) principles have received cogent criticism. These programmes tend to locate responsibility for crime and managing risk in the offender, thereby emphasizing individual responsibility and free choice while ignoring the structural inequalities that contribute to offending (Hannah-Moffat, 2005; Moore and Hannah-Moffat, 2005; Pollack, 2005; Genders and Player, 2022). These programmes fit well with a wider 'responsibilization strategy' that serves to transfer responsibility for crime control from state actors to private individuals and groups (Garland, 2001, 127). They also comport well with prison regimes that are built upon the assumption that prisoners are rational actors who can be disciplined through carrot-and-stick management strategies (Hancock and Jewkes, 2011; Khan, 2022). In turn, they leave little room for acknowledging the contribution of wider social problems, such as poverty, abuse, and a lack of legitimate opportunities, to crime rates (Moore and Hannah-Moffat, 2005, 94; Maurutto and Hannah-Moffat, 2006).

Trauma-informed practices, by contrast, recognize the role of abuse and social deprivation in producing problematic behaviours and the role that relationships in custody can play in either reinforcing or helping people to break out of these behaviours (Jones, 2018). Practices of trauma-informed custody and trauma-based interventions on the OPD Pathway therefore recognize, at least to some extent, the structural factors that contribute to crime. These practices further acknowledge the role of trusting relationships in facilitating desistance and the role of punitive behaviours and attitudes in provoking or reinforcing 'difficult' behaviours (Jones, 2018; Jeffcote, Gerko, and Nicklin, 2018). Literature emerging from the OPD Pathway acknowledges that imprisonment is often traumatizing, and that people leaving prison face multiple barriers to a crime-free life. These include poverty, substance abuse, homelessness, stigma, and, for those subject to Multi-Agency Public Protection Arrangements (MAPPA), requirements to disclose past sexual or violent offending to potential employers, partners, and training organizations (Jeffcote, Gerko, and Nicklin, 2018).

Despite this revolutionary potential, a conflict between the therapeutic approach of the OPD Pathway and a punitive and control-oriented prison culture can be discerned. The OPD Pathway implicitly recognizes this conflict in its policies on psychologically informed planned environments

(PIPEs). PIPEs are intended to provide 'a safe and facilitating environment that can retain the benefits gained from treatment, test offenders to see whether behavioural changes are retained and support offenders to progress through the system' (Department of Health and NOMS 2011a, para 59). This implies that a return to mainstream prison locations risks undoing the progress made in therapy and, by extension, that the prison environment is not supportive of lasting change. In a recent evaluation of PIPEs, staff and residents raised concerned that the benefits of the PIPE, which included better behaviour on behalf of residents and better relationships between residents and staff, were at risk of being undone by time spent in the ordinary prison system (Kuester et al, 2022, 29).

Small-scale studies of OPD Pathway prison units have also reported tensions between the interests of security, discipline, and therapy. These tensions echo the culture clash seen under the DSPD Programme between the therapeutic ethos of treatment units and a wider prison culture that cautions against 'pampering' prisoners (Liebling, 2013). McMurran and Delight's (2017) study of a Pathway prison progression unit in a high security prison in London found that the psychological approach of the unit and trusting relationships between prisoners and staff were difficult to maintain. These difficulties were largely attributed to the prison environment: ' "security restrictions" curtailing purposeful activities, visits, and community contact and "stigmatising beliefs about personality disorder" in the wider prison' (McMurran and Delight, 2017, 254).

A study examining working relationships between staff on 'Unit A'— an OPD Pathway treatment unit in a high security prison—reported that prison officers working in Unit A were given the derogatory label of 'care bears' by officers working in the wider prison (Cooke et al, 2017). In addition, both disciplinary and clinical staff in Unit A saw the security protocols and hierarchical structure of the host prison as impeding the therapeutic work of the unit. Tensions arose between disciplinary staff and clinical staff from 'deselections': decisions to remove prisoners from the unit for misbehaviour. These tensions centred around disagreements between clinical staff, who wanted to take a therapeutic approach, and disciplinary staff, who wanted to remove challenging prisoners from the unit (Cooke et al, 2017; see also Hadden et al, 2016). The authors of the study attributed these differences to the professional cultures of clinical staff and prison cultures:

> it may be that the very nature of discussing offenders and to try to understand their behaviour is not in keeping with the prison ethos of mistakes

must be punished regardless of the underlying cause; indeed it could be part of the wider existing societal ethos of punishment rather than treatment being effective and appropriate for offenders (Cooke et al, 2017, 859).

Unit A closed before the end of its contract and moved to a lower security prison—an outcome that the authors of the study attributed to a lack of support for the unit from its host prison (Cooke et al, 2017). The closure of Unit A further suggests that the compatibility of penal power with rehabilitative interventions that purport to reduce reoffending risk is not absolute. To operate within prisons, rehabilitative strategies must not threaten the institution's power to control and discipline troublesome prisoners, or expose prisons to their greatest threat: riots and escapes. As was the case under the DSPD Programme, therapeutic units may be forced to adapt their practices to the security protocols of their host institutions. Or, like Unit A, they may be pushed out of high security prisons if they are perceived to pose too much of a threat.

The evidence suggests that tensions between trauma-informed care and the disciplinary ethos of the prison are gradually being resolved in favour of the latter. Treatment programmes under the OPD Pathway have adapted the concept of trauma-informed care to fit the dominant narrative that offenders are ultimately responsible for their own behaviour and that the onus is on them to improve it. An example of this is Kaizen: a treatment programme for high-risk men with psychopathic traits and a history of violent or sexual offending.[9]

Kaizen is based on RNR principles and emphasizes personal choice, autonomy, and building participants' motivation to change. Kaizen does not seek to treat trauma directly, nor does it seek to change participants' personalities. Rather, trauma is viewed as a 'responsivity' factor that can impede engagement in interventions that are designed to equip participants with the skills and attitudes needed to behave pro-socially (Henfrey, 2018). Kaizen is designed to be delivered in a 'trauma-informed manner' that seeks to validate participants' negative feelings, to avoid re-traumatizing them, and to encourage practitioners to support participants and to enable

---

[9] Kaizen has replaced Chromis: a treatment programme developed under the DSPD Programme for men (Henfrey, 2018). Kaizen and Horizon have replaced the long-running, prison-based Sex Offender Treatment Programme (SOTP) (McCartan et al, 2018). For an analysis of Chromis, see O'Loughlin (2019).

them to manage their own trauma symptoms (Henfrey, 2018). Kaizen is strengths-based, and seeks to respond to the critique that the RNR model focuses on participants' deficits rather than building on their existing abilities (Marshall, 2019; Jones, 2020).

While Kaizen seeks to be sensitive to trauma, it nevertheless places responsibility for managing its consequences onto the individual and focuses on skills-teaching and encouraging offenders to take responsibility for managing their own risks. Thus, its therapeutic model brackets off consideration of the structural barriers to desistance and the detrimental impacts of imprisonment on prisoners' life chances. Given that Chromis was based on a similar therapeutic model and participation increased self-harming amongst prisoners (de Motte et al, 2017), it is concerning that Kaizen is being rolled out without a full evaluation of its effectiveness or its impact on prisoners (McCartan et al, 2018).

On a more fundamental level, the OPD Pathway demonstrates that therapeutic programmes that are underpinned by radical theories can nevertheless be shaped by the prevailing criminal justice conception of crime as the product of individual choices. While some initiatives may acknowledge the structural factors and adverse life experiences that contribute to crime and problematic behaviours in prisons, they operate in a wider prison system that does not give offenders the tools they require to make a success of their lives on the outside. Trauma-informed care under the OPD Pathway therefore appears as a sticking plaster on a prison system that can be retraumatizing and damaging, and that implicitly or explicitly assumes that the individual alone bears responsibility for their past, present, and future behaviour. Without a more fundamental rethink of the way in which the criminal justice system is organized, positive initiatives that can enhance the wellbeing and behaviour of participants and their relationships with staff are likely to struggle to achieve more than piecemeal and fragile gains. In addition, as set out below, there is a risk that trauma-specific interventions will subject participants on the Pathway to further harm.

5.4 The Risks of the Trauma-informed Model

As Genders and Player (2014, 451) argue, the use of therapeutic interventions with serious offenders with personal histories of being victimized, socially disadvantaged, and excluded can render them more vulnerable to physical and psychological harm in a prison environment. Prisoners are at a particular risk of harm if they leave trauma-based programmes before completion due to the vulnerabilities generated by participation in treatments that encourage them to face their traumas and to open up to staff and other prisoners (Genders and Player, 2022). While the evidence from the OPD Pathway suggests that it is valued for its contribution to fostering a safer and more supportive environment for prisoners and staff, it operates within a wider system that poses significant risks to prisoner safety. Trauma-based interventions also pose a risk of re-traumatizing participants as they bring them face-to-face with their past traumas (Blagden et al, 2023, 1047). Group-based therapies that involve discussion of offences against children can also be re-traumatizing for participants who have experienced childhood abuse (Blagden et al, 2023, 1047). These processes must be carefully managed to avoid causing harm to participants.

Prisoners who return to unsafe prison environments part way through trauma-based interventions after deselection from the OPD Pathway may be particularly at risk of suicide or self-harm in an overstretched system. The current state of safety in prisons in England and Wales demonstrates that the state is failing to protect the basic rights of prisoners (House of Commons Health and Social Care Committee, 2018; European Committee for the Prevention of Torture and Inhuman or Degrading Treatment or Punishment, 2020; Criminal Justice Joint Inspection, 2021a; 2021b). Rates of self-inflicted death amongst prisoners reached record levels in 2016 and rates of assaults and self-harm incidents reached record levels in 2019 (Ministry of Justice, 2018a; 2020). While rates of self-harm amongst male prisoners have since declined slightly, rates amongst female prisoners overtook 2019 levels in 2022 (Ministry of Justice, 2023a, 10). While there was a sharp decrease in assaults during 2020 due to Covid-19 restrictions, rates of assault in women's prisons have since overtaken 2019 levels (Ministry of Justice, 2023a, 12).

As was the case under the DSPD Programme discussed in Chapter 4, selection for the OPD Pathway may have the effect of increasing the period that prisoners spend in detention. Recently, decisions by Category A Review Teams to refuse to recommend downgrading prisoners' security categories on the grounds that they have not addressed risk factors relating to their personality have been upheld on judicial review.[10] In addition, the Parole Board has refused to recommend prisoners for transfer to open conditions

---

[10] *R (Unwin) v Secretary of State for Justice* [2021] EWHC 1503 (Admin); *R (Bruton) v Parole Board of England and Wales and Secretary of State for Justice* [2022] EWHC 1692 (Admin).

or for release on the grounds that they had not addressed personality traits or factors that were said by prison psychologists to be linked to their risk of reoffending.[11]

Given the results of the NEON study, selection for the OPD Pathway may impede, rather than facilitate, the journey of prisoners serving indeterminate sentences towards release. Prisoners may be required to complete interventions under the OPD Pathway that are not based in sufficient evidence to convince the Parole Board that their risk has been reduced. For prisoners serving determinate sentences, selection for the OPD Pathway may open the door to preventive detention in hospital under the MHA 1983. In the absence of robust evidence that current treatments are effective in reducing reoffending risk, patients detained on the grounds of personality disorder are likely to face a long battle to secure their discharge from hospital.

While there is some evidence that incapacitation through imprisonment can reduce overall crime rates, very high levels of imprisonment would be necessary to achieve just a small impact on crime (McGuire, 2018, 527). The impact of incapacitation may also be reversed by the criminogenic effects of imprisonment, as studies have shown that people who have served prison sentences are more likely to reoffend than those who have served community sentences (McGuire, 2018, 528). This suggests that the strategy of handing down increasingly lengthy prison sentences and pursuing rehabilitation in prisons seen in England and Wales will have little impact on crime rates.

Developing the evidence base for interventions with personality disorder and offending behaviour may, to some extent, address these concerns. On the one hand, convincingly demonstrating that certain treatment programmes that purport to reduce reoffending are *not* effective in achieving that goal would support the removal of requirements to engage with such programmes as a precondition to release. On the other hand, if programmes are convincingly demonstrated to reduce recidivism risk, then successful completion should provide prisoners with a more straightforward route to release. Similarly, finding effective programmes that can enhance the wellbeing of participants and reduce incidents of violence and self-harm within institutions could contribute to more humane and productive uses of

---

[11] *R (Samuel) v Parole Board for England and Wales and Secretary of State for Justice* [2020] EWHC 42 (Admin); *R (Debono) v Parole Board for England and Wales and Secretary of State for Justice* [2020] EWHC 655 (Admin).

custody. As set out in this chapter and in the previous chapter, developing a robust evidence base for current treatments has proven problematic. While the OPD Pathway strategy 2023–2028 sets out that developing large-scale, independent evaluations of the Pathway is a priority, the design and details of these evaluations remain to be seen (HM Prison and Probation Service and NHS, 2023, 48).

Another way forward would be to delink participation in rehabilitative interventions from progress towards release from prison and to provide interventions on a voluntary basis. As Egardo Rotman (1990; 1986) argues, rehabilitation can have a place within a prison system largely based on retributive punishment, as it can mitigate some of the damaging effects of incarceration on prisoners, and has the potential to improve their prospects of a crime-free and productive life post-release. He further argues that the authorities should abstain from forcing unwilling prisoners to participate in rehabilitative interventions. As set out in Chapters 2 and 4 of this book, coercive approaches to rehabilitation often prove counter-productive. Such a system would, however, demand greater tolerance of the risks posed by the release and re-integration of serious offenders. It may also provide less symbolic reassurance than indeterminate sentences for those deemed to pose a risk. These proposals are fleshed out further in Chapter 8, after considering the current legal framework for protecting the rights of the public and those of the individual.

5.5 Conclusion

The growing importance of trauma-informed care on the OPD Pathway seems to present a counter-trend to the criminal justice system's focus on placing the responsibility for crime squarely with offenders. However, the criteria for entry onto the OPD Pathway, coupled with a failure to robustly monitor the wellbeing of offenders, suggests that improving wellbeing takes second place to the goal of managing disruptive prisoners. The OPD Pathway further suggests a tendency to pathologize 'difficult' prisoner behaviour and to place responsibility on the individual for managing both their risk of reoffending and the symptoms of trauma. The inclusion of individuals without a formal diagnosis in the Pathway is problematic, and continuing uncertainties regarding treatment effectiveness may mean that a stigmatizing label will be attached to participants without a sufficient means of removing it. Conversely, the focus on 'high risk, high harm' may result in some individuals being excluded from services that could benefit them.

The evidence emerging from the OPD Pathway suggest that the radical potential of trauma-informed practice is being compromised in favour of the goals of the criminal justice system. This limits the extent to which the OPD Pathway can resist the harmful impact of imprisonment on mental health and on a person's prospects outside the prison. A better way forward may be to reduce reliance on indeterminate prison sentences as a means of managing risk and to offer rehabilitative treatments on a voluntary basis. Such a system would also require a more robust limit on the proportionality of detention to the punishment deserved for an offence. Moving towards a system predicated on voluntary participation in rehabilitation for prisoners could help to counteract the problems of coercion and give prisoners a greater hope of release. But such a system would require fostering an atmosphere of tolerance of risk amongst practitioners and counteracting the public blame culture that tends to follow high profile cases of reoffending. These suggestions are returned to in Chapter 8, which sketches an alternative approach based on the findings of this book.

6
Preventive Detention and Human Rights

6.1 Introduction

This chapter turns to consider whether the jurisprudence of the European Court of Human Rights (ECtHR) can provide adequate safeguards against the risks to prisoners' rights identified in Chapters 4 and 5 of this book.[1] It focuses on the Court's jurisprudence on two rights that mirror those underlying the DSPD proposals: the offender's 'right to rehabilitation' (van Zyl Smit et al, 2014) and the public's 'right to security' (Lazarus, 2007; 2012a; 2012b; 2015). The ECtHR's case law on the 'right to rehabilitation' is based on two rights protected by the European Convention on Human Rights (ECHR): the right not to be subjected to inhuman and degrading treatment or punishment or torture under Article 3 and the right to liberty under Article 5. What may be termed a limited 'right to security' for the public primarily derives from the positive duty of the state under Article 2 to protect those under its jurisdiction from 'real and immediate' risks of death (Lazarus, 2007; 2012a; 2012b; 2015).[2] While there is a considerable academic literature on each right, they tend to be considered in isolation from each other. This chapter brings the literature and case law on each right together to interrogate how the ECtHR understands the relationship between them, and how this understanding impacts upon prisoners serving risk-based indeterminate sentences who are labelled with a personality disorder.

The analysis presented demonstrates that the ECtHR takes for granted many of the problematic assumptions that underlie recourse to preventive

---

[1] This chapter is adapted from O'Loughlin, A (2021a) 'Risk reduction and redemption: An interpretive account of the right to rehabilitation in the jurisprudence of the European Court of Human Rights', *Oxford Journal of Legal Studies*, 41(2), 510–38.
[2] This positive duty was established in *Osman v UK* [1998] ECHR 101; (2000) 29 EHRR 245.

detention measures for 'dangerous' offenders. While Article 3 protects an absolute right, the public's 'right to security' commonly takes precedence over the offender's 'right to rehabilitation' in the ECtHR's case law. In part, this is due to the very high threshold the ECtHR sets for finding violations of Article 3. In addition, the ECtHR takes for granted that states can adequately protect prisoners' rights under Articles 3 and 5 by providing them with access to rehabilitative interventions and regularly reviewing the grounds for their detention. Consequently, the case law of the ECtHR does not provide an adequate response to the risks of excessive punishment and arbitrary detention posed by risk-based sentences.

This chapter further presents an analysis of two conceptual frameworks deployed by the ECtHR for understanding what rehabilitation requires of prisoners serving indeterminate sentences. In its case law on life and imprisonment for public protection (IPP) sentences, the ECtHR deploys a concept of *rehabilitation as risk reduction*. This concept takes for granted the disputed logic underlying the dominant risk–need–responsivity (RNR) model of offender rehabilitation: that recidivism risk can reliably be assessed and reduced through targeted treatment programmes. In its case law on whole life orders, the ECtHR relies upon a concept of *rehabilitation as redemption*. This reflects the older idea that offending is a sign of bad character, but that people can atone for their crimes by working hard to change themselves. Both frameworks place the onus on prisoners to demonstrate that they have achieved rehabilitation and are eligible for release. Moreover, rehabilitation as redemption seems to invite decision-makers to assess prisoners' suitability for release using judgements about their characters. Both concepts pose a particular challenge for offenders who are diagnosed with personality disorders that are associated with unpredictability and untrustworthiness. Where courts assess risk of reoffending primarily by reference to a person's criminal past and presumed tendencies, chances of release are likely to be very slim. The concept of rehabilitation as risk reduction also poses challenges for offenders diagnosed with personality disorders that are linked to a risk of reoffending, given the paucity of evidence for effective treatments discussed in Chapter 2.

6.2 Two Concepts of Rehabilitation

As set out in Chapter 3, civil servants and politicians in the Home Office and Department of Health were concerned 'to get the right balance between the human rights of individuals and the right of the public to be protected from these very dangerous people' (Boateng and Sharland 1999, 7). Implicit in the DSPD proposals was the idea that, in discharging its duty to protect the public by removing the liberty of the 'dangerous', the state incurs a duty to provide detainees with the means to regain their liberty. This idea has since been framed by the ECtHR as the 'right to rehabilitation': a right for prisoners detained on the grounds of risk to the public to be provided with risk-reducing rehabilitative interventions that will allow them, eventually, to return to society (van Zyl Smit et al, 2014). Under the DSPD proposals, where such interventions were not found to reduce risk, there would be 'no alternative but to continue to detain [the DSPD group] indefinitely if the public is to be properly protected' (Home Office and Department of Health, 1999, 9). This idea reflects the priority that is often given to the public's 'right to security' over the right to liberty of supposedly 'dangerous' individuals (Ramsay, 2012a).

There is a growing body of scholarship on the state's positive duty to provide prisoners with opportunities for rehabilitation (van Zyl Smit et al, 2014; Meijer, 2017; Martufi, 2018; Annison and O'Loughlin, 2019) and the principle of human dignity that underpins the right to a hope of release in *Vinter and others v UK*[3] for prisoners sentenced to whole life orders has received extensive analysis (Mavronicola, 2014; 2015; Almenara and van Zyl Smit, 2015; Dyer, 2016; Vannier, 2016). However, there have been few attempts to analyse what exactly the ECtHR means by 'rehabilitation'—a term with a long history and multiple meanings (Raynor and Robinson, 2005; McNeill, 2012; Meijer, 2017). In addition, scant attention has been paid to the penal theories that underlie the ECtHR's case law on the right to rehabilitation[4] and the competing right of the public to security.

As set out below, the Court's concept of rehabilitation in respect of life-sentenced prisoners is not unitary but takes two principal forms: *rehabilitation as risk reduction* and *rehabilitation as redemption*. Both concepts place the onus on the prisoner to demonstrate that they have succeeded in achieving rehabilitation in order to progress towards release. As prisoners serving risk-based sentences are required to demonstrate progress in rehabilitation to progress towards release, the right to rehabilitation essentially consists of a right to do what the state requires of them if they wish to have any chance of regaining their liberty. Thus, the positive language

---

[3] (2016) 63 EHRR 1.
[4] Notable exceptions are Rogan (2018) and Dagan (2020).

of rehabilitation tends to obscure the fundamental imbalance of power between the prisoner and the state.

Rehabilitation as risk reduction

While the ECtHR recognizes that grossly disproportionate punishments can contravene Article 3, it sets a high threshold for violations. In the seminal case of *Weeks v UK*,[5] the ECtHR declined to find a violation of Article 3 in respect of an applicant who had received a discretionary life sentence for armed robbery when he was aged just 17. During the course of the offence, the applicant had threatened the owner of a pet shop with a starting pistol loaded with blanks and stole 35 pence. Despite the relatively minor nature of his offence, the ECtHR held that the sentencing court's concern for public safety and the applicant's rehabilitation, coupled with the fact that the court hoped for an early release, justified the imposition of discretionary life sentence on a minor. Without these justifications, the sentence would have constituted grossly disproportionate punishment in violation of Article 3.

In its subsequent case law, the ECtHR has not robustly challenged the use of indeterminate sentences for 'dangerous' offenders that impose a level of punishment that is disproportionate to the seriousness of the offence committed. Instead, the Court has focused its energy on challenging the failure of governments to provide adequate rehabilitative interventions for prisoners serving IPP or life sentences under Article 3 or Article 5(1)(a). In so doing, the Court takes for granted the premise that access to rehabilitative interventions will ensure the timely release of prisoners who are deemed to be 'dangerous'.

In *James Wells and Lee v UK*,[6] three IPP[7] prisoners challenged the legality of their detention in prison after the expiry of their punitive tariffs. The Fourth Section of the ECtHR held that detention after conviction by a competent court under Article 5(1)(a) required a sufficient causal connection and 'a relationship of *proportionality* between the ground of detention

---

[5] [1987] ECHR 3.
[6] [2012] ECHR 1706. Hereafter, *James*.
[7] See Chapter 1 for further discussion of the IPP sentence. The sentence has since been abolished by the Legal Aid, Sentencing and Punishment of Offenders Act 2012 so that no more can be handed down. This did not, however, affect those already subject to the sentence.

relied upon and the detention in question.'[8] The Court held that, after the expiry of their punitive tariffs, the detention of IPP prisoners was solely based on the risks they posed. This detention would be arbitrary and unlawful unless there were:

> special measures, instruments or institutions in place . . . aimed at reducing the danger they present and at limiting the duration of their detention to what is strictly necessary in order to prevent them from committing further offences.[9]

These principles were derived partly from the purpose of the IPP sentence as expressed by UK politicians[10] and partly from the ECtHR's case law on preventive detention in other jurisdictions.[11] While the ECtHR voiced its disapproval of the statutory presumption of dangerousness that led to an IPP sentence, it did not evaluate the proportionality of the punishment imposed by the appellants' sentences. Rather, it assessed whether the appellants' detention was proportionate to the need to protect the public from harm. The ECtHR therefore did not challenge the core premise of risk-based sentences like the IPP: that risk to the public justifies preventive detention. Instead, the ECtHR found that the failure of the UK Government to provide the prisoners with the requisite rehabilitative programmes violated their right not to be subject to arbitrary detention under Article 5. The ECtHR did not question the effectiveness of the rehabilitative treatments on offer, and took for granted that a combination of rehabilitative intervention and regular risk assessments would be sufficient to ensure the prisoners' detention remained lawful post-tariff.

In the subsequent case of *Murray v Netherlands*,[12] the applicant alleged that the Dutch authorities had deprived him of any prospect of release by failing to provide him with any psychiatric treatment and that his life sentence was therefore irreducible and violated Article 3.[13] The Grand Chamber held that, while 'the Convention does not guarantee, as such, a

---

[8] *James* (n 6), [195].
[9] ibid, [194].
[10] ibid, [152].
[11] The proportionality principle in *James* was derived from the cases of *M v Germany* [2010] 51 EHRR 41 and *Grosskopf v Germany* (2011) 53 EHRR 7. See *James* (n 6), [194]. For further discussion of this case law and of the domestic case law on the IPP, see Annison and O'Loughlin (2019).
[12] (2017) 64 EHRR 3.
[13] *Murray* (n 12), [91].

right to rehabilitation', the ECtHR's case law entailed a positive duty on the state to enable a life prisoner 'to make such progress towards rehabilitation that it offers him or her the hope of one day being eligible for parole or conditional release'.[14] Judge Pinto de Albuquerque went further in his partly concurring opinion, arguing that, according to the Court's case law, prisoners had 'a vested and enforceable right to be paroled if and when the legal requisites of parole are present'.[15] Such a right would be consistent with the principle in *Murray* that 'a prisoner cannot be detained unless there are legitimate penological grounds for incarceration, which include punishment, deterrence, public protection and rehabilitation'.[16]

James[17] and *Murray* offer a similar vision of the positive change life-sentenced prisoners will need to demonstrate to earn a right to parole. These cases are based on a 'correctional' (Raynor and Robinson, 2005, 5) or 'psychological' (McNeill, 2012, 18) model of rehabilitation that assumes 'that positive change, however conceived, can be brought about by subjecting offenders to particular interventions, programmes or regimes' (Raynor and Robinson, 2005, 5). A similar vision of rehabilitation underpins treatment programmes delivered on the DSPD Programme and the OPD Pathway that are based on RNR principles.[18]

Both *James* and *Murray* show the influence of the RNR model of offender rehabilitation. In *James*, the Court drew on the Committee of Ministers' Recommendation of 9 October 2003 to establish rehabilitation as the aim of prison sentences.[19] The Recommendation was influenced by the RNR model and emphasizes that life prisoners should receive sentence plans that 'include a risk and needs assessment ... and interventions and participation in programmes designed to address risks and needs so as to reduce disruptive behaviour in prison and re-offending after release'.[20]

As the Court noted in *James*, the primary means for IPP prisoners in England and Wales to progress towards release is to follow their sentence plan.[21] Thus, providing 'a real opportunity for rehabilitation'[22] for the

---

[14] ibid, [103]. See Meijer (2017) for further analysis of this positive obligation.
[15] *Murray* (n 12), Partly Concurring Opinion of Judge Pinto De Albuquerque, [OII-14].
[16] *Murray* (n 12), [100].
[17] n 6.
[18] See Chapters 2, 4, and 5.
[19] *James* (n 6), [159]–[161].
[20] ibid, [161].
[21] For an overview of the aims and practice of sentence planning in England and Wales, see NOMS (2014).
[22] *James* (n 6), [209].

applicants in *James* required 'reasonable opportunities to undertake courses aimed at helping them to address their offending behaviour and the risks they posed'.[23] In *Murray* the Grand Chamber seemed to endorse a wider view of rehabilitation, holding that rehabilitation involved 'resocialisation through the fostering of personal responsibility'[24] and social reintegration.[25] As in *James*, however, the state's positive duties were primarily confined in *Murray* to providing life prisoners with any treatment needed to reduce their risk of re-offending.[26] States could meet this duty by 'setting up and periodically reviewing an individualized programme that will encourage the sentenced prisoner to develop himself or herself to be able to lead a responsible and crime-free life'.[27]

The Grand Chamber recognized a broader concept of rehabilitation under Article 8 in *Khoroshenko v Russia*.[28] In *Khoroshenko*, the Court acknowledged the importance of maintaining family ties not only for rehabilitation but also to counteract the detrimental effects of imprisonment and facilitate social reintegration upon release.[29] Restrictions on contact with family had to be proportionate to a legitimate aim and to strike a fair balance between punishment and rehabilitation.

In their joint concurring opinion in *Khoroshenko*, Judges Pinto de Albuquerque and Turković explicitly portrayed rehabilitation as noncoercive. They asserted that 'a sentence plan aimed at a particular prisoner's resocialisation is a proposal made to him or her. The rehabilitative terminology should not have any connotation of forced treatment.'[30] Similarly in *Murray*, Judge Pinto de Albuquerque argued that 'resocialisation is no longer understood, as in the classical medical analogy, as a "treatment" or "cure" of the prisoner, aimed at the reformation of the prisoner's character, but as a less ambitious, yet more realistic task: his or her preparation for a law-abiding life after prison'.[31]

These statements neglect the coercion underlying offers of rehabilitation tied to a prospect of release. The prisoner's 'right to rehabilitation' must be

---

[23] ibid, [218].
[24] *Murray* (n 12), [70].
[25] ibid, [102].
[26] ibid, [108]–[109] and [110]–[111].
[27] ibid, [103].
[28] App no. 41418/04 (ECtHR, 30 June 2015).
[29] *Khoroshenko* (n 28), [144].
[30] ibid, Joint Concurring Opinion of Judges Pinto de Albuquerque and Turković, fn 11.
[31] *Murray* (n 12), Partly Concurring Opinion of Judge Pinto de Albuquerque, fn 1, referring to his partly dissenting opinion in *Öcalan v Turkey (No 2)* [2014] ECHR 24069/03.

understood in light of the unequal relationship between the prisoner and the state. The prisoner has a right to opportunities for rehabilitation because, without them, the prisoner has no hope of regaining liberty, and the state, through the sentence plan, dictates what it requires of the prisoner. From this perspective, the right to rehabilitation looks more like a duty to engage with rehabilitative opportunities if one wishes to have any prospect of being released.[32]

The ECtHR in *James* did not fundamentally challenge the legitimacy of imposing an indeterminate prison sentence based on judgements of dangerousness, and nor did it challenge the assumption that access to relevant rehabilitative courses or psychiatric treatment would enable the applicants to progress towards release. Thus, in *James* and *Murray*, as in *Khoroshenko*, the ECtHR merely tweaked the conditions in which a life or indeterminate sentence should be served without challenging the justifications for imposing such sentences. Furthermore, the Court's uncritical acceptance of sentence planning and RNR principles in *Murray* and *James* left little room for prisoners to challenge the requirements of their sentence plans or the problematic risk assessments that underpin them. These problems are considered in the next section.

Risk and character in rehabilitation as risk reduction

Commentators have argued that contemporary rehabilitation policies seek to change offenders' behaviours rather than their characters (Ryan, 2015). However, some of the criminogenic needs that are targeted by rehabilitative programmes, such as pro-criminal attitudes or an antisocial personality pattern (Bonta and Andrews, 2007), could be viewed as character traits. This raises the question of what role character continues to play in rehabilitation as risk reduction. Drawing on the RNR framework and Nicola Lacey's work on character responsibility, I argue below that offending and character are only contingently related in rehabilitation as risk reduction. Nevertheless, character judgements can come into play in practice when assessing risk. This suggests that the ECtHR was incorrect to assume in *James*

---

[32] Here I draw on Peter Ramsay's (2012b, 214–15) argument that the test for release under an IPP effectively places the onus on the prisoner to demonstrate to the Parole Board that he is safe. Ramsay argues that this is effectively an obligation to reassure other citizens that he does not pose a threat to their security.

and *Murray* that modern risk assessment methods are an objective measure of the need to detain a given person.

Lacey (2016) defines character responsibility as the view that the underlying rationale for conviction and punishment is bad or antisocial character, and that criminal conduct itself is a symptom of bad character. Consequently, character responsibility 'invites us to condemn not merely the sin but also, and fundamentally, the sinner' (Lacey, 2016, 35). Character is also implicated in judgements of risk using the logic that criminal character causes criminal behaviour, and that a propensity for criminal behaviour can therefore be inferred from past offending. While these sentiments appear at odds with a criminal law that seeks primarily to punish offenders for what they have voluntarily done rather than for what kind of person they are, Lacey (2011) argues that character-based attributions of criminal responsibility have enjoyed something of a renaissance in recent times. This renaissance can be seen in the introduction of preventive measures, such as the IPP, that are imposed in response to a person's history of violent or sexual offending (Lacey, 2011).

While Lacey's work focuses on character responsibility in the criminal law, the spectrum of criminal responsibility she develops can also help us to understand the role played by the character in post-conviction decisions, including sentencing and execution of sentence (Lacey, 2016, 63–64). As Lacey (2016) argues, 'a welter of information' about character can be taken into account in sentencing and parole decision-making. This 'stretches well beyond past criminal record, encompassing judgments or information about lifestyle, attitudes, and compliance with probation or prison discipline' (Lacey, 2016, 63–64).

At one extreme of Lacey's spectrum of character responsibility is 'character essentialism' or 'character determinism': 'a view of human character . . . and of identity as fixed, or at least as relatively stable' that 'regards character as determining conduct' (Lacey, 2016, 35). At the other extreme is the view that a criminal conviction does not necessarily mark out a stable propensity for crime (Lacey, 2016, 35–36). Between each extreme are 'intermediate positions in which criminal conduct expressing vicious characteristics gives rise to a (stronger or weaker) presumption of bad character in the sense of propensity' (Lacey, 2016, 36).

While a personality disorder diagnosis is not exactly the same as a judgement of bad character, the process of determining whether a person has a personality disorder has some parallels with character judgements. In the DSM-5-TR and ICD-11, personality disorder traits are indicated by specific behaviours that are engaged in so often that they suggest innate qualities of the person. Thus, under the diagnostic criteria for borderline personality disorder (BPD) in DSM-5-TR, 'difficulty controlling anger' is inferred from 'frequent displays of temper' or 'recurrent physical fights' (APA, 2022, 753). In ICD-11, 'dissociality' is indicated by behaviour that is 'deceptive, manipulative and exploitative of others' (WHO, 2022, sec. 6D11.2).

As set out in Chapter 2, while it has not been reliably established whether a personality disorder *causes* behaviour, both personality and personality disorder are regarded as influencing behaviour. The psychiatric construct of personality disorder is based on the idea that personality traits, such as impulsivity or aggression, can be inferred from a person's behaviour. In troublingly circular logic, this behaviour is then attributed to the existence of specific personality traits. Like character, these traits are thought to be enduring, or at least relatively stable. As a result, a personality disorder diagnosis carries with it the suggestion that a person can be expected to act in troublesome ways in future. This is part of the reason why the diagnosis is so stigmatizing, and why a diagnosis is often experienced as a judgement that one is simply a bad person. As set out in Chapter 4, personality disorder can also become a lens that colours others' perceptions of a person's behaviour, so that even seemingly cooperative conduct can be interpreted as an attempt at manipulation and as a confirmation of personality disorder traits.

While a strong presumption of criminal propensity underlies the imposition of an IPP sentence, character and offending are only contingently related in the RNR model. To some extent, the RNR model views offending as a product of poor self-control and antisocial attitudes: personality traits that may be understood as character defects. However, the RNR model identifies a much broader range of risk factors, and RNR programmes only target personality traits where this is expected to reduce the person's likelihood of re-offending. While offending behaviour programmes modelled on RNR principles have been characterized as 'normalizing' or 're-moralizing' (see Rose, 2000; Pollack, 2005; and Robinson, 2008), their aim is not necessarily to transform the person's character or identity. Rather, their goal is to reduce risk by helping 'offenders to take . . . control of their lives and behaviour and to make more pro-social choices by helping them to learn necessary skills such as listening and communication, critical and creative thinking, problem-solving, self-management and self-control' (Raynor and Robinson, 2009, 12). Kaizen, a treatment programme on the OPD Pathway that is based on RNR principles (Henfrey, 2018),[33] views personality traits as responsivity factors that are to be worked around, or worked with, rather than changed.

While RNR principles do not necessarily assume a strong connection between personality disorder and risk, empirical studies demonstrate that practitioners' subjective judgements about the offender's character play a significant role in risk assessment in practice. While Parole Board members in England and Wales thoroughly review the evidence presented to them, they also draw on 'gut reaction', 'instinct', 'experience' 'intuition', 'common sense' and their 'impressions' of the prisoner when it comes to making release decisions (Jacobson and Hough, 2010, 28).

A study of Parole Board decision-making conducted in the 1990s found that 'in cases in which "further work" on offending behaviour in prison was not given as the reason for refusal [to grant parole], the issue usually came down to whether to trust the prisoner or not' (Hood and Shute, 2000, 56). Parole Board members also used negative character judgements about sexual offenders when assessing their eligibility for parole, including 'a man of violence', 'a thoroughly unpleasant character from a thoroughly unpleasant family', and 'a bully, a really dangerous man' (Hood et al, 2002, 373; 382; 385). This reasoning reflects the assumptions of character essentialism: that a person's character can be inferred from their past behaviour and that bad character indicates a propensity for offending. Such judgements are unlikely to be an accurate reflection of a person's probability of offending given the low predictive accuracy of professional judgement, considered in Chapter 2. They also encourage the notion that serious offenders are unlikely to change.

These assumptions can also be seen in the perception of Mental Health Review Tribunal (MHRT) members that personality disorder is an enduring or fixed characteristic of patients with the diagnosis, and that the perception that reoffending by those in the DSPD group was 'high, almost inevitable' (Trebilcock and Weaver, 2010b, 67).[34] Where, as in the DSPD Programme and the OPD Pathway, dangerousness is assumed to be linked to a personality disorder, counteracting judgements of dangerousness is likely to be a very difficult task.

In *James*, the ECtHR failed to recognize that even the best available objective measures of risk are a poor measure of the 'need' to detain an

---

[33] See Chapter 4.
[34] See Chapter 4.

individual to prevent an offence from occurring. As set out in Chapter 2, empirical studies show that the actuarial risk assessment instruments (ARAIs) used in prisons and probation are reasonably good at predicting re-offending at the group level. When it comes to predicting which individuals will re-offend, however, their accuracy is much more limited. This is because they return a high proportion of false positives (individuals identified as high risk who do not re-offend) and false negatives (individuals identified as low risk who do re-offend) (Szmukler, 2003; Fazel et al, 2012). These problems are exacerbated when the instrument is used to predict rare events, like serious offending, that have a low base rate in the population (Szmukler, 2003).

Judge Pinto de Albuquerque in *Öcalan v Turkey (No. 2)* demonstrated acute awareness of the problems associated with ARAIs, and he was critical of the assumption that dangerous offenders could be reliably identified and that they ought to be excluded from the community. His concept of resocialization as 'preparation for a law-abiding life after prison'[35] more closely resembles social reintegration and resettlement efforts than the risk-focused RNR model. Nevertheless, in *Murray*, Judge Pinto de Albuquerque strongly advocated for a duty on states to provide prisoners with sentence plans based on RNR principles. RNR assessments are, however, underpinned by the same 'highly problematic prediction scales'[36] he criticized in *Öcalan (No. 2)*.

Moreover, it is doubtful that prisons are suitable sites for rehabilitation given that they are coercive environments in which prisoners' rights are curtailed and prison staff fulfil both custodial and therapeutic roles.[37] Furthermore, there is a danger in requiring RNR assessments for all prisoners as 'unmet treatment needs are easily elided with risk' in the RNR model (O'Loughlin, 2019, 630. See also Hannah-Moffat 2005; 2015a; 2016). As shown in Chapter 4, offenders serving determinate sentences who fail to progress through treatment programmes targeting their risk factors for offending may find themselves subject to restrictive measures on the grounds that they continue to pose a risk to the public. Or, if they meet the requisite criteria, they may be detained in hospital on the grounds of unsound mind under mental health law.[38]

The idea that engaging in offending behaviour programmes presents a straightforward means of demonstrating reduced risk of re-offending can

---

[35] *Öcalan (No 2)* (n 31), Partly Dissenting Opinion of Judge Pinto De Albuquerque, fn 22.
[36] ibid, [6].
[37] See Chapters 4 and 5.
[38] See Chapter 7.

also be challenged. As set out in Chapter 2, there is a lack of robust evidence that prison-based offending behaviour programmes reduce serious violent or sexual recidivism, although they may have some impact on general recidivism. As set out in Chapters 4 and 5, there is a paucity of robust evidence to demonstrate the effectiveness, or ineffectiveness, of current treatments that aim to reduce the risk of serious sexual or violent offending amongst offenders with personality disorders. As a result, providing prisoners with such interventions may not be sufficient to curb the excessive use of preventive detention.

There is evidence that criminal justice practitioners are sceptical about the effectiveness of common offending behaviour programmes in reducing risk amongst serious offenders (Jacobson and Hough, 2010). This scepticism is likely to have increased in the wake of the finding that participation in the widely-used prison-based Sex Offender Treatment Programme (SOTP) may have *increased* reoffending amongst the treated group (Mews, Di Bella, and Purver, 2017). As shown in Chapter 4, where a personality disorder is linked with a judgement of dangerousness, it is particularly difficult for offenders to demonstrate suitability for release by engaging with treatment programmes. This is because efforts to comply with treatment may be interpreted as an attempt to manipulate decision-makers and as confirmation of dangerousness and deceitfulness.

Rehabilitation as redemption

In *James* and *Murray*, the ECtHR took for granted that risk assessments were a good objective measure of reoffending risk and failed to interrogate the potential for character judgements to influence release decisions. In *Vinter*, it went further and seemed to call upon decision-makers to evaluate progress in rehabilitation by examining changes in the person's character. In *Vinter*, three prisoners subject to whole life sentences argued that the very limited grounds for release by the Justice Secretary meant their sentences were irreducible, depriving them of any hope of freedom and violating Article 3. Whole life prisoners can only be released by the Justice Secretary where 'exceptional circumstances exist which justify the prisoner's release on compassionate grounds.'[39] At the time *Vinter* was decided by the ECtHR,

---

[39] Crime (Sentences) Act 1997, s 30(1).

'exceptional circumstances' was defined by Prison Service Order (PSO) 4700 as follows:

> the prisoner is suffering from a terminal illness and death is likely to occur very shortly . . . is bedridden or similarly incapacitated, for example, those paralysed or suffering from a severe stroke; and the risk of re-offending (particularly of a sexual or violent nature) is minimal; and further imprisonment would reduce the prisoner's life expectancy; and there are adequate arrangements for the prisoner's care and treatment outside prison; and early release will bring some significant benefit to the prisoner or his/her family.[40]

The Grand Chamber's judgment in *Vinter* affirmed that a prisoner cannot not be detained unless there are legitimate penological grounds for their detention, including 'punishment, deterrence, public protection and rehabilitation,'[41] and that the balance between these grounds can shift during the sentence. Such shifts can only be evaluated by a review of the grounds for the detention at an appropriate point.[42] The Court placed particular emphasis on the rehabilitative purpose of prison sentences and on the need for states to offer prisoners 'the possibility of rehabilitation and the prospect of release if that rehabilitation is achieved.'[43] After *Vinter*, therefore, Article 3 was to be:

> interpreted as requiring reducibility of the sentence, in the sense of a review which allows the domestic authorities to consider whether any changes in the life prisoner are so significant, and such progress towards rehabilitation has been made in the course of the sentence, as to mean that continued detention can no longer be justified on legitimate penological grounds.[44]

In *Vinter*, the Grand Chamber found that the applicants' whole life sentences were irreducible because PSO 4700 did not provide a real prospect of release. In doing so, it rejected the UK Government's argument that the Justice Secretary's duty to act in conformity with Article 3 was sufficient.

---

[40] Quoted by the Grand Chamber in *Vinter* (n 3), [43].
[41] ibid, [111].
[42] ibid.
[43] ibid, [114].
[44] ibid, [199].

PSO 4700 was recently cancelled by HM Prison and Probation Service and replaced by a new policy entitled Early Release on Compassionate Grounds (ERCG). The new policy allows applications for release on grounds including a prisoner's health or social care needs, tragic family circumstances, and exceptional circumstances based on Article 3 of the ECHR. The grounds for an application based on Article 3 use the wording in *Vinter*: 'circumstances which have arisen since the imposition of the sentence which render the punishment originally imposed no longer justifiable on penological grounds' (Ministry of Justice and HM Prison & Probation Service, 2022, para 4.41). The policy applies in respect of prisoners serving determinate, IPP, life sentences, and civil imprisonment. Thus, while the UK Government initially resisted the judgment in *Vinter*, the case has since prompted a welcome reversal in policy.

Previous accounts of *Vinter* have highlighted that purely retributive whole life sentences that eliminate any prospect of release are incompatible with the principle of human dignity underpinning Article 3 (Dyer, 2016; Vannier, 2016; Martufi, 2018). Natasa Mavronicola (2014, 303) argues that, after *Vinter*, all life sentences should adhere to the tariff structure. However, this claim does not tally with the ECtHR's comment in *Vinter* that a whole life sentence can be 'condign' punishment (appropriate to the crime; fitting and deserved)[45] at the time of its imposition.[46] The Court further affirmed in *Vinter* that 'a life sentence does not become irreducible by the mere fact that in practice it may be served in full'.[47] This implies that, while the ECtHR rejected the argument that retributive punishment justifies whole life detention without review, it did not absolutely reject punishment as a justification for a person serving a whole life sentence until its end. To demonstrate this argument, it is necessary to dig deeper into the Court's concept of 'atonement' in *Vinter*.

The meaning of atonement

Little attention has been paid in previous accounts to the principle in *Vinter* that prisoners serving whole life sentences should have the opportunity to 'atone' for their offences through rehabilitation:

---

[45] Definition of 'condign' in the *Oxford Dictionary of English*, 3rd edn (Stevenson, 2015).
[46] *Vinter* (n 3), [112].
[47] ibid, [108].

> If . . . a prisoner is incarcerated without any prospect of release and without the possibility of having his life sentence reviewed, there is the risk that he can never atone for his offence: whatever the prisoner does in prison, however exceptional his progress towards rehabilitation, his punishment remains fixed and unreviewable. If anything, the punishment becomes greater with time: the longer the prisoner lives, the longer his sentence. Thus, even when a whole life sentence is condign punishment at the time of its imposition, with the passage of time it becomes . . . a poor guarantee of just and proportionate punishment.[48]

This passage implies that if a prisoner sufficiently atones for their crimes by changing themselves, they will no longer deserve to be detained for their whole life. Judge Power-Forde made this rationale more explicit in her concurring opinion:

> Those who commit the most abhorrent and egregious of acts and who inflict untold suffering upon others, nevertheless retain their fundamental humanity and carry within themselves the capacity to change. Long and deserved though their prison sentences may be, they retain the right to hope that, someday, they may have atoned for the wrongs which they have committed.[49]

Andrew Dyer (2016, 579) has branded as 'illogical' the implication in *Vinter* that a whole life sentence can be a fitting punishment at sentencing but can subsequently become unjust. Dyer assumes, however, that retributive punishment can only be backward-looking and desert-based. This is reflected in his argument that 'the sentence necessitated by punitive considerations [is] exactly the same at the time of sentencing as at any other time during the sentence' (Dyer, 2016, 579). I argue, however, that the Court in *Vinter* endorses a different rationale for retributive punishment. This focuses on the qualities of the offender, which are amenable to change, rather than on those of the crime, which are not. This reasoning is consistent with an understanding of atonement as a moral transformation that entails a character-based theory of offending. This concept has its roots in Kantian moral philosophy and sees atonement as freeing the offender from punishment. In this sense, the Grand Chamber in *Vinter* conceives of

---

[48] ibid, [112].
[49] ibid, Concurring Opinion of Judge Power-Forde, [OII-2].

rehabilitation as a process of redemption. To demonstrate this argument, I compare the Court's vision of atonement in *Vinter* with theories of atonement in law and philosophy below.

The primary meaning of atonement is 'making amends for a wrong or injury'.[50] The idea in *Vinter* that one can 'atone' by changing oneself may therefore strike readers as odd. However, as Linda Radzik (2009, 21) demonstrates, atonement in law and philosophy commonly carries three separate meanings: 'atonement as the repayment of a moral debt, atonement as moral transformation, and atonement as the reconciliation of a relationship'. *Vinter* does not explicitly require reparation or reconciliation before a life-sentenced prisoner can earn a right to release. Instead, the judgement focuses on changes in the prisoner themselves and reflects a theory of atonement as a moral transformation.

Atonement as a moral transformation 'is most commonly expressed in a demand for repentance, a regretful turning away from the wrongful path, and a recommitment to the right and the good' (Radzik, 2009, 21–22). On one reading, repentant wrongdoers not only commit themselves to be good in future—they can even undergo 'a change of identity that frees them from their guilt' (Radzik, 2009, 21–22). This idea has its roots in Kant's (1960) theory of punishment. For Kant, before a wrongdoer has had a 'change of heart', he is deserving of punishment as an agent who has freely chosen his actions. However, after his change of heart 'the penalty cannot be considered appropriate to his new quality . . . for he is now leading a new life and is morally another person' (Radzik, 2009, 67).

Atonement as a moral transformation further implies that offenders atone for their crimes by changing their very characters. This is an active process whereby:

> Repentant persons reject their former actions, habits, thoughts, or character traits in favour of a new set of values, commitments, dispositions, and intentions. Repentance is not a mere change in one's future course . . . It is a repudiation of one's past as wrongful and as a mistake for which one acknowledges responsibility and blameworthiness (Radzik, 2009, 67).

This implies that repentant wrongdoers not only atone for their past crimes but also turn away from committing crime in future. In *Marcello*

---

[50] Definition of 'atonement' in the *Oxford Dictionary of English* (Stevenson, 2015).

Viola v Italy (No.2), [51] the First Section of the ECtHR made the relationship between character and offending more explicit than in *Vinter*. It stated that the process of rehabilitation presents an opportunity for the prisoner to 'critically review his criminal career and to rebuild his personality.'[52] This implies a much more holistic and deeply transformational process than the concern with merely addressing risk factors for offending seen in the concept of rehabilitation as risk reduction in *James* and *Murray*.

Like Kant's theory of punishment, Judge Power-Forde's opinion in *Vinter* implies that atonement is achieved by exercising one's human capacity for change. Power-Forde's argument is reminiscent of Kant's 'change of heart' and similarly implies that, by working on themselves, a former offender can change so profoundly that they no longer deserve punishment despite the gravity of their crimes.

Further scrutiny of *Murray* and *Vinter* suggests that the Court's attitude towards the relationship between character and offending falls in the middle of Lacey's spectrum of character responsibility, some distance from the pessimism of character essentialism. Human dignity in *Vinter* entails, inter alia, an optimistic view of offenders' potential for self-improvement. This may be traced back to the concept of human dignity in German constitutional law. In the *Life Imprisonment*[53] case, the German Federal Constitutional Court affirmed that the primacy of human dignity in the German constitution is 'based on the conception of human persons as spiritual-moral beings endowed with the freedom to determine and develop themselves.'[54] This notion is reflected in the Grand Chamber's ruling in *Murray* that states cannot avoid their Article 3 obligations by claiming that a prisoner is incapable of change.[55]

While Radzik focuses her account of atonement as repayment on compensation for victims (Radzik, 2009, 21), Zedner (1994) argues that theories of reparative justice recognize that an offender can 'pay back' by reforming themselves. Thus, 'evidence of a change in attitude, some expression of remorse that indicates that the victim's rights will be respected in the future' may be enough for reparation (Zedner, 1994, 234–35). This change may be achieved by engaging with rehabilitative interventions such as training or

---

[51] App no 45106/04, ECtHR 13 June 2019 (First Section).
[52] *Marcello Viola* (n 51), [125]. This judgment is not available in English. Quotations have been translated from the French version of the judgment by the author.
[53] (1977) 45 BVerfGE 187 IV(c).
[54] Quotation from translation of the judgment in Kommers and Miller (2012), 365.
[55] *Murray* (n 12), [62] and [111].

counselling (Zedner, 1994, 235). While *Vinter* does not explicitly address reparation, it could be consistent with an account of atonement as reparation primarily achieved through self-transformation. *Vinter* does not, however, seem to require reconciliation of relationships.

The concept of atonement as a moral transformation or the repayment of a moral debt through self-transformation can help explain why the ECtHR is willing to accept a whole life order as 'condign' punishment at the time of its imposition but not after the offender has made progress in rehabilitation. A backward-looking retributive justification for punishment that focuses solely on the gravity of the offence would require the offender to serve a whole life sentence to its end. This justification underpinned Lord Scott's statement in *Wellington* that 'if a whole life sentence ... is a just punishment for the crime, the prisoner atones by serving his sentence'.[56] The focus in *Vinter*, however, on the need to consider positive changes in the offender suggests that it subscribes instead to a present-centred normative justification for retributive punishment. This justification focuses on the blameworthiness of the offender, conceived of as amenable to change, rather than on the blameworthiness of the act.

While the Court in *Vinter* suggested that progress in rehabilitation was the primary basis for a prospect of release, other changes in the prisoner could be relevant to reviews of detention. The idea in *Vinter* that punishment under a whole life sentence can become greater with time[57] suggests that reviews should consider natural changes, such as aging or illness, that can make punishment weigh more heavily on the offender. In this respect, the Court was likely influenced by the German Federal Constitutional Court's *War Criminal* case.[58]

While *Vinter* has been welcomed for turning the tide against whole life sentences (van Zyl Smit, 2014, 62), the concept of rehabilitation as redemption at its centre implies a character-based justification for punishment that sits uncomfortably with liberal criminal law principles. The focus in *Vinter* on atonement as a justification for release suggests that a prisoner who fails to atone for their offences by reforming themselves could legitimately be detained for their whole life, provided that regular reviews of the purpose of

---

[56] R. (Wellington) v Secretary of State for the Home Department [2008] UKHL 72, [46]. Referred to by the Grand Chamber in *Vinter* (n 3), [57].
[57] *Vinter* (n 3), [111].
[58] BVerfGE 72, 105 24 April 1986--2 BvR 1146/85. Discussed by the Grand Chamber in *Vinter* (n 3), [70]. On the influence of German law on the Grand Chamber's reasoning in *Vinter*, see Meijer (2017, 148) and van Zyl Smit and Appleton (2019, 22).

detention were provided. In *Vinter*, therefore, the Court missed its chance to set definitive, universal, and principled limits on the use of whole life sentences. Rather than interrogating the proportionality of the prisoner's punishment to the crime, it invited states to engage in the much more difficult, and subjective, task of assessing changes in their character.

The concept of rehabilitation as redemption in *Vinter* places a heavy responsibility on the prisoner to demonstrate a change in personality so profound that they no longer deserve punishment regardless of the heinousness of their offence(s). While *Vinter* does not condone forcible treatments or harsh punishments designed to reform prisoners' characters, it does legitimize a subtler form of coercion that places the burden on the prisoner to engage with rehabilitation in order to progress towards release.

An aspect of *Vinter* that has received surprisingly little analysis is the principle that 'States have a *duty* under the Convention to take measures for the protection of the public from violent crime' that may be fulfilled by 'continuing to detain . . . life sentenced prisoners for as long as they remain dangerous.'[59] In the ECtHR context, the prisoner's right to rehabilitation is limited by the competing right of the public to security. The cases of *Mastromatteo v Italy*[60] and *Maiorano and others v Italy*[61] demonstrate the weakness of the Court's commitment to rehabilitation in the face of serious reoffending by released prisoners. As set out below, in *Maiorano*, the Court itself used character-based judgements of risk to evaluate a decision by the Italian authorities to release a serious offender.

6.3 The Right to Security and the Limits of the Right to Rehabilitation

As set out in Chapter 3, the Home Office referred to human rights principles to justify the New Labour's plans for the DSPD group. Mike Boyle, then head of the Mental Health Unit at the Home Office, drew on the ECtHR's decision in *Osman v UK*[62] to assert that the ECHR imposed on the state 'an obligation to protect the public from predictable dangers that individuals may cause' (Select Committee on Health, 2000, para 636). This rhetorical

---

[59] *Vinter* (n 3), [108]. Emphasis added.
[60] [2002] ECHR 694.
[61] App no 28634/06, ECtHR 15 Dec 2009.
[62] *Osman* (n 2).

obligation can be characterized as the corollary of the 'right to security' often claimed by politicians on behalf of the public.

The measures that could be taken to protect the public's purported 'right to security' are potentially unending (Lazarus, 2012b, 106). However, the rule in *Osman* did not oblige the government to preventively detain people who were thought to be likely to commit acts of physical or sexual violence against unknown members of the public. Rather, *Osman* established a much narrower positive duty on state authorities to 'take preventive operational measures to protect an individual whose life is at risk from the criminal acts of another individual.'[63] The authorities would be in violation of this duty if they 'knew or ought to have known at the time of the existence of a *real and immediate risk to the life of an identified individual or individuals*' but 'failed to take measures within the scope of their powers which, judged reasonably, might have been expected to avoid that risk.'[64]

The ECtHR has sought to impose limits on this right by anchoring it to the right to life under Article 2 and setting a high threshold for violations.[65] Liora Lazarus argues that *Osman* and subsequent cases limit the state's positive obligations to 'the development of structures and institutions capable of responding to and minimising "critical and pervasive threats" to human safety' (Lazarus, 2012b, 106). However, her analysis misses the implications of the Grand Chamber's decision in *Mastromatteo*, which significantly expanded the scope of the state's duty in respect of released prisoners. As set out below, the ECtHR recognizes two versions of the 'right to security'. The first is the right to protection from 'critical and pervasive threats' to physical safety described by Lazarus (2012b, 106). The second version is a much more expansive right to protection from the potential acts of released prisoners convicted of violent offences, established in *Mastromatteo* and *Maiorano*.[66] Both versions are grounded in the state's positive obligation to protect the right to life under Article 2 of the ECHR.

---

[63] ibid, [115].
[64] ibid, [116]. Emphasis added.
[65] The Grand Chamber has established an additional positive duty under Article 3 for states to protect children from ill-treatment at the hands of third parties: *Z and others v UK* (2002) 34 EHRR 3. The corresponding right to protection may also be conceptualized as a right to security. Here, I focus on the Court's Article 2 jurisprudence as this is more developed than the Article 3 jurisprudence.
[66] Both cases are regarded as leading authorities on the state's positive duty to protect life under Article 2 and are frequently cited by the ECtHR. See *Murray* (n 12), *Khoroshenko* (n 28), and *Vinter* (n 3).

In *Mastromatteo*, the applicant's son had been shot dead by a prisoner who was escaping the scene of a bank robbery the prisoner had committed with two accomplices after all three had absconded while on prison leave. The applicant alleged that the Italian State had failed to protect his son's life by granting leave to three 'very dangerous habitual criminals'.[67] The Grand Chamber extended the *Osman* duty to embrace an obligation for the state 'to afford *general protection to society* against the *potential* acts of one or of several persons serving a prison sentence for a violent crime'.[68] It was careful, however, to recognize that the progressive social reintegration of prisoners was a 'legitimate aim' of the state[69] and to reiterate the requirement in *Osman* that the state's duty to protect life must

> be interpreted in a way which does not impose an impossible or disproportionate burden on the authorities, bearing in mind the difficulties involved in policing modern societies, the unpredictability of human conduct and the operational choices which must be made in terms of priorities and resources.[70]

In *Mastromatteo*, the Grand Chamber was satisfied that the Italian authorities had appropriate systems in place to protect the public given very few prisoners re-offended or escaped while on leave.[71] It also took seriously the need to consider the unpredictability of human conduct by judging the reasonableness of the decision to release the prisoners based on the evidence available to the Italian authorities at the time it was made, rather than with the benefit of hindsight. The Court concluded that 'there was nothing in the material before the national authorities to alert them to the fact that the release of [the prisoners] would pose a real and immediate threat to life'[72] and there was therefore no violation of Article 2.

The partly dissenting judgment of Judge Bonello in *Mastromatteo* points to the road not travelled by the majority. While Bonello recognized that there was no 'compelling causal link between the failures by the State and the death of the victim'[73] he nevertheless branded the Italian judges' decision

---

[67] *Mastromatteo* (n 60), [56].
[68] ibid, [69]. Emphasis added.
[69] ibid, [72].
[70] ibid, [68], citing *Osman* (n 2), [11].
[71] *Mastromatteo* (n 60), [72].
[72] ibid, [76].
[73] ibid, Partly Dissenting Opinion of Judge Bonello, [4].

to grant temporary release as 'misinformed'[74] and a 'fatal blunder'.[75] In so doing, he gave in to the temptations of outcome bias: a common tendency for people to rate decision-making quality as poor when told that the outcome of a decision was bad (Baron and Hershey, 1988). This is clear from Bonello's argument that 'the stark killing of young Mastromatteo goes some way to confirming that the judges who authorized the release of the criminals made shabby use of the discretion which Italian law entrusted them to exercise'.[76]

Furthermore, Bonello's judgment demonstrates hindsight bias—the tendency for people's judgements about the probability of an outcome to be influenced by information about the actual outcome (Fischhoff, 1975; Szmukler, 2000). This can be seen from his claim that the death of the applicant's son demonstrated that the Italian judges were mistaken in deciding that 'the State owed faith and credit to those who deserved diffidence and scepticism'.[77]

While Bonello's opinion could be dismissed as the view of one judge, his narrative demonstrates the temptations of character essentialism: the commonly held view that convicted offenders are untrustworthy and have 'immutable and essentially flawed natures' (Maruna, 2001, 4). Bonello referred to the prisoners as 'reoffenders already convicted of murder, attempted murder, complicity in attempted murder, and armed robbery, one a card-carrying member of the elite league of "socially dangerous"'.[78] For Bonello, the fact they went on to collectively commit robbery and murder could only confirm that character judgement.

Whereas the Grand Chamber in *Mastromatteo* avoided these temptations, the positive duty it created left the door open to the Second Section of the ECtHR to find a breach of Article 2 in *Maiorano*. In that case, the applicants were the family members of two women raped and murdered in 2005 by Angelo Izzo: a life-sentenced prisoner on day release. While the ECtHR mentioned the limits set on the positive duty to protect life in *Mastromatteo*, it neglected the injunction to bear in mind 'the unpredictability of human conduct'[79] in reaching its judgment. Although less explicit than Bonello's

---

[74] ibid, [17].
[75] ibid, [16].
[76] ibid, [19].
[77] ibid.
[78] ibid, [18].
[79] *Osman* (n 2), [116].

judgment, the reasoning in *Maiorano* illustrates the same tendencies towards outcome bias, hindsight bias, and character essentialism.

Izzo had been convicted in 1975 of kidnapping, rape, murder, and attempted murder in respect of two female victims. He had a history of violent behaviour in prison and of violating the terms of prison leave. By 2005, however, Izzo was 50 years old,[80] he had not been involved in a violent incident for nearly 30 years, and he had been out on temporary release on several occasions without incident.[81] Prison psychologists were enthusiastic about Izzo's progress, reporting that his personality had improved and matured, that he regretted his violent past, and that he wanted to atone and make reparation for his crimes.[82]

The ECtHR, however, placed greater weight on Izzo's violent history than on more recent evidence of improvement. It was unpersuaded by the Italian government's argument that 'the mere possibility that a person who had killed once could kill again' could not, in itself, constitute a 'real and immediate' risk to life.[83] Instead, the Court held that Izzo was a 'dangerous' 'repeat offender' convicted of 'exceptionally brutal crimes' (Registrar of the European Court of Human Rights, 2009, 3) who had a 'tendency to disrespect the law and authority'.[84] It concluded that, given Izzo's 'personality, his substantial criminal record and the evidence indicating that he was a danger to society', the authorities had failed to exercise due diligence in releasing him.[85] While the Court approved of Italy's measures of social reintegration for prisoners and its safeguards in general, it held that they had not been adequately followed on this occasion.

Maiorano implies that states ought to err on the side of caution in granting prisoners leave from prison or in moving them to open prison conditions. Consequently, the public's right to security can limit not only the prisoner's right to release on parole but also their access to opportunities for

---

[80] Empirical studies have consistently demonstrated that the prevalence and incidence of offending amongst the population both drop sharply from young adulthood onwards, although a small minority continue in their criminal careers. See Moffitt (1993).

[81] Temporary release schemes are associated with reductions in reoffending (Cheliotis, 2008). A study by the UK Ministry of Justice found a 3.1 per cent lower reoffending rate amongst individuals with 25 or more releases on temporary licence (ROTLs) compared to those with fewer than 25 (Hillier and Mews, 2018).

[82] *Maiorano* (n 61), [27], [90], and [114]. Quotations have been translated into English from the French version of the judgment by the author. An English summary of the case is available from the Registrar of the European Court of Human Rights (2009).

[83] *Maiorano* (n 61), [89].

[84] ibid, [118].

[85] ibid, [121].

rehabilitation. The positive obligations doctrine could therefore generate a chilling effect for the right to rehabilitation if the ECtHR continues to judge the quality of decisions on outcome rather than on process.

The fact that the Court so easily dismissed the evidence supporting the decision to grant Izzo temporary release indicates that it was sceptical that such a serious offender could change. However, given the Court's optimism towards the possibility for even those convicted of the most heinous crimes to change for the better in *Vinter*, it is unlikely that the Court, as a general principle, adopts this view. Nevertheless, both *Vinter* and *Maiorano* invite parole decision-makers to use judgements about prisoners' characters to assess their suitability for release. The narrative of character essentialism in *Maiorano* suggests that, in practice, offenders serving life sentences for very serious crimes will find it very difficult to demonstrate suitability for parole.

The Court's confidence in *Maiorano* in the idea that judges can (and should) distinguish between those offenders who have truly achieved rehabilitation and those who have not conflicts with its injunction in *Osman* and *Mastromatteo* to bear in mind the unpredictability of human conduct. It is, however, consistent with the Court's confidence in *James* and *Vinter* in the ability of parole decision-makers to determine when a prisoner can be released. This confidence does not adequately take into account the limits of our current capabilities to predict reoffending. Furthermore, it overlooks the weaknesses of the evidence base for the effectiveness of interventions to reduce serious reoffending.

6.4 The Duty to Engage in Rehabilitation

So far, I have argued that two key premises underpinned the DSPD proposals and the broader use of indeterminate prison sentences with offenders who are thought to be dangerous. First, that the public has a right to security and that the state has a duty to take coercive measures against third parties to protect that right. Second, that the rights of patients or prisoners affected by coercive measures can also be protected by giving them access to suitable rehabilitative interventions. The case law considered in this chapter demonstrates that the 'right to rehabilitation' can be better understood as a duty rather than a right. This is because as prisoners who are subject to preventive detention on the grounds of risk have little choice but to engage with rehabilitative interventions if they want to have any chance of release. The language of rights conceals the coercive nature of the bargain struck between the interests of the public and those of the (potential) offender. *Maiorano* further demonstrates a tendency for character judgements based on a person's past record of offending to tip the balance in favour of the public's right to security when it comes to courts deciding whether to give a person greater freedom in the interest of their rehabilitation.

As highlighted in Chapter 4, in England and Wales, the duty for prisoners to engage with treatments that practitioners believe are linked with their risk of reoffending has been given the status of an administrative requirement. Where a prisoner is found to require treatment for personality disorder or personality traits, refusing to engage with treatment can become a barrier to onward progress. For example, in *Samuel* [86] the Parole Board stated that a post-tariff prisoner serving a sentence of detention for public protection bore the responsibility for addressing his risk factors. If he did not apply for a therapeutic community or personality disorder unit he was 'likely to remain in custody'.[87]

Meeting the duty to engage in rehabilitation may also be characterized as a condition of citizenship. As Zedner argues, 'irregular citizens', including sexual and violent offenders, are 'consigned to a probationary or provisional status' as 'citizenship rights of participation and protection are made conditional upon compliance with prescribed norms and upon conformity with specified requirements' (Zedner, 2010, 389). Those who fail to comply are 'barred temporarily or indefinitely from full citizenship' through exclusionary measures (Zedner, 2010, 390). Appeals to rehabilitation as a means of avoiding disproportionate punishment thus conceal the unequal and coercive nature of the 'balance' being struck between the 'law-abiding' citizen and the 'dangerous' offender, who is constructed as an irregular or non-citizen.

In *Vinter*, the ECtHR presented rehabilitation and periodic review of detention as a means of avoiding the disproportionate punishment that would otherwise be imposed by indefinite detention under a whole life tariff. However, in the framework of the ECHR, the right not to be subjected to inhuman or degrading treatment or punishment, enshrined in Article 3, is an unqualified right. This implies that there should be no trade-off between the prisoner's Article 3 rights and the state's duty to protect potential victims from violations of Article 2 and 3. In *Maiorano*, however, the security

---

[86] R. (Samuel) v Parole Board for England and Wales and Secretary of State for Justice [2020] EWHC 42 (Admin).
[87] ibid, 13.

of the public took priority over the right of the offender to social reintegration and states were permitted to detain indefinitely those who are deemed to pose too high a risk.

In this way, the ECtHR's acceptance of the premise that rehabilitation will lead to release prevents it from scrutinizing the potential for risk-based indeterminate sentences to lead to disproportionate punishment. These sentences include the now-abolished IPP sentence and its replacement: the life sentence for dangerous offenders, available under s 285 of the Sentencing Act 2020.[88] The tendency for the Court to cast rehabilitation in a positive light further leads it to overlook the risks of harm that coercive rehabilitative interventions pose. As set out in Chapters 4 and 5 of this book, participation in rehabilitative programmes can expose prisoners to a risk of harm, including through self-harm or suicide.

6.5 Conclusion

The extensive coercive powers taken against 'dangerous' offenders discussed in this chapter exploit the mobile boundaries of a human rights framework that prioritizes the public's 'right to security' over the rights of individuals to liberty or to protection from disproportionate punishment. At first glance, the ECtHR's case law on the right to rehabilitation appears to be progressive and protective of prisoners' rights. The ECtHR's case law on the right to security, however, demonstrates that the Court is willing to sacrifice the right of offenders to social re-integration to the pursuit of public protection.

It has further been argued that the Court's concept of rehabilitation for life-sentenced prisoners is not unitary but takes two principal forms. Rehabilitation as risk reduction requires prisoners to engage with interventions that seek to reduce their risk factors for reoffending. Rehabilitation as redemption, by contrast, requires a transformation in the person's very identity that frees them from further punishment. Nevertheless, both forms of rehabilitation place the onus on the offender to earn their right to release rather than on the state to justify their continued detention. Rather than interrogating the proportionality of the prisoner's punishment to their crime, the Court invites states to engage in the much more difficult, and

---

[88] See Chapter 1 for further details of this sentence.

subjective, task of assessing changes in the prisoner's character. This offers weak protection to prisoners from the excesses of preventive detention and punishment. It is particularly problematic for offenders who are labelled as both dangerous and suffering from a personality disorder, given that a diagnosis of antisocial personality disorder or psychopathy is often associated with traits of aggression, impulsivity, and untrustworthiness.[89]

Moreover, the Court's failure to challenge the assumptions underpinning life sentences risks further entrenching the trends of punitiveness and risk aversion it has tried to resist. There is a mismatch between the Court's awareness in *Mastromatteo* of the unpredictability of human conduct and its confidence in *James*, *Vinter*, and *Maiorano* in the capacity for judges to distinguish between dangerous offenders and those who are safe to release. The pursuit of security therefore has the potential to significantly limit opportunities for prisoners to demonstrate their suitability for release by restricting rehabilitation opportunities that accord greater freedom to the prisoner. The Court should recognize the coercive context in which the 'right to rehabilitation' operates and the imbalance of power between the state and prisoners who have little choice but to conform if they wish to have any prospect of release. The final chapter of this book considers ways in which the current framework could provide greater recognition of the rights of prisoners who are labelled as dangerous.

---

[89] See Chapters 2–5.

7
Culpability, Responsibility, and Personality Disorder

7.1 Introduction

Offenders with personality disorder can straddle both the mental health and criminal justice systems. As set out in Chapter 3, the question of which system ought to take responsibility for them is longstanding. While much of the literature on personality disorder and the criminal law focuses on the insanity doctrine, this chapter takes sentencing as its starting point. Very few offenders successfully plead not guilty by reason of insanity, and evidence of mental disorder is more likely to make a difference at sentencing. 'Dangerous' offenders with personality disorders have come to be governed by a combination of indeterminate or extended determinate sentences, wholly therapeutic hospital orders, or partly punitive hybrid orders under the Mental Health Act (MHA) 1983. It has largely been left to sentencing judges to decide whether individual offenders belong in the criminal justice system or in the mental health system, or whether they should be managed by both. But it remains a possibility for the Justice Secretary to transfer sentenced prisoners to hospital under the MHA 1983. Prisoners may therefore be detained in hospital beyond their sentence in the name of protecting the public.

Loughnan and Ward (2014, 33) argue that sentencing powers under the MHA 1983 have the effect of 'side-stepping the question of responsibility altogether and going straight to the issue of dangerousness and treatment'. However, the analysis of leading cases from the Court of Appeal (Criminal Division) presented in this chapter demonstrates that the issue of responsibility or culpability is often determinative at sentencing. Drawing on insights from legal history and Cyrus Tata's (2019) concept of 'case-cleansing', I show that, by borrowing mental incapacity doctrines from the trial stage, sentencing judges can reassert the law's authority to punish offenders who have been found criminally responsible despite their mental disorders. In addition, judges have borrowed and reshaped the 'treatability' criterion from the original MHA 1983[1] to prevent patients from being discharged from hospital while they still pose a risk to the public. Both types of borrowing tend to push judges towards punitive disposals, and this can close off consideration of the damaging impact such disposals can have on individuals who are vulnerable to serious harm in prison.

A personality disorder diagnosis therefore presents a double disadvantage for criminal defendants. They are often deemed sufficiently mentally well to be punished for their offences, yet can be deemed sufficiently mentally unwell to justify detention and coerced treatment under mental health law. Drawing on the literature on 'coercive human rights' (Mavronicola and Lavrysen, 2020), I demonstrate that human rights law does not require judges to prioritize protecting the public and punishing culpable offenders over protecting offenders from harm in prison. By making use of the full range of alternatives to imprisonment, sentencing judges can protect the rights of offenders while also meeting the state's duties towards the public and victims.

7.2 Law and Personality Disorder

The literature on personality disorder and criminal responsibility is dominated by debates about how the law ought to respond to the emotional and volitional deficits associated with personality disorder. Neuroscientific research suggests that individuals diagnosed with antisocial personality disorder (ASPD) or psychopathy experience difficulties in exercising self-control, learning from experience, empathizing with others, and understanding moral reasons for restraint (Fine and Kennett, 2004; Glannon, 2008; Morse, 2008b; Glenn and Raine, 2014; Pickard, 2015). Some commentators argue that, in certain circumstances, evidence that these impairments prevented a person from obeying the law ought to ground a full defence (Morse, 2008b; Penney, 2012). Others argue that such evidence ought to reduce criminal responsibility by degrees, rather than excluding

---

[1] The treatability requirement applied under the MHA 1983 as originally enacted to offenders who met the legal criteria for 'psychopathic disorder' and reserved hospital orders for those individuals for whom treatment in hospital was 'likely to alleviate or prevent a deterioration of his condition'. The MHA 2007 replaced this requirement with the less stringent requirement that appropriate medical treatment must be available to the patient in hospital.

it completely (Sisti and Caplan, 2012; Glenn and Raine, 2014). Others still argue that such evidence ought to be grounds for sentence mitigation alone (Glannon, 2008).

While these debates continue, offenders diagnosed with personality disorders are typically held accountable by the criminal law (Peay, 2011b, 232–34). As Hanna Pickard (2015, 16) shows, individuals with personality disorders are often deemed mentally well enough to be punished under the criminal law but not well enough under mental health law to decide whether to accept treatment or whether to end their own lives.[2] Thus, she argues, an offender with personality disorder seems to get a 'raw deal': 'whichever way he turns, he is subjected to the strong arm of the law'.

Building on these observations, the discussion below demonstrates that 'dangerous' individuals with personality disorder often do not enjoy the protections from punishment accorded by the criminal law to those who suffer from mental disorder. Yet, if they are thought to pose a risk to others, they often do not benefit from the protections from detention and involuntary treatment without their consent accorded by mental health law to those who have no mental disorder. Mental health law will be returned to later in this chapter. First, the approach of the substantive criminal law to determining criminal responsibility and its implications for offenders diagnosed with personality disorders are drawn out.

Mental incapacity doctrines

The doctrines of insanity and diminished responsibility evolved to make only limited concessions to psychiatric evidence that not all offenders satisfy the ideal of the rational actor of criminal law. Using these concepts to evaluate culpability at sentencing can therefore be expected to push judges towards handing down punitive sentences. As both doctrines favour defendants with psychotic symptoms, their use at the sentencing stage is likely to inflate assessments of the culpability of offenders with personality disorders. The analysis of the leading sentencing cases presented below bears this out. In some cases, however, the Court of Appeal has taken a more

---

[2] This is because personality disorder constitutes a 'mental disorder' under s 1(1) of the MHA 1983 and, in general, treatment can be imposed upon detained patients under s 63 of the MHA 1983 without their consent and regardless of their decision-making capacity. Certain treatments are subject to additional safeguards and require consent and/or a second medical opinion (MHA 1983, ss 57–58A).

flexible approach. This approach has the potential to form a more principled basis for sentencing offenders with mental disorders that can better reflect their culpability and take into account the risks that imprisonment can pose to their mental health and physical safety.

There are two dominant theories of the normative basis for criminal responsibility: the reason-based account and the agency/authorship account (Berger, 2012). The first holds that criminal responsibility derives from 'the subject's capacity for practical reasoning—her capacity to bring rationality to bear on the situations that she confronts and using that reason based assessment as a guide for her actions' (Berger, 2012, 124). For example, Stephen J. Morse (2008a, 7) argues that the law's normative force is predicated on its subjects having at least a minimal level of capacity to 'understand good reasons for action, including the relevant facts and rules' and to conform to the law's requirements through 'intentional action or forbearance'. The agency/authorship account 'focuses on whether an act can be fairly attributed to an individual as the author of an autonomous and authentic human life' (Berger, 2012, 125). Thus, according to Victor Tadros, responsible agents are 'agents who are capable of believing and acting in the light of reasons that they adopt as their own' (Tadros, 2007, 138).

In practice, however, the criminal law treats as responsible many individuals who do not conform to these ideals. The insanity doctrine is a concession to only a very limited range of impairments that affect a person's ability to act autonomously or in accordance with practical reasoning. According to the *M'Naghten* rules, a person is insane if, at the time of the offence, he (or she) was:

> labouring under such a defect of reason, from disease of the mind, as not to know the nature and quality of the act he was doing; or, if he did know it, that he did not know he was doing what was wrong.[3]

The insanity plea is of general application[4] and, if successful, results in the 'special verdict' of 'not guilty by reason of insanity'.[5] The special verdict avoids a criminal conviction but disposals are available to the court to

---

[3] *Queen v M'Naghten*, 8 Eng Rep 718 [1843].
[4] *Loake v DPP* [2017] EWHC 2855 (Admin), [54].
[5] Trial of Lunatics Act 1883, s 2.

ensure that the person receives treatment and remains under the control of the state.[6]

The *M'Naghten* rules exclude individuals who were aware of the physical circumstances and consequences of their act[7] and those who knew that what they are doing was legally wrong, even if they did not understand that it was morally wrong.[8] In other words, the rules serve to 'exclude the vast majority of mentally disordered persons from the realm of the insanity doctrine' (Mackay, 1995, 100). The question of whether a person with a mental disorder ought to be punished therefore often falls to be decided at sentencing.

The narrow scope of the insanity rules is the result of efforts by judges in the mid-nineteenth century to protect legal attributions of criminal responsibility from both common-sense and expert understandings of 'madness' (Eigen 1995; 1999). These understandings threatened the authority of the criminal law to govern through deterrence, and the authority of courts to determine questions of criminal liability (Eigen, 1995; see also Smith, 1998 and Wiener, 2003).[9] The insanity rules therefore tend to strictly limit the extent to which evidence of mental disorder can impact upon findings of criminal responsibility at the trial stage.

The doctrine of diminished responsibility responds to a broader range of impairments than insanity. Currently, a defendant charged with murder can plead guilty to manslaughter by reason of diminished responsibility if they can show that, at the time of the killing, they were 'suffering from an abnormality of mental functioning' that 'arose from a recognised medical condition' and that this abnormality 'substantially impaired' their ability 'to . . . understand the nature of [their] conduct; to form a rational judgment [or] to exercise self-control'. The impairment must also provide 'an explanation for [their] acts and omissions in doing or being a party to the killing'. An abnormality of mental functioning 'provides an explanation for

---

[6] Originally, those found insane would be detained indefinitely in a psychiatric hospital. Now, section 5 of the Criminal Procedure (Insanity) Act 1964 provides that courts may choose between making (a) a hospital order (with or without a restriction order); (b) a supervision order; or (c) an order for absolute discharge. Where the charge is murder, the court is bound to impose a hospital order with a restriction order.
[7] *R v Codère* (1917) 12 Cr App R 21.
[8] *R v Windle* [1952] 2 QB 826; *R v Johnson* [2007] EWCA Crim 1978; *R v Keal* [2022] EWCA Crim 341.
[9] There have long been disagreements amongst both legal and medical experts as to how the law of insanity ought to operate, and courts in the nineteenth century frequently stretched the rules. See Eigen (1995), Wiener (2003), Smith (1998), Loughnan (2012), and Loughnan and Ward (2014) for a fuller account than space allows here.

D's conduct if it causes, or is a significant contributory factor in causing, D to carry out that conduct'.[10]

While the test of one's ability to understand the nature of one's conduct in diminished responsibility is similarly demanding to the nature and quality limb of *M'Naghten*, the level of impairment need only be 'substantial', not total (Mackay, 2018). The 'rational judgment' limb of diminished responsibility is much broader than the wrongfulness limb of *M'Naghten* and seems to allow consideration of the defendant's ability to assess the moral wrongfulness of their conduct.[11] Unlike insanity, diminished responsibility takes into account substantial impairments of self-control. Consequently, diminished responsibility can be expected to be more responsive to the volitional and emotional deficits associated with personality disorder.[12] However, unlike insanity, a successful plea of diminished responsibility does not entirely eliminate criminal responsibility but results in a manslaughter conviction.

The limited scope of diminished responsibility is attributable to its historical development. The doctrine originally emerged in Scotland in the second half of the nineteenth century (Loughnan, 2012, 230–32). It was adapted and incorporated into the law of England and Wales through the Homicide Act 1957, largely to bring greater flexibility to the law of insanity at a time when a murder conviction carried the death penalty (Loughnan and Ward, 2014).

Given these differences, insanity and diminished responsibility present conflicting theories as to how mental disorder or incapacity affects criminal responsibility. While insanity recognizes that only certain cognitive deficits can *eliminate* criminal responsibility, diminished responsibility holds that both volitional and cognitive deficits can *reduce* criminal responsibility by degrees (Peay, 2016, 154). As a successful plea of diminished responsibility results in a manslaughter conviction, it does not entirely exclude criminal responsibility (Peay, 2016). Diminished *culpability* would be a more accurate description of the doctrine: the offender is held *responsible* for the killing but his or her *culpability* falls short of that required for a murder conviction (Howard, H, 2015; Peay, 2016). This is the case even where a person's behaviour has been *caused* by their mental disorder, and where it

---

[10] Homicide Act 1957, s 2, as amended by s 52(1) of the Coroners and Justice Act 2009.
[11] *R v Conroy* [2017] EWCA Crim 81; [2017] 2 Cr App R 26.
[12] See Chapter 2 on the characteristics associated with psychopathy, ASPD, and BPD.

could therefore be questioned whether the person's conduct was voluntary (Mackay and Hughes, 2021).[13]

As both doctrines tend to strictly limit the extent to which evidence of incapacity can affect findings of responsibility at the trial stage, judges using these doctrines at the sentencing stage are likely to overestimate culpability. This is because judges are likely to overlook psychiatric evidence at sentencing that does not fit within the insanity or diminished responsibility rules but that nevertheless casts doubt on the appropriateness of punishment. The use of these doctrines at sentencing is also likely to confine the use of hospital orders under s 37 of the MHA 1983 to individuals who have been found insane or guilty of manslaughter by reason of diminished responsibility. This would go against the legislative purpose of the order, which is to provide an alternative to imprisonment for offenders convicted of any imprisonable offence other than murder (O'Loughlin, 2021b).

Using the mental incapacity doctrines at sentencing is particularly likely to lead judges to overlook the deficits associated with personality disorder. This is because, both according to the letter of the law and in practice, the doctrine of insanity tends to favour defendants affected by delusions or hallucinations associated with schizophrenia (Mackay, 1990; Kearns and Mackay, 1999). While a personality disorder constitutes a 'disease of the mind', offenders with personality disorders typically have a good cognitive understanding of legal rules and of the nature of their own actions (Morse, 2008b; Peay, 2011b). Despite their difficulties in restraining themselves, responding emotionally to moral reasons or empathizing with others, such individuals typically have a good grasp of reality. Although borderline personality disorder (BPD) can be associated with 'paranoid ideation or severe dissociative symptoms', this is not a feature of ASPD or psychopathy.

This can be seen from the latest available statistics. Between 1975 and 1988, just three people with a primary diagnosis of personality disorder successfully pleaded not guilty by reason of insanity in England and Wales (Law Commission, 2012, para 3.58). Between 1997 and 2001,[14] there were no successful insanity pleas based on this diagnosis (Mackay et al, 2006, 400). Juries in diminished responsibility cases similarly favour defendants affected by schizophrenia, and successful defendants with personality

---

[13] That is to say, unless the causal connection is so strong that the defendant is found insane or is found not to satisfy the *actus reus* or *mens rea* requirements of murder.
[14] At the time of writing, this was the latest period for which data broken down by diagnosis was available.

disorder who plead diminished responsibility more frequently receive a prison sentence than those diagnosed with schizophrenia (Mackay and Mitchell, 2017, Table 8).

A further doctrine that features in the sentencing case law is the prior fault doctrine, which is based on 'the idea that an individual should not be able to rely on a defence when he or she has culpably brought about the condition that forms the basis of that defence' (Loughnan and Wake, 2014, 113). For example, an individual cannot deny responsibility at trial if they voluntarily consumed alcohol or dangerous drugs before committing the offence.[15] This doctrine is based on policy considerations rather than on any coherent theory of the impact that intoxication has on a person's ability to understand good reasons for action or to act autonomously. Using this doctrine at sentencing can therefore also be expected to lead judges to overestimate culpability.

7.3 Sentencing and Mental Disorder

The insanity doctrine is not the only means through which a convicted offender can avoid punishment. Where the relevant criteria are met, a sentencing court may choose to forgo punishment entirely in favour of treatment by handing down a hospital order in place of a prison sentence under s 37 of the MHA 1983. Despite the significant practical importance of sentencing, analyses of the interactions between psychiatric expert witnesses and judges tend to focus on the trial stage.[16] In addition, there is a tendency to portray the trial and sentencing stages as animated by different conceptions of offenders. A classical conception of offenders as 'freewill rational beings' is commonly associated with the trial stage, while a positivist conception of offenders and a focus on pathology is associated with the post-trial stage (Bottoms, 1977, 92). However, as the sentencing case law discussed below demonstrates, judges often draw on concepts from the trial stage to make decisions about criminal culpability at the sentencing stage. Drawing on Cyrus Tata's (2019) concept of 'case-cleansing' and the historical development of the mental incapacity doctrines, I suggest that this is a means for

---

[15] *DPP v Majewski* [1977] AC 443. See Loughnan and Wake (2014) for further discussion of the case law.
[16] See, in particular, on the history of mental incapacity doctrines: Lacey (2001; 2016); Loughnan (2007; 2012); and on the role of psychiatric expert witnesses, Ward (1997; 2006; 2017); and Loughnan and Ward (2014).

judges to resist the threat that psychiatric evidence poses to the legitimacy of a criminal conviction and the punishment that follows. While this threat has been safely contained at the trial stage, it can re-emerge when psychiatric evidence is called to support a disposal under the MHA 1983.

The next section outlines the options available to judges sentencing an offender who suffers from mental disorder and draws out the principles governing the leading sentencing cases from the Court of Appeal (Criminal Division). While case law encourages judges to draw on concepts of rationality at the sentencing stage, the Court of Appeal has taken a more flexible approach in deciding several individual appeals against sentence. These cases demonstrate that considerations of the offender's welfare and public protection can take priority over punishing culpable offenders.

Sentencing Disposals and Principles

When it comes to sentencing, judges are expected to weigh several factors in the balance: the offender's culpability, the degree of harm caused by the offence, and any aggravating or mitigating factors (Sentencing Council of England and Wales, 2019). They are further required to choose a sentence that speaks to the legislative aims of sentencing: punishment, reduction of crime (including by deterrence), reform and rehabilitation, the protection of the public, and reparation.[17] There is no hierarchy between these aims and no statutory guidance on the relative weight judges ought to accord to them.

Judges in England and Wales can choose from a wide range of disposals when sentencing an offender with a mental disorder or impairment. Some disposals involve detention, including an indeterminate or determinate prison sentence, with the possibility of a transfer to hospital under s 47 of the MHA 1983; a hospital order under s 37 of the MHA 1983 (with or without restrictions under s 41); and a hospital and limitation direction under s 45A of the MHA 1983 coupled with a prison sentence (also known as a hybrid order). Other disposals include guardianship orders under s 37 of the MHA 1983 and mental health treatment requirements imposed as part of a community order or suspended sentence order.[18]

The judge's choice of disposal has a significant influence on how the person is subsequently dealt with. In short, it determines whether they go

---

[17] Sentencing Act 2020, s 57.
[18] Available under Schedule 9, Part 9 of the Sentencing Act 2020.

straight to hospital, straight to prison, or remain in the community. If the order is for detention, the disposal determines (1) which authorities be tasked with deciding when to release the person and the criteria they will apply; (2) which authorities will be responsible for monitoring the person in the community; (3) whether the person will be subject to recall to hospital or to prison; and (4) on what grounds the person can be recalled.

Despite the significance of this decision, little statutory guidance is available to assist judges in choosing between disposals. Judges are reliant on the guidance handed down by the Court of Appeal (Criminal Division) in the leading cases of *Vowles and others*[19] and *Edwards and others*[20] and the Sentencing Guideline for Courts Sentencing Offenders with Mental Disorders, Developmental Disorders, or Neurological Impairments (Sentencing Council of England and Wales, 2020). These cases focus on the judge's choice between sentences of imprisonment, hybrid orders under s 45A, and hospital orders under ss 37/41 of the MHA 1983. The differences between these orders are set out below, followed by an analysis of the principles drawn from the leading cases.

Hospital orders are available under s 37 of the MHA 1983 where a Crown Court or a Magistrates' Court is sentencing an offender convicted of any imprisonable offence, except murder.[21] To make a hospital order, the court must be satisfied, on the written or oral evidence of two doctors, that the person 'is suffering from mental disorder . . . of a nature or degree which makes it appropriate for him to be detained in a hospital for medical treatment and appropriate medical treatment is available for him'.[22] Mental disorder is defined broadly as 'any disorder or disability of the mind'[23] and includes personality disorder. While in hospital, the person can be given treatment for mental disorder without their consent, subject to criteria and safeguards.[24] Importantly, this power to treat without consent is not available in prison.[25]

---

[19] [2015] EWCA Crim 45, [2015] 1 WLR 5131, [2015] 2 WLUK 161.
[20] [2018] EWCA Crim 595; [2018] 4 WLR 64; [2018] 2 Cr App R (S) 17.
[21] A hospital order is not available where the sentence is 'fixed by law' (s 37(1), MHA 1983). The only sentence that is fixed by law is the mandatory life sentence for murder (s 1, Murder (Abolition of Death Penalty) Act 1965; Sentencing Act 2020, s 275).
[22] MHA 1983, s 37.2(a). The MHA 1983 uses male pronouns throughout but applies regardless of gender.
[23] MHA 1983 s 1(2).
[24] MHA 1983, ss 56 and 63. The safeguards are contained in ss 57–58A.
[25] This is because the MHA 1983 does not apply in prisons. Prisoners who lack capacity to make a decision regarding medical treatment, including mental health treatment, can, however, be treated in prison under the Mental Capacity Act 2005 if this is in their best interests. See Department for Constitutional Affairs (2007).

A Crown Court may make the patient subject to 'restrictions' under s 41 if necessary to protect the public from serious harm. Restricted patients may not take leave of absence or be transferred to another hospital without the assent of the Justice Secretary and can only be discharged from hospital by the Justice Secretary or by the First Tier Tribunal (Mental Health) in England or the Mental Health Tribunal for Wales.

The Tribunal has a duty to discharge a hospital order patient under s 72(1)(b) of the MHA 1983 if it is *not* satisfied:

> (i) that he is then suffering from mental disorder or from mental disorder of a nature or degree which makes it appropriate for him to be liable to be detained in a hospital for medical treatment; or (ii) that it is necessary for the health and safety of the patient or for the protection of other persons that he should receive such treatment; or (iia) that appropriate medical treatment is available for him.

Tribunals therefore have the power to discharge restricted patients without the agreement of the Justice Secretary, and the Tribunal may be obliged to discharge a patient even if it judges that they still pose a risk to the public. The only exception is where the patient is concurrently serving a prison sentence. Restricted patients may be discharged by the Justice Secretary or by a Tribunal absolutely or subject to conditions.[26] Conditionally discharged restricted patients can be recalled to hospital by the Justice Secretary.[27]

Alternatively, Crown Courts have the power to make a hospital and limitation direction (also known as a hybrid order). Under s 45A of the MHA 1983, a hospital direction, placing the offender in a specific hospital, and a limitation direction, subjecting them to restrictions, may be attached to any custodial sentence.[28] The hybrid order criteria under s 45A(2) are very similar to the s 37 hospital order criteria.

A court may instead choose to hand down a prison sentence and to leave it to the Justice Secretary to transfer the prisoner to hospital under s 47. The Justice Secretary may do so if satisfied based on reports from two

---

[26] The Justice Secretary's discharge powers are contained in MHA 1983, s 42(2) and the Tribunal's discharge powers are contained in MHA 1983, s 73(1)–(2).

[27] MHA 1983, s 73(2).

[28] Originally, s 45A orders were available only for offenders suffering from 'psychopathic disorder' under the MHA 1983. After the MHA 2007 came into force they became available for convicted offenders suffering from any disorder or disability of the mind.

medical practitioners that the prisoner is suffering from a mental disorder 'of a nature or degree which makes it appropriate for him to be detained in a hospital for medical treatment' and 'that appropriate medical treatment is available for him'.[29] A transfer direction has the same effect as a hospital order[30] and the Justice Secretary can make the prisoner subject to restrictions under s 49.

The timing and conditions of release for s 45A and ss 47/49 patients depends on the terms of their prison sentences. While their sentences remain in force, the Tribunal has no power to discharge these patients from hospital, even if the MHA 1983 detention criteria are no longer met. Such patients may only be discharged by the Justice Secretary, who may transfer them to prison.[31] Patients whose prison sentences have lapsed remain in hospital until discharged by a Tribunal.[32]

Given the above, hospital order patients enjoy stronger liberty protections than those accorded to prisoners or patients serving indeterminate prison sentences. This is because a hospital order patient must be discharged by a Tribunal if it is not satisfied that any one of the criteria in s 72(1)(b) are met, even if they are still believed to present a risk to the public. A patient subject to a hospital order with restrictions can only be recalled to hospital if the Justice Secretary possesses recent medical evidence from which it can reasonably be concluded that all three criteria in s 72(1)(b) are met.[33] By contrast, a person serving an indeterminate sentence can only be released where the Parole Board is satisfied that their detention 'is no longer necessary for the protection of the public'.[34] A prisoner released on licence can be recalled to prison on risk grounds alone (Ministry of Justice and HM Prison & Probation Service, 2023, para 4.2.1).

In a context of little statutory guidance, judges have developed a concept of 'partial culpability' to determine the choice of sentence in cases in which a person is eligible for an order under the MHA 1983 or a prison sentence alone (Peay, 2015, 12). This concept derives from the partial defence

---

[29] MHA 1983, s 47(1).
[30] MHA 1983, s 47(2).
[31] MHA 1983, s 50(1).
[32] This is because s 45 orders and ss 47/49 orders have the same effect, and the restrictions lapse upon the expiry of a determinate prison sentence (MHA 1983 s 50(2)). Once the restrictions lapse, the patient's detention continues as if under a s 37 hospital order (Ministry of Justice and HM Prison & Probation Service, 2017, 6).
[33] *R (M) v Secretary of State for the Home Department* [2007] EWCA Civ 687.
[34] Crime Sentences Act 1997, s 28(6)(b). As set out in Chapter 6, it is also possible for those serving indeterminate sentences to be released on compassionate grounds.

of diminished responsibility and its use at sentencing can be traced back to the Court of Appeal's 1989 decision in *Birch*.[35] While the Court in *Birch* did not favour prison sentences for offenders with mental disorders, its reasoning has come to underpin subsequent sentencing decisions that prioritize punishment and the use of indeterminate prison sentences to protect the public.

The Court of Appeal observed in *Birch* that the choice of prison as an alternative to hospital could arise for a mentally disordered offender in two rather different scenarios:

> (1) If the offender is dangerous and no suitable secure hospital accommodation is available . . . [and] (2) Where the sentencer considers that notwithstanding the offender's mental disorder there was an element of culpability in the offence which merits punishment. This may happen where there is no connection between the mental disorder and the offence, or where the defendant's responsibility for the offence is 'diminished' but not wholly extinguished.[36]

The Court was nevertheless wary of using prison sentences solely to manage risk. It held that: 'in the absence of any question of culpability and punishment, the judge should not impose a sentence of imprisonment simply to ensure that if the [Tribunal] . . . is . . . constrained to order a discharge, the offender will return to prison rather than be set free'.[37] It further implied that a hospital order would be suitable where treatment in hospital was expected to reduce risk, remarking that purpose of the order was to ensure the offender would receive treatment 'in the hope and expectation of course that the result will be to avoid the commission by the offender of further criminal acts'.[38]

While the Court in *Birch* recognized that there was no requirement for a 'causal connection' between the index offence and the disorder for a hospital order to be made,[39] its reasoning suggested that a hospital order may not be suitable where there was no connection at all, and where there was therefore an element of culpability. However, the Court was wary of the

---

[35] (1989) 11 Cr App R (S) 202; (1990) 90 Cr App R 78.
[36] ibid, [64].
[37] ibid, [65], following *R v Howell* (1985) 7 Cr App R (S.) 360.
[38] ibid, [36].
[39] ibid, [57].

use of prison sentences to punish offenders with mental disorders, holding that 'even where there is culpability, the right way to deal with a dangerous and disordered person is to make [a hospital order with restrictions] under sections 37 and 41'.[40]

Over time, *Birch* was reinterpreted in line with the increasing pressure on judges to respond to political demands for harsher punishments and greater protection for the public noted in the sentencing literature (see Hough et al, 2003; Ashworth and Player, 2005). In *Drew*,[41] the House of Lords declined to depart from the preference in *Birch* for hospital orders. Nevertheless, it held that it was not 'wrong in principle to impose a punitive sentence of imprisonment on a mentally disordered defendant who was criminally responsible and fit to be tried'.[42] The House of Lords was concerned that Tribunals were obliged to discharge hospital order patients where the medical criteria for their detention were no longer met and regardless of risk to the public.[43] It therefore called on courts to give 'appropriate weight' to the regime governing release and recall.[44] The Court of Appeal in *Welsh*[45] consolidated this approach, holding that it was bound to take public confidence into account when choosing between a hospital order with restrictions and life imprisonment. For the Court, public confidence could 'only be satisfied by ensuring that the issue is resolved in a way which best protects the public and reflects the gravity of the offence'.[46]

The Court of Appeal's 2015 decision in *Vowles*[47] shifted further towards a preference for punishment. Two key themes emerged from *Vowles*:

> the first is that the court should ensure that a mentally disordered offender is punished for any element or particle of responsibility for her or his wrongdoing; the second is that the court should focus on finding the sentence or disposal with the most suitable release provisions, taking account of the risk presented by D (Ashworth and Mackay, 2015, 545).

---

[40] ibid, [64], following *R v Mbatha* (1985) 7 Cr App R (S) 373.
[41] [2003] 1 WLR 1213.
[42] ibid, [17].
[43] ibid, [21].
[44] ibid, [22].
[45] *R v Welsh* [2011] 2 Cr App R (S) 68.
[46] ibid, [14].
[47] n 19. *Vowles* united six appeals against sentence and the judgment was delivered by the Lord Chief Justice. *Vowles* therefore has the characteristics of a 'guidance judgment': a decision by an upper court made in the absence of a sentencing guideline that is intended to hand down binding guidance to lower courts on sentencing (see Ashworth and Kelly, 2022, 1.5.3.2).

In *Vowles*, the Court of Appeal seemed to establish a presumption in favour of hybrid orders under s 45A of the MHA 1983, holding that 'there must always be sound reasons for departing from the usual course of imposing a penal sentence'.[48] *Vowles* further emphasized that the choice between a hospital order and a sentence with a penal element should not turn on 'clinical advantage' but on 'whether successful medical treatment is expected to reduce the risk to the public' (Ashworth and Mackay, 2015, 546). As Peay (2016) highlighted, given the possibility for offenders who received hybrid orders to be later transferred to or recalled to prison, *Vowles* seemed likely to exacerbate the 'notorious' 'difficulties caused to prison managements by the presence and behaviour of those who are subject to serious mental disorder' noted by the House of Lords in *Drew*.[49]

However, while the guidance in *Vowles* seemed to advise judges to prioritize hybrid orders, the Court did not follow this order of priority when deciding the individual appeals before it (Peay, 2015). Other elements of the guidance suggested that the Court did not intend to entirely erode the place of hospital orders with restrictions. Part of the guidance suggested that judges should take a more flexible approach to determining sentence and have regard to four factors:

> (1) the extent to which the offender needs treatment for the mental disorder from which the offender suffers, (2) the extent to which the offending is attributable to the mental disorder, (3) the extent to which punishment is required, and (4) the protection of the public including the regime for deciding release and the regime after release.[50]

Another part of the guidance suggested that judges should have regard to the causal connection between the defendant's mental disorder and their offending, and that a hospital order with restrictions would be appropriate where:

> (1) the mental disorder is treatable; (2) once treated there is no evidence [the offender] would be in any way dangerous; and (3) the offending is entirely due to that mental disorder.[51]

---

[48] *Vowles* (n 19), [51].
[49] *Drew*, (n 42), [22].
[50] *Vowles* (n 19), [51]. For further discussion and analysis of *Vowles*, see Peay (2016); Ashworth and Mackay (2015); and O'Loughlin (2021b).
[51] *Vowles* (n 19), [54(iii)].

This causal connection approach can be traced back to the influence of the diminished responsibility doctrine on *Birch*, and the reasoning of the Court of Appeal in deciding the individual appeals before it in *Vowles* fit most closely with this approach. This is despite the fact that diminished responsibility would not have been available at trial to any of the six appellants in *Vowles*.[52] In applying this approach, the Court tended to find in favour of a hospital order with restrictions where it found that an appellant's index offence and risk of reoffending was causally connected to a treatable mental disorder.[53] Where the connection was unclear and/or treatability uncertain, the Court tended to leave the appellant's prison sentence in place to reflect their culpability and to ensure they would be released via the Parole Board.[54]

In *Edwards*,[55] the Court of Appeal sought to clarify the confusion that had arisen from the inconsistencies in *Vowles*. The Court of Appeal expanded the circumstances in which a hospital order with restrictions would be warranted, holding that 'sound reasons' for departure from the 'usual course' of a prison sentence may include:

> the nature of the offence and the limited nature of any penal element (if imposed) and the fact that the offending was very substantially (albeit not wholly) attributable to the offender's illness.[56]

Nevertheless, *Edwards* again seemed to reserve hospital orders for defendants whose culpability was very low and for whom treatment could be expected to significantly reduce risk of reoffending. An application of the prior fault doctrine can also be seen in *Edwards*. The Court of Appeal inferred culpability from the failure of the appellant, Regina Edwards, to take her medication, holding that she 'must have had some (albeit limited) awareness of the consequences of taking her medication erratically' given she had previously been violent towards family members.[57]

---

[52] The appellants in *Vowles* had variously been convicted of arson (Vowles); theft, robbery, and obtaining property by deception (Barnes); attempted robbery and assault with intent to resist arrest (Coleman); wounding with intent (Odiowei); seven offences of arson, one offence of criminal damage, and one offence of threats to kill (Irving); and wounding with intent to cause grievous bodily harm (McDougall). None of the appellants were charged with murder.
[53] See the successful appeals of McDougall and Coleman.
[54] See the unsuccessful appeals of Vowles and Irving.
[55] *Edwards* (n 20).
[56] ibid, [12].
[57] ibid, [49].

While based on the Court of Appeal's case law, the Sentencing Council's (2020) Sentencing Guideline for Courts Sentencing Offenders with Mental Disorders, Developmental Disorders, or Neurological Impairments does not fully endorse the *Vowles* causal connection approach. Rather, it specifies that 'culpability will only be reduced if there is *sufficient* connection between the offender's impairment or disorder and the offending behaviour' (Sentencing Council of England and Wales, 2020, paras 10–11).[58] Nevertheless, the guideline advises judges to consider factors loosely based on the diminished responsibility doctrine when assessing culpability:

> At the time of the offence did the offender's impairment or disorder impair their ability:
> - to exercise appropriate judgement,
> - to make rational choices,
> - to understand the nature and consequences of their actions?
> (Sentencing Council of England and Wales, 2020, para 15).

This further suggests that the Sentencing Council regards rational reasoning or conduct at the time of the offence as suggestive of culpability. The sentencing guideline further suggests courts should assess culpability in light of 'wilful' failures to take prescribed medication or evidence that the offender took alcohol, non-prescribed or illicit drugs at the time of the offence while being aware that this would worsen their mental impairment or disorder (Sentencing Council of England and Wales, 2020, para 15). Consequently, both *Edwards* and the guideline use the logic of the prior fault doctrine to suggest that judges should examine whether fault may be attributed to the defendant for precipitating or failing to prevent the deterioration of their mental state prior to the commission of the offence.

As set out in the next two sections, the Court of Appeal has adopted rather different interpretations of these principles in subsequent individual appeals against sentence. In earlier work, I identified two distinct strands in the case law after *Vowles*: a punitive strand and a therapeutic strand (O'Loughlin, 2021b). Cases in the first strand adopted a prescriptive interpretation of *Vowles* and tended to prioritize punishment over the therapeutic interests of the offender. Cases in the second strand followed the more flexible four-factor approach in *Vowles* and tended to de-prioritize

---

[58] Emphasis added.

punishment while giving as much weight to the defendant's therapeutic interests as the needs of public protection allow. Below, I build on this analysis by demonstrating that these two strands of case law represent two different methods for judges to resolve conflicts between psychiatric evidence presented at sentencing and determinations of criminal responsibility from the trial stage. Later, I turn to consider the relevance of 'treatability' in the sentencing case law and post-sentence.

The punitive strand

A distinguishing feature of several cases in the first strand is judicial reliance on doctrines from the trial stage when determining culpability at the sentencing stage and a focus on finding elements of rationality or fault in the defendant's conduct. This tendency, coupled with political pressure on judges to prioritise punishment and public protection, can help to explain the emphasis on punishment and managing risk in this strand of case law in a process that has parallels with Cyrus Tata's (2019) concept of 'case-cleansing'.

Tata argues that defence lawyers and pre-sentence report writers 'cleanse' criminal cases of anomalous or ambiguous features that threaten legal ideals prior to sentencing. These ideals include 'freedom of choice; the presumption of innocence; participation in one's own case; consistency balanced with attendance to the unique individual' (Tata, 2019, 670). Denials of guilt or denials of culpability despite a guilty plea can conflict with these ideals. Legal actors therefore try to translate such anomalies into more acceptable categories (Tata, 2019, 670).

The case law in the punitive strand suggests that anomalous features of cases can be reintroduced at sentencing stage by psychiatric evidence in support of a disposal under the MHA 1983. Such evidence can cast doubt on the offender's capacity to control their actions or to act rationally, thereby seeming to contradict a conviction for a very serious offence. Judges respond by borrowing concepts from the trial stage in order to protect two legal ideals from the challenge of psychiatric evidence: the image of the rational offender and the legitimacy of punishing an offender who has admitted guilt or been found responsible at trial. Borrowing these concepts tends to push sentencing in a punitive direction because, as set out earlier, the mental incapacity doctrines tend to limit the extent to which mental disorder can reduce or eliminate criminal responsibility.

As set out earlier, the logic of diminished responsibility was borrowed by the Court of Appeal in *Vowles* via the earlier case of *Birch* to help to determine the suitability of a hospital order with restrictions at sentencing. The Court's use of the phrase ' "diminished" but not wholly extinguished' in *Birch*[59] was unfortunate. As diminished responsibility is a partial defence and results in a manslaughter conviction it cannot 'wholly extinguish' criminal responsibility. *Birch* was open to the interpretation that a hospital order would only be suitable for individuals whose responsibility (and therefore culpability) was 'wholly extinguished'. There was a further risk that *Birch* would be interpreted as *requiring* a prison sentence in such circumstances. While both interpretations would frustrate the legislative purpose of the hospital order, as set out above, they can help to explain the outcomes of the punitive strand post-*Vowles*.[60]

In *Graciano*,[61] the appellant appealed against a life sentence and s 45A order imposed after he was found guilty of manslaughter by reason of diminished responsibility. The Court of Appeal placed significant weight on evidence that the appellant's behaviour in attacking the victim was apparently purposeful and gave less weight to psychiatric evidence that he was in the midst of a psychotic episode at the time. It held that his culpability had not 'been entirely extinguished by his mental disorder (paranoid schizophrenia) such as would be the case with a finding of insanity'.[62] Furthermore, it approved the sentencing judge's finding that there were 'significant elements of rationality' in his behaviour at the time of the killing.[63] It concluded that the appellant retained 'a significant degree of culpability' and left his life sentence in place.[64] In so doing, the Court seemed to automatically infer culpability from the failure of the insanity defence, despite psychiatric evidence that the appellant's mental disorder was a 'significant contributory factor and even an explanation' for the killing.[65]

Martens[66] also involved an appeal against a life sentence and s 45A order. The appellant had pleaded guilty to causing grievous bodily harm with

---

[59] n 35, [64].
[60] Similar reasoning to the cases in the punitive strand can be seen in the earlier cases of *R v Staines* [2006] EWCA Crim 15 and *R v Fox* [2011] EWCA Crim 3299.
[61] [2015] EWCA Crim 980.
[62] *Graciano* (n 61), [21].
[63] ibid, [22].
[64] ibid, [22]–[23].
[65] ibid, [22].
[66] [2015] EWCA Crim 1645.

intent and was convicted at trial of attempted murder. The Court of Appeal inferred culpability from the appellant's guilty plea and gave less weight to psychiatric evidence that the offence would not have occurred if he had not been ill. This differential weighing of evidence may be attributed to the fact that the appellant's guilty plea seemed to conflict with the psychiatric evidence on appeal that his offending was largely attributable to his mental disorder. Furthermore, the Court gave little weight to psychiatric evidence that the appellant was likely to return to prison during his sentence, and that this would trigger a serious deterioration in his condition. Instead, it decided that it was 'quite open' to the mental health or prison authorities 'to provide suitable mental health care'.[67] Thus, the Court of Appeal in *Martens* reasserted the legitimacy of punishing an offender who had admitted he was guilty of a serious offence by using inferences of culpability from findings at the trial stage to resist the implication of the psychiatric evidence that the appellant's culpability was low and that imprisonment would go against his interests.

In view of the law, the Court of Appeal in *Graciano* and *Martens* was not bound to maintain the appellants' prison sentences. There is no legislative requirement for courts to punish offenders who are not found insane or who plead guilty, and judges are not obliged to prioritize punishment over the other purposes of sentencing.[68] Moreover, it is doubtful that a guilty plea should be taken as evidence of culpability. Defendants are not routinely screened for their capacity to plead guilty, and some with mental disorders or disabilities may be induced to plead guilty by the prospect of a lesser sentence despite having grounds for raising a defence or being found unfit to plead (Peay and Player, 2018).

By examining elements of rationality in the appellants' conduct or inferring culpability from a guilty plea, the Court of Appeal in each case seemed to disregard evidence that the appellants did not fit with the ideal, rational subject of the trial stage, and to resist the implication that the long-established mental incapacity doctrines do not adequately respond to evidence of mental disorder. These cases further suggest judicial resistance to the idea that a convicted offender may not be a suitable subject for punishment, despite a conviction for a very serious violent offence.

Reliance on the prior fault doctrine at sentencing may also be understood as means through which judges can resist evidence that undermines

---

[67] ibid, [39].
[68] Sentencing Act 2020, s 57.

policy-based distinctions between deserving and undeserving defendants at the trial stage. While both the sentencing guideline and the Court of Appeal's judgment in *Edwards* recognize that mental disorder can play a part in decisions to stop taking medication, the prior fault doctrine is problematic. It is difficult to draw a clear moral distinction between culpable and non-culpable defendants based on their reasons for failing to take medication, as these reasons are often complex and range from stigma to side effects (Loughnan and Wake, 2014, 131). In addition, it is difficult to attribute direct causation between a failure to take medication and an offence, as other factors are likely to have been at play at the time of the offending.

The influence of mental incapacity doctrines can also be seen after the introduction of the 2020 sentencing guideline. In *Skana*,[69] a woman appealed against a life sentence and s 45A order imposed after she was convicted of manslaughter by reason of diminished responsibility for killing a 7-year-old girl in a public park. At sentencing, the judge used the logic of the insanity defence to infer culpability, stating that he 'was satisfied that Ms Skana knew that what she intended to do and which she went on to do was wrong'.[70] Her inability to offer a 'narrative' to explain the killing further led the judge to infer significant responsibility from her seemingly purposeful actions before and after the offence.

In *Lundy*,[71] the appellant challenged a life sentence and s 45A order imposed following his conviction for wounding with intent. His sentencing judge drew on the logic of insanity and diminished responsibility to infer culpability, holding that the appellant, at the time of the offence, 'was aware of his actions and able to exercise choice and control over them' and 'was aware . . . of the criminal nature of his wrongdoing'.[72] While the sentencing judge recognized that the appellant did not offend while his mental health was stable, the Court of Appeal nevertheless held that appropriate medical management in the community required a life licence.[73] The Court held, without referring to any evidence, that the appellant's licence conditions would ensure the supervision of his mental health and medication and minimize the risk of serious harm to the public.[74]

---

[69] *R v Skana* [2022] EWCA Crim 186.
[70] ibid, [16].
[71] *R v Lundy* [2021] EWCA Crim 1922.
[72] ibid, [7].
[73] ibid, [24].
[74] ibid, [23].

Byrne[75] involved an appeal against two life sentences and s 45A orders imposed for manslaughter by reason of diminished responsibility and attempted murder. The Court of Appeal approved the sentencing judge's finding that the appellant retained a high level of culpability despite psychiatric evidence that his retained responsibility was minimal. The Court of Appeal refused to disturb his sentences despite psychiatric evidence that the appellant could not be compelled to accept medication in prison and that his mental health would deteriorate as a result (Wortley, 2023).

As these cases demonstrate, if a judge infers *culpability* from a finding of criminal *responsibility* from the trial stage, this is likely to lead to a punitive result. This is the case not only for offenders with personality disorders but for offenders with a wide range of mental disorders. Similarly, using the logic of insanity and diminished responsibility to determine culpability at the sentencing stage, even where these defences were unavailable at trial, is likely to lead judges to overestimate culpability. This is because these doctrines were designed to make only limited concessions to the challenge that psychiatric evidence posed to the authority of the criminal law. Using these doctrines at the sentencing stage may be understood as an attempt by judges to reconcile inconsistencies between the fact of a criminal conviction and psychiatric evidence at the sentencing stage that casts doubt on the appropriateness of the offender's conviction and punishment.

This reasoning poses risks to the safety of vulnerable offenders. For those suffering from mental disorder, imprisonment can 'exacerbate mental ill health, heighten vulnerability and increase the risk of self-harm and suicide' (Bradley, 2009, 7). As set out in Chapter 2, there is a heightened risk of suicide amongst those diagnosed with ASPD, and prisoners diagnosed with BPD are at a particularly high risk of suicide and self-harm in prison (Favril et al, 2020; 2022). As set out below, sentencing judges can, and should, take into account the risks that punitive sentences pose to vulnerable individuals.

The therapeutic strand

In an equally authoritative line of case law, the Court of Appeal steered away from the rigid application of doctrines from the trial stage to determine culpability and instead adopted the flexible four-factor approach in

---

[75] *R v Byrne* [2022] EWCA Crim 1630.

Vowles (O'Loughlin, 2021b). Rather than seeing itself as bound to punish offenders who had been found criminally responsible, the Court decided the appeals in *Hoppe*[76] and *Turner*[77] based on clear psychiatric evidence that the appellants' offending was related to their personality disorders, that they were responding to treatment, and that imprisonment would not be in their interests nor in the public interest. A lesser emphasis on punishment allowed the Court to give greater weight to the appellants' welfare and to substitute hospital orders with restrictions for their prison sentences. By contrast to *Martens*, the Court also took into account the likely adverse impact of imprisonment on their mental health.

The Court of Appeal based its decision in *Ahmed*[78] on similar reasoning. While the Court held that the appellant's responsibility for manslaughter was 'diminished, not entirely eliminated',[79] it substituted a hospital order with restrictions for his prison sentence. This was on the basis that the appellant needed continuing hospital treatment in his own interests and in the interests of public protection. Shockingly, the Court heard evidence that the appellant's treatment in prison during the six years he had already served of his sentence had caused him to develop PTSD. The appellant had not been given his medication in prison and, when he became violent, he was repeatedly placed in isolation.

Khan[80] demonstrates that concern for an offender's welfare can trump the need for punishment event where his culpability was entirely unaffected by his mental disorder. In *Khan*, the Court of Appeal accepted undisputed psychiatric evidence that if the appellant returned to prison he would be at serious risk of suicide. It concluded that culpability could not be determinative of the disposal and substituted a hospital order for his prison sentence. This was despite finding that the offences of dishonesty he had committed were unrelated to his mental disorder.

This trend has continued following the decision in *Edwards* and the publication of the sentencing guideline.[81] In *Miller*,[82] the Court of Appeal was

---

[76] *R v Hoppe* [2016] EWCA Crim 2258.
[77] *R v Turner* [2015] EWCA Crim 1249.
[78] *R v Ahmed* [2016] EWCA Crim 670; [2016] MHLR 282 (CA (Crim Div)).
[79] ibid, [28].
[80] *R v Khan* [2017] EWCA Crim 174.
[81] See the cases of: *R v Fisher* [2019] EWCA Crim 1066; *R v Westwood* [2020] EWCA Crim 598; *R v Stredwick* [2020] EWCA Crim 650; *R v Nelson* [2020] EWCA Crim 1615; *R v Crerand* [2022] EWCA Crim 962.
[82] *R v Miller* [2021] EWCA Crim 1955.

willing to consider the adverse impact that the very possibility of a return to prison would have on the appellant's mental health. Directly contradicting the finding in *Lundy*, it held that:

> the conditions which may be attached to conditional discharge from a section 37/41 order will make it possible to require the applicant to maintain appropriate medication, which could not be made a condition of a release from prison on licence.[83]

While this strand of case law is not based on human rights principles, it has the potential to develop into a more coherent and rights-respecting sentencing framework. Ideas for this framework are sketched out later. First, the implications of the *Vowles* approach to treatability for offenders with personality disorders at sentencing and post-sentence are drawn out.

7.4 Treatability at Sentencing and Post-sentence

In *Vowles*, the Court of Appeal suggested that judges should determine sentence with reference to the defendant's 'treatability'. However, when it comes to the transfer of prisoners to psychiatric hospital under s 47 of the MHA 1983 or decisions to discharge patients from hospital, the much broader 'appropriate medical treatment' test is applied. Consequently, like a personality disorder diagnosis itself, the malleable concept of 'treatability' can present a double disadvantage for defendants. They may be found to be insufficiently 'treatable' to warrant a hospital disposal at sentencing, yet a lower standard applies when it comes to decisions to detain them in hospital post-sentence in the interests of public protection.

The concept of 'treatability' deployed in *Vowles* was shaped by two concerns. The first concern was to avoid saddling psychiatrists with patients who had little prospect of recovery or discharge from hospital.[84] The second was to prevent patients who were no longer detainable under the MHA 1983 but who still posed a risk to the public from being discharged from

---

[83] The Court of Appeal similarly found in *R v Nelson (Keith)* [2020] EWCA Crim 1615, [38], that the Parole Board would not impose adherence to medication as a licence condition. The Court based this finding on the evidence given by a psychiatrist.

[84] As set out in Chapter 3, this concern originally animated the introduction of an earlier version of the treatability requirement for patients in the psychopathic disorder category under the MHA 1959.

hospital. Drawing on psychiatric evidence, the Court of Appeal advised judges that a hospital order with restrictions was more likely to be appropriate for defendants primarily diagnosed with 'severe mental illness' than for those with a personality disorder. This was because it was 'more likely' that severe mental illness would 'have a direct bearing on the offender's culpability' and would 'be more responsive to treatment in a hospital' than a personality disorder.[85] As a result, the Court advised that a hybrid order was more suitable for defendants with personality disorder.[86]

Despite this guidance, its decisions in *Hoppe* and *Turner* demonstrate that the Court of Appeal does not assume that certain disorders are untreatable. The psychiatric evidence in both cases demonstrates greater willingness amongst psychiatrists to accept patients diagnosed with BPD for treatment in hospital. This development is likely attributable to advances in care and treatment for BPD.[87] It suggests that psychiatrists, and therefore the courts, are now distinguishing between different forms of personality disorder and their prognoses. These cases therefore demonstrate that the interface between psychiatry and the law is porous, and that sentencing law has the potential to evolve in line with psychiatric understandings of mental disorder. Relying on the limited and inflexible mental incapacity doctrines at sentencing is likely to stymie this potential.

The risk-focused concept of treatability in *Vowles* nevertheless has the potential to create unfairness for individuals with disorders that are not clearly causally linked to their offending or straightforwardly treatable. Those with ASPD or psychopathic traits are less likely to be deemed 'treatable' due to uncertainties regarding the causal connection between personality disorder and offending, and a poor evidence base for the effectiveness of treatment.[88] Such offenders may therefore be excluded from therapeutic disposals even though their disorder may have played a role in their offending and they may be at risk of harm in prison.

The *Vowles* test of treatability is much more stringent than the appropriate medical treatment test set out in the MHA 1983. According to that test, there is no need to show in advance that treatment is likely to have particular effect, so long as the *purpose* of treatment is to 'alleviate, or prevent a worsening of, the disorder or one or more of its symptoms or manifestations'

---

[85] *Vowles* (n 19), [50].
[86] ibid.
[87] See Chapter 2.
[88] See Chapter 2.

(Department of Health, 2015, para 23.4).[89] According to the MHA 1983, the same test applies at sentencing as when the Justice Secretary is deciding whether to transfer a prisoner to hospital under s 47 and when a Tribunal is deciding whether to discharge a detained patient from hospital.[90]

The appropriate treatment test poses little barrier to detention in hospital on public protection grounds, even where treatment has little prospect of success. While the *Mental Health Act 1983 Code of Practice* states that 'simply detaining someone, even in a hospital, does not constitute medical treatment' it also states that 'for some patients with persistent and severe mental disorders, management of the undesirable effects of their disorder may be the most that can realistically be hoped for' (Department of Health, 2015, paras 23.18 and 23.16). In *WH v Llanarth Court Hospital*,[91] the Upper Tribunal recognized that, for a personality disorder patient, 'it may in some circumstances be difficult to distinguish appropriate treatment from mere detention'.[92] It held that the key to this problem was that 'the purpose of treatment must be to benefit the patient . . . even though the outcome of such treatment may have little or no beneficial effect on the patient'.[93]

The mismatch between the *Vowles* test of treatability and the appropriate medical treatment test has the potential to generate unfair results. A person may conceivably be given a prison sentence on the grounds of culpability and 'untreatability' only to be transferred to and detained in hospital towards the end of their sentence on the grounds that they pose a risk to the public, are suffering from a personality disorder, and that appropriate treatment is 'available' to them in hospital.[94] This will not necessarily be true in all cases, as courts may decide not to make an order under the MHA 1983 for reasons other than doubtful treatability. Or a defendant may prefer the certainty of a determinate prison sentence and choose not to seek a hospital order. Nevertheless, the statutory test at sentencing is whether appropriate medical treatment is available, not whether that treatment can be expected to reduce risk of reoffending.

The combination of doctrines derived from the trial stage and the risk-based treatability test in *Vowles* is likely to disadvantage other groups

---

[89] MHA 1983, s 145(4).
[90] MHA 1983, s 72(1)(b).
[91] *WH v Llanarth Court Hospital (Partnerships in Care)* [2015] UKUT 0695 (AAC).
[92] ibid, [56].
[93] ibid, [56].
[94] See the criteria for civil detention for treatment under s 3 of the MHA 1983 and the criteria for orders transferring prisoners from prison to hospital under s 47 of the MHA 1983.

beyond those with personality disorder. Individuals diagnosed with any psychiatric disorder who consumed alcohol or drugs, or failed to take their medication before the offence, or who displayed seemingly purposeful behaviour may be found by judges to be deserving of punishment at sentencing. Where their disorders are not clearly causally linked to their offending, or where treatment is problematic, they may find themselves subject to a prison sentence that goes against their therapeutic interests. While a s 45A order may mean that such defendants do not immediately go to prison, they will remain at risk of being inappropriately transferred to or recalled to prison for the remainder of their sentence.

7.5 Sentencing and Human Rights

While the case law considered so far does not explicitly use the language of rights and duties, the punitive strand seems to reflect the tendency for the contemporary criminal law to prioritize the rights of unknown potential victims over those of identified offenders noted in Chapters 3–5 of this book.[95] While human rights law affords protection to individuals from the criminal law by placing limits on penal power, the criminal law is often also invoked as a tool for protecting the human rights of potential victims or as a means of redressing human rights violations. Thus, human rights act both as a 'shield' and a 'sword' in the criminal law context (Tulkens, 2011; Mavronicola and Lavrysen, 2020).

In line with the 'sword' function, it could be argued that the priority placed on punishment and prison sentences in the punitive strand of sentencing case law is justified by the state's positive duties to protect potential victims and to punish offenders who have violated the fundamental rights of others. This is the justification underlying the ECtHR's coercive human rights doctrine under Articles 2 and 3 of the ECHR (Mavronicola and Lavrysen, 2020). However, the 'shield' function requires limits to be set in accordance with the duties the state owes under the same Articles to people in its custody.

The state's duties towards victims and potential victims cannot require it to violate its duties towards offenders. Sentencing courts, as public authorities, have a positive duty under Article 3 to protect convicted offenders

---

[95] On this tendency in the broader criminal law context, see Ramsay (2012a, 206) and Ashworth and Zedner (2014, 150).

from inhuman or degrading treatment or punishment in prison.[96] Sentencing courts should examine whether a prison sentence poses a real risk of breaching the Article 3 rights of an offender with a physical or mental disorder or disability:

> first, where there is evidence that the practical operation of existing arrangements is insufficient to protect the offender's rights; secondly, where there is medical evidence that imprisonment would breach art. 3 regardless of any possible arrangements (O'Loughlin, 2021b).[97]

A similar duty can be inferred from the duty of the state to do all it reasonably can to protect prisoners from 'real and immediate' risks of suicide.[98] However, the Court of Appeal has not connected these human rights principles to its case law on sentencing mentally disordered offenders. While the decision in *Khan* to prioritize the appellant's welfare is justifiable under Articles 2 and 3 of the ECHR, the Court of Appeal was cautious to confine its reasoning to the particular facts of that case (O'Loughlin, 2021b).

Similarly, the 2020 sentencing guideline fails to adequately recognize human rights principles. On the one hand, the guideline acknowledges that mental disorder can be taken into account at sentencing even where it was not linked to the commission of the offence. Thus, courts should bear in mind that 'an offender's impairment or disorder may mean that a custodial sentence weighs more heavily on them' and that 'custody can exacerbate the effects of impairments or disorders' (Sentencing Council of England and Wales, 2020, para 22). On the other hand, the guideline downplays the court's duty to respond to evidence that a custodial sentence will be detrimental to an offender's mental health or physical safety. Thus, it states that 'impairments or disorders can only be taken into account in a limited way so far as the impact of custody is concerned' (Sentencing Council of England and Wales, 2020, para 22).

Existing human rights principles can be drawn upon to develop a sentencing framework that can more fully reconcile the rights of offenders and victims. The state's positive duties to protect potential victims under Articles 2 and 3 are typically limited by a standard of reasonableness (Mavronicola,

---

[96] *Price v UK* (2002) 34 E.H.R.R. 53.
[97] See *R v Hetherington* [2009] EWCA Crim 1186; *R v Qazi* [2010] EWCA Crim 2579; [2011] 2 Cr App R (S) 8.
[98] *Keenan v UK* (2001) 33 EHRR 38; *Renolde v France* (2009) EHRR 42.

2017a; 2017b) and by offenders' negative human rights (Lazarus, 2020).[99] While it is possible for the positive and negative duties conferred by the same right to conflict, the state's duty to take positive measures to protect one person's rights under Article 2 or 3 cannot entail a duty to violate another person's absolute right under Article 3 (Mavronicola, 2012). Thus, there is no duty to torture a kidnapper in order to extract information about the whereabouts of a missing child who may be facing ill-treatment or death (Mavronicola, 2012, 732).[100] For the same reason, the state is not obliged to detain a vulnerable person under dangerous conditions in order to meet its positive duty to protect the lives of members of the public. Given Article 3 protects an absolute right, [101] it would be reasonable for the state to seek alternative measures that would not violate the offender's rights.

While the right to life under Article 2 is a fundamental and basic right, it is not absolute (Mavronicola, 2017b). However, the permissibility of the use of lethal force by state agents is limited to circumstances in which such action is absolutely necessary to protect a person from unlawful violence.[102] This exception is unlikely to extend to the much more speculative risks of future violence that are in consideration at sentencing. Moreover, the state has a duty to protect vulnerable people in custody from 'real and immediate' risks of suicide.[103] Where imprisonment poses such a risk, sentencing courts must take reasonable steps to mitigate this risk, including by examining alternative disposals.

In respect of the rights of victims of past offences, Article 2 confers a positive duty on member states to establish 'effective criminal-law provisions to deter the commission of offences against the person'. [104] This duty has been described as a duty to criminalize (Lavrysen, 2020). In *Öneryildiz v Turkey*,[105] the Grand Chamber made clear that the duty to criminalize entails a duty to punish:

> where lives have been lost in circumstances potentially engaging the responsibility of the State, [Article 2] entails a duty for the State to

---

[99] See further *Z and others v UK* (2002) 34 EHRR 3, [73]. See Chapter 6 for further discussion of the positive duty to protect life under Article 2 established by the ECtHR in *Osman v UK* [1998] ECHR 101; (2000) 29 EHRR 245.
[100] As Mavronicola (2012) remarks, this seems to be the approach taken by the ECtHR in *Gäfgen v Germany* [2010] 6 WLUK 4; (2011) 52 EHRR 1.
[101] *Chahal v UK* (1997) 23 EHRR 413; *Tyrer v UK* [1978] ECHR 2. See Mavronicola (2012).
[102] Article 2(2).
[103] *Keenan* and *Renolde* (n 98).
[104] *Osman v UK* [1998] ECHR 101; (2000) 29 EHRR 245, [115].
[105] *Öneryildiz v Turkey (No 2)* [2004] 11 WLUK 785; (2005) 41 EHRR 20, [91].

ensure, by all means at its disposal, an adequate response–judicial or otherwise–so that the legislative and administrative framework set up to protect the right to life is properly implemented and any breaches of that right are repressed and punished.

However, this duty does not 'entail the right for an applicant to have third parties prosecuted or sentenced for a criminal offence or an absolute obligation for all prosecutions to result in conviction, or indeed in a particular sentence'.[106]

The ECtHR's case law in respect of the duty to criminalize has been subject to significant criticism. As Laurens Lavrysen (2020) points out, the principle in *Öneryildiz* that there is no right to a particular sentence conflicts with the Court's finding that Turkey had violated the procedural obligation to protect life on the grounds, inter alia, that the 'derisory fines' issued to the officials responsible for failing to protect life were not an adequate deterrent.[107] In subsequent cases, the ECtHR has held that, while 'substantial deference' was due to national courts in the choice of appropriate sanctions for ill-treatment and homicide by state agents, it would 'intervene in cases of manifest disproportion between the gravity of the act and the punishment imposed'.[108] As Mattia Pinto (2020) argues, this case law risks encouraging states to pursue harsher punishments and to expand the remit of their criminal justice systems.

This willingness of the ECtHR to interrogate the proportionality of punishment to the gravity of offences in its case law on the duty to criminalize contrasts with its reluctance to do so in respect of risk-based sentences or whole life tariffs as considered in the previous chapter. Again, this suggests a tendency to prioritize the rights of victims over the rights of convicted offenders. Taken together, both the coercive human rights doctrine and the right to rehabilitation jurisprudence suggest a reluctance on behalf of the Court to challenge extreme punishments on desert grounds and even a willingness to push states to increase punishment. While the role of the ECtHR should not extend to determining the correct punishment in individual cases, as it lacks both the authority and capacity to do so (Mavronicola, 2020, 192), the Court should devise a more coherent and even-handed set of principles.

---

[106] ibid, [96].
[107] ibid, [116]–[118].
[108] *Nikolova and Velichkova v Bulgaria* [2007] 12 WLUK 663; (2009) 48 EHRR 40, [62]. Approved by the Grand Chamber in *Gäfgen* (n 100), [123].

Nevertheless, according to human rights principles, the duty to punish cannot entail an obligation to violate an offender's absolute right under Article 3. What is more, given the margin of appreciation, states are permitted to implement frameworks for mitigation of sentence or alternatives to imprisonment. That is, provided that these are based on reasonable grounds and do not give rise to a culture of impunity or result from state collusion with perpetrators or amount to systemic dysfunction (see Lavrysen, 2020). Where an offender's rights under Article 2 or 3 are in jeopardy, there is an obligation to take reasonable steps to mitigate that risk, and this may include making alternative disposals to ensure that their mental health needs will be met.

It is worth noting that there is a danger in recommending hospital orders as an alternative to prison sentences in cases of serious offending. Hospital orders may be experienced as an additional punishment by those who are subject to them (Stanton-Ife, 2012). Thus, there is a need to move away from the view that detention, whether in hospital or in a prison, is required as a response to serious crimes. The final chapter of this book builds on these findings to put forward suggestions for a more coherent and rights-based framework.

7.6 Conclusion

Reserving hospital orders for offenders whose culpability is very low or absent and whose risk of reoffending is causally connected to a treatable mental disorder is not warranted by sentencing legislation. Rather, the Court of Appeal in *Vowles* and other cases has chosen to narrow the scope of hospital orders by importing concepts from criminal law doctrines and from the former MHA 1983 into its sentencing case law. This tendency can be understood as a response by judges to the threat that psychiatric evidence can pose to the criminal law's authority to punish convicted offenders. While these threats have largely been contained at the trial stage, the longstanding tensions between legal and psychiatric understandings of the impact of mental disorder on criminal responsibility continue to play out at the sentencing stage.

The doctrines of insanity and diminished responsibility are compromises that were developed by judges as limited concessions to the reality that not all offenders fit the model of the rational actor. These doctrines are not based on any one coherent theory of how mental disorder impacts upon criminal responsibility or culpability. Rather, they were designed as strictly limited concessions to psychiatric evidence that not all criminal defendants fit the ideal image of the rational criminal actor. Borrowing from these doctrines at sentencing can therefore be expected to push sentencing in a punitive direction. This judicial borrowing is particularly likely to disadvantage defendants with personality disorder, as both doctrines tend to favour defendants affected by psychotic disorders. Inferring culpability from a guilty plea or using the prior fault doctrine at sentencing is also likely to lead judges to overestimate culpability.

For defendants with personality disorders, the malleable concept of appropriate medical treatment can present a double disadvantage: their mental disorders may be found to be insufficiently 'treatable' to warrant a hospital disposal at sentencing, yet a lower standard applies when it comes to decisions to detain them in hospital in the interests of public protection. The same is true for defendants with other psychiatric disorders where the connection between their offending and disorder is unclear or where treatment is problematic.

A different approach is possible. Judges are not obliged to prioritize punishment over the other purposes of sentencing, and the flexible four-factor approach in *Vowles* can allow judges to take into account the needs of the offender alongside public protection. In human rights terms, the state's positive duties under Articles 2 and 3 of the ECtHR towards victims or potential victims cannot entail a duty for states to violate an offender's absolute right under Article 3. Courts must also take reasonable steps to avoid exposing an offender to a real and immediate risk of suicide in prison to meet the state's duties under Article 2. Where there is a real risk of a prison sentence violating a defendant's rights, courts should consider alternatives to punishment.

8
Reflections

8.1 Introduction

This chapter draws together the explanatory and normative claims made in this book and returns to four puzzles or paradoxes identified in Chapter 1 to show the implications of this study for legal and criminological theory. The first set of puzzles emerges from the history of the DSPD Programme and the OPD Pathway. How can we understand the continuation of a faith in the transformative power of rehabilitative interventions with 'dangerous' offenders in a policy context that prioritizes the interests of potential victims over those of convicted offenders? And how can we account for the survival of a treatment programme for 'dangerous' offenders that has not yet been able to demonstrate that it can reduce serious reoffending?

A second set of puzzles arises from the contradictory constructions of 'dangerous' offenders with personality disorders. The requirement that a 'dangerous' individual must engage with rehabilitative programmes to have any chance of release implies that such individuals are capable of change. Yet the labels of 'dangerousness' and personality disorder encourage decision-makers to regard their efforts to change with scepticism.

A third set of puzzles emerges from the mental incapacity doctrines in the criminal law and the law of sentencing. The existence of indeterminate sentences for 'dangerous' people implies that they are incapable of restraining themselves from offending: a judgement that sits uneasily with the finding that they are also responsible for their past offending (Ashworth and Zedner, 2014, 149). The combination of criminal law and mental health law raises a further paradox. How can a person be sufficiently mentally well to be held criminally responsible and deserving of punishment, yet be so unwell that they can be detained under mental health law and denied the right to refuse treatment for their mental disorder?

A final set of puzzles concerns human rights. The first of these is the paradox of liberty: 'that a major justification for taking preventive powers is to secure or enhance the liberty of individuals, but that one possible effect of such powers is to deprive some individuals of their liberty' (Ashworth and Zedner, 2014, 201). As set out in Chapter 1, this puzzle is also a paradox of security: by taking measures to protect the public from 'dangerous' individuals, the state exposes those it considers 'dangerous' to a risk of harm.

This chapter then turns to consider responses to these paradoxes. It advances modest suggestions for a new legal framework that builds on the findings of this study and on the literature on preventive justice (Ashworth and Zedner, 2014; 2019; Zedner and Ashworth, 2019) and coercive human rights (Mavronicola and Lavrysen, 2020). Resolving the problem of 'dangerous' offenders will ultimately require the political will to build public tolerance of the limits of the state's capacity to prevent private individuals within its jurisdiction from harming others.

8.2 The Survival, and Revival, of Rehabilitation

As set out in Chapter 1, the emergence of the DSPD Programme and the OPD Pathway presents somewhat of a puzzle for contemporary criminological theory. Both initiatives demonstrate a faith in the power of rehabilitative interventions to transform 'dangerous' offenders. This faith that seems at odds with the idea that such offenders are viewed by the public or by those in power as monsters who must be segregated from society (see Bottoms, 1977; Rutherford, 1997; 2006; Simon, 1998; Seddon, 2008). Both initiatives further demonstrate the survival of a belief in the welfarist ideal that rehabilitation will enable even the most serious offenders to rejoin society as productive citizens. As Chapter 3 has shown, even prior to the DSPD Programme, mental health practitioners held a range of views regarding the treatability of personality disorder, and efforts were underway to develop treatments for 'psychopaths' by the 1940s.

The Mental Health Act (MHA) 1959 sought to strike a compromise between liberal criminal law principles that militated against detention without conviction and the principle that the state should endeavour to protect the public from 'dangerous' individuals. Nevertheless, objections to the detention of 'psychopaths' in psychiatric hospitals resurfaced repeatedly. These objections were not only based on the thinness of the evidence base for the effective treatment of personality disorder. Rather, the 'treatability' criterion could be used to exclude patients from services who were thought to be too disruptive, too dangerous, or to be so likely to reoffend that they threatened the reputation of mental health authorities. Despite this, psychiatric hospitals did accumulate significant numbers of 'psychopathic' patients who were not benefiting from treatment but who were thought to be too dangerous to discharge (see Boynton, 1980; Dell and Robertson, 1988; Fallon et al, 1999a).

While the DSPD initiative represented an attempt to break free from these failures, it neverthless went on to repeat some of them. As Chapters 3 and 4 have shown, the DSPD proposals were heavily reliant on the discovery of more effective treatments as a means of striking a better balance between the competing rights of the public and 'dangerous' individuals. However, in the rush to be 'seen to be doing something', policymakers seemed to disregard some important lessons from the past. In particular, using mental health law to preventively detain 'dangerous' prisoners is likely to lead to disgruntled patients resisting treatment, and concentrating the most disruptive prisoners in one unit is likely to generate high rates of staff burnout and turnover and to limit the possibilities for therapeutic intervention.

The history of the DSPD initiative further demonstrates that the rehabilitative ideal continues to resonate with politicians and policymakers who are looking for ways to render the 'troubling and distasteful practice' (Loader, 2006, 565) of punishment easier for liberal governments to swallow. The promise of rehabilitation serves a useful rhetorical function for criminal justice policymakers and politicians by seeming to offer a means of reconciling political pressures to respond to public fears of victimization with rule of law principles. These principles include the prohibition on the retrospective application of criminal penalties that are harsher than those available at the time of the offence and the principle that a person should only be detained under mental health law if treatment is expected to enable them to regain their freedom. By constructing rehabilitation as something that can enhance the wellbeing of offenders, protect their right to liberty, *and* protect the public, policymakers and legislators can present coercive preventive detention measures as both humane and necessary.

The types of treatment deployed under the DSPD Programme and the OPD Pathway further contradict the idea that 'dangerous' offenders are primarily seen as pathological monsters driven by innate criminal tendencies. The treatment programmes developed under the DSPD Programme and the OPD Pathway drew on existing psychological therapies that seek to equip offenders with the skills they require to lead a law-abiding life. The use of these treatments implies that criminal justice actors conceive of offenders with personality disorders as capable of learning to govern their own behaviour.

This development tracks the evolution of the construct of personality disorder, charted in Chapter 2 towards a spectrum of human personality that extends from the 'normal' to the 'abnormal'. Rather than seeking to change participants' personalities, initiatives like Kaizen, a treatment programme on the OPD Pathway, seek to work around problematic traits and to equip participants with tools for managing the consequences of their disorders and past traumas (see McCartan et al, 2018; Henfrey, 2018).

The OPD Pathway further suggests a movement towards viewing difficult, violent, or high-risk prisoners as traumatized victims who have developed unhelpful ways of coping with stress and relating to others. This generates a conflict between prison and probation cultures that take a punitive approach to transgressions and trauma-informed therapeutic cultures that see punishment as potentially re-traumatizing and counterproductive. Treatment programmes that construct offending and rehabilitation as the sole responsibility of the individual fit well with the wider ideology of prison and probation systems. By contrast, services that recognize the role of trauma in offending and rule-breaking behaviours in prison recognize, at least to some extent, the role of structural inequalities, abuse, and social deprivation in crime. Where trauma-informed care or treatment can de-escalate violence or self-harm within prisons, these strategies are likely to garner support from prison administrations. However, rehabilitative strategies must not expose prisons to their greatest threat: riots and escapes.

The OPD Pathway further suggests a blurring of the boundaries between prisoners with personality disorder and prisoners who are simply difficult to manage. Psychological explanations for offending or difficult behaviour are becoming more mainstream and are applied by psychologists and criminal justice practitioners to an ever-broader cohort of people in prisons and on probation. The OPD Pathway seems to presage an evolution towards viewing *all* disruptive or difficult prisoners through the lens of personality disorder and trauma. This movement is apt to attribute the failings of prisons to 'difficult' prisoners, and to draw attention away from the structural factors that contribute to violence and self-harm in prison. These include chronic overcrowding, a shortage of experienced staff, and underinvestment in prisoner mental health.

The case study of the DSPD Programme and the OPD Pathway further demonstrates that rehabilitative programmes in prisons are valued not only for their promise to reduce serious reoffending, but also for their potential to contribute to other key priorities of the prison. These include: maintaining external security; upholding internal order and control; and providing a safe and 'decent' environment for prisoners (Crewe, 2009, 26). The OPD Pathway has achieved some successes in improving relationships between staff and prisoners and creating a sense amongst participants that their wellbeing and behaviour have both improved (Moran et al, 2022). These gains are fragile in a criminal justice system that prioritizes risk management, punishment, and control, and is insufficiently protective of the basic rights of prisoners (see also Genders and Player, 2014 and Player, 2017).

8.3 Contradictory Constructions of the Dangerous Subject

As set out in Chapter 3, referral to the DSPD Programme could have the effect of delaying release for prisoners. This effect operated through two mechanisms: longer stays on indeterminate sentences, and extensions to detention through transfers to hospital under mental health law. These legal mechanisms are still in operation under the OPD Pathway. While the OPD Pathway has undertaken work to enable prisoners to progress towards release, the continuing paucity of robust evidence that it reduces risk of reoffending may not be sufficient to counteract the personality disorder double bind.

As set out in Chapter 4, this double bind results from a combination of two factors. The first is the requirement for offenders subject to preventive detention to earn the trust of decision-makers by engaging with treatment and demonstrating positive change. The second is the assumption that 'dangerous' offenders with personality disorders are both unlikely to change and likely to try to deceive others into believing they have changed to secure release. Combined with a culture of risk aversion and scepticism regarding the effectiveness of treatment amongst key decision-makers, this double bind is likely to make it extremely difficult for those offenders it affects to secure release from detention.

As highlighted in Chapter 7, the criminal law treats 'dangerous' offenders with personality disorders *as if* they are fully responsible for their past offending, even though they may not have been in full control of their actions at the time of their offence. Indeterminate sentencing powers and the parole process further treat such offenders *as if* they are both capable of and responsible for reforming themselves. The burden of demonstrating change rests with the individual, who may struggle to meet it. Thus, the legal framework overlooks the fact that some offenders may not respond to the experience of punishment and efforts at their rehabilitation in the expected ways (see also Peay, 2011b).

The analysis of the case law of the European Court of Human Rights (ECtHR) on the 'right to rehabilitation' presented in Chapter 6 demonstrates the continuation of a character-based understanding of rehabilitation as a process of redemption that requires one to become a new person. This process is likely to be undermined by character-based judgements of criminal propensity and untrustworthiness. These judgements often reflect the assumptions of character essentialism: that a person's character can be inferred from their past behaviour and that their character determines their conduct (Lacey, 2016, 35). There is evidence that such assumptions affect Parole Board decision-making (see Hood and Shute, 2000; Hood et al, 2002). Their influence can also be seen in the tendency discussed in Chapter 4 for Mental Health Review Tribunal[1] members to view offending by the DSPD group as 'almost inevitable' and to see personality disorder as an enduring or fixed characteristic (Trebilcock and Weaver, 2010b, 67). This view is further reflected in a tendency discussed in Chapters 4 and 5 for prison psychologists, Category A Review Teams, and Parole Boards to interpret a prisoner's seeming cooperation with treatment as a form of manipulation that confirms their untrustworthiness.

While a personality disorder diagnosis is not the same as a judgement of bad character, there are significant parallels between the two. On the one hand, the new psychiatric models of personality disorder seen in the DSM-5 and the ICD-11 have retreated from the idea that personality disorder traits are lifelong and pervasive. On the other hand, the personality disorder double bind and the persistence of character-based concepts of offending and rehabilitation suggest that the idea that behaviour is determined by personality and that personality is unlikely to change has proven enduring. It was suggested in Chapter 4 that a more robust programme of research has the potential to redress this double bind by confirming whether rehabilitative programmes are achieving their goals. However, given that coercive treatment strategies are unlikely to succeed with offenders, and may subject

---

[1] Now known as the First Tier Tribunal (Mental Health) in England and the Mental Health Tribunal for Wales.

them to further harm, a better way forward may be to delink progress in rehabilitation from release from detention. This suggestion is returned to below.

8.4 Responsibility, Dangerousness, and the Criminal Law

As set out in Chapter 7, the criminal law typically constructs 'dangerous' offenders with personality disorders as responsible for their past offending. This is likely to be because people with personality disorder traits are typically in control of their behaviour and the pattern of their offending does not fit easily with legal or lay notions of insanity. The sentencing case law discussed in Chapter 7 further suggests that offenders with antisocial personality disorder (ASPD) or psychopathic traits are more likely to be punished for their offences than offenders affected by schizophrenia. This is particularly likely when sentencing courts draw on findings of criminal responsibility from the trial stage to infer culpability at the sentencing stage. A hospital order with restrictions is unlikely to be handed down by courts that apply a risk-based test of 'treatability' at sentencing, as it is not clear that treating people with ASPD or psychopathic traits in hospital will reduce their risk of reoffending. If they are judged to be dangerous they are also likely to be subjected to preventive detention through an indeterminate prison sentence.

As Ashworth and Zedner (2014) argue, the existence of preventive detention for 'dangerous' people convicted of criminal offences presents a puzzle. How can we 'square the tacit denial of responsibility entailed in saying that an individual is incapable of restraining their dangerous violent or sexual impulses with the judgement that the same individual can justly be held responsible for past criminal conduct' (Ashworth and Zedner, 2014, 149). This puzzle is twofold. First, it poses an explanatory question: how do we explain the coexistence of seemingly contradictory images of the same offender under the criminal law? Second, it poses a normative question: is the criminal law justified in treating the same offender differently at different points in the criminal justice system? I address the explanatory problem below before turning to examine the normative case for consistency.

Ashworth and Zedner (2014, 150) suggest that the seeming inconsistency inherent in the judgement that a person is criminally responsible yet dangerous is attributable to the different premises that underlie decisions at the trial and sentencing stages:

> Whereas conviction for a crime past rests upon the claim that the individual acted culpably at a particular point in time, the decision to detain preventively . . . relies upon the assertion that the character traits of the detainee are enduring and predictable.

They further suggest that two different assumptions may underlie the judgement that an individual poses a 'significant risk of serious harm' to the public. Either that the person 'does not have the capacity to choose to do right' or that 'he will not in fact exercise that capacity to restrain himself' (Ashworth and Zedner, 2014, 150).

On an explanatory level, the seeming tension between criminal responsibility and dangerousness arguably results from the collapsing of three different meanings of 'responsible'. The first meaning is responsible in the sense of 'answerable or liable to be called to account'[2] by the criminal law. The second meaning is responsible in the more everyday sense of 'capable of fulfilling an obligation or duty; reliable, trustworthy, sensible'.[3] The third sense is responsible in the sense of 'morally accountable for one's actions; capable of rational conduct'.[4] As set out below, different concepts of responsibility underlie the judgement that a person is criminally responsible and the judgement that they are dangerous.

As set out in Chapter 7, the law treats as criminally responsible individuals who lack the capacity for practical reason or responsible agency: the criteria that criminal law theorists argue are required for moral responsibility (Berger, 2012; Morse, 1999; 2008a; Tadros, 2007). This is because the test for insanity is so stringent that most people with mental disorders cannot satisfy it (Mackay, 1995). The doctrine of diminished responsibility is somewhat less demanding and recognizes that impaired volitional and cognitive capacities can reduce criminal responsibility. However, it applies only to murder cases and a successful plea results in a conviction for manslaughter. Consequently, the criminal law can hold a person responsible for their past actions despite evidence that their capacity to conform to the law was significantly impaired, or even absent. Consequently, a criminal

---

[2] *Oxford Dictionary of English*, 3rd edn (Stevenson, 2015), 'responsible', 3(b).
[3] ibid, 'responsible', 1(b).
[4] ibid, 'responsible', 3(c).

conviction implies that a person has been found legally *answerable* for their past crimes, even though they may not have been fully *responsible* in the moral sense. A criminal conviction therefore does not necessarily imply the judgment that a person was, at the time of the offence, fully rational or fully in control of their actions.

At the point of sentencing when a judgment of dangerousness is made, this judgment can be understood as implying that the person has criminal tendencies and that they cannot be depended upon not to repeat their offences. Rather than implying a denial of the finding of answerability from the trial stage, a judgment of dangerousness at sentencing relies upon a different concept of responsibility. The dangerous person is judged to be irresponsible in the everyday sense of untrustworthy or unreliable: it is assumed that they cannot be trusted to abide by the law. If such a person were to commit an offence, the judgement that they were dangerous would not, in itself, preclude them from being held answerable for it under the criminal law.

The law therefore tends to obscure the deeper question of whether offenders with traits of impulsivity and impaired capacities for moral reasoning or emotional understanding *should* be held responsible for their offences. As set out in Chapter 7, culpability is often inferred by judges at sentencing from findings of criminal responsibility at the trial stage or from evidence of rationality at the sentencing stage. However, the mental incapacity doctrines are not a good measure of culpability as they are designed to strictly limit the impact of psychiatric evidence on findings of criminal responsibility at the trial stage. Together, they do not form a coherent theory of how mental disorder affects culpability. The use of these doctrines at the sentencing stage can therefore be expected to ratchet up punishment.

On a normative level, the answerable-yet-dangerous puzzle seems to result from a sense that the criminal law should not hold a person answerable for past offending that resulted from a genuine inability to exercise control over their conduct. According to this account, a person who had the capacity for choice and control at the time of the offence would also have the capacity to act differently next time. The law should therefore give the person a second chance, rather than take preventive action that denies them the opportunity to do better. However, the law as it stands does not work in this way. Bringing the law in line would require a much wider-ranging reform of the basis for criminal responsibility. Suggestions for such a reform are set out further below.

8.5 Responsibility, Capacity, and Treatability under Mental Health Law

As set out in Chapter 7, a personality disorder diagnosis seems to result in a double disadvantage for defendants diagnosed with personality disorders. While it is unusual for a person with a personality disorder to be found not guilty by reason of insanity, they can nevertheless be deprived of their liberty under mental health law after serving their punishment. At first glance, this possibility seems to raise a problem. How can a person be deemed sufficiently mentally well to be justly punished under the criminal law, yet be deemed sufficiently mentally unwell to justify depriving them of their liberty under mental health law?

Ashworth and Zedner (2019, 140) highlight a similar apparent tension between findings of criminal responsibility and civil commitment laws in the US:

> the alleged inconsistency between finding the individual not to be mentally disordered at the point of conviction and sentence, and yet finding the individual to be suffering from a form of personality disorder sufficient to render him or her so dangerous as to require indefinite commitment.

Based on a critique of the US Supreme Court ruling in *Kansas v Hendricks*,[5] Morse (1998, 259) argues that this tension is a paradox:

> It is utterly paradoxical to claim that a sexually violent predator is sufficiently responsible to deserve the stigma and punishment of criminal incarceration, but that the predator is not sufficiently responsible to be permitted the usual freedom from involuntary civil commitment that even the very predictably dangerous but responsible agents retain because our society wishes to maximise the liberty and dignity of all citizens.

While Morse recognizes that the standards for responsibility in criminal law and civil commitment do not necessarily have to be symmetrical,

---

[5] 521 US 346 (1997). In that case, the US Supreme Court ruled that post-sentence civil commitment laws for 'sexually violent predators' were intended to prevent harm to the public rather than to punish the person. It therefore held that the power to detain a 'sexually violent predator' was a civil law power rather than a criminal law power.

his argument conflates the different meanings of 'responsible' discussed earlier. As set out above, a person can be held fully answerable in the legal sense for an offence without necessarily having had the capacity to obey the law.

Morse (1998) further conflates the capacity requirement underlying judgments of criminal responsibility with the requirement in some involuntary commitment laws that the person must lack the capacity to make decisions regarding their own care and treatment. Morse contends that Hendricks was both 'fully responsible according to even the most permissive cognitive standard for criminal responsibility' and 'fully capable of making rational decisions about his own treatment' (Morse, 1998, 258). He concludes that, once Hendricks had completed his sentence, he deserved no further punishment as 'he was a responsible agent who did not qualify for traditional involuntary civil commitment' (Morse, 1998, 258).

However, the requirements of capacity for crime are not the same as the requirements of capacity to make decisions regarding one's care and treatment. Typically, evaluations of decision-making capacity in healthcare law focus on the person's ability to retain, understand, use, and weigh relevant information to come to a decision regarding treatment, and on their ability to communicate that decision (Appelbaum and Grisso, 1988).[6] The insanity rules only examine whether the person knew what they were doing in a basic physical sense, and whether they knew it was wrong in the legal sense. Consequently, a person may be found to lack the capacity to make decisions about their care and treatment whilst nevertheless being found to have had the capacity to commit a criminal offence, or vice versa.

Even if we were to introduce a test for capacity for crime modelled on healthcare law, decision-making capacity would nevertheless be decision-specific. One may have capacity to make one decision but not another (Peay, 2011b; Pickard, 2015). It would therefore be possible for a person to lack the capacity to make decisions about their care and treatment whilst having had the capacity to commit a crime at the time it occurred. This is not necessarily inconsistent, because the content, context, and time frame of each decision would be very different.[7]

---

[6] See, in England and Wales, the Mental Capacity Act 2005, s 3.
[7] At present in England and Wales, there is no requirement for a person to lack capacity before they can be detained under the MHA 1983. Commentators have argued that people should not be detained under mental health law unless they also lack capacity to make decisions about their care and treatment (Szmukler et al, 2014). These proposals have not been implemented in England and Wales.

Where the law of England and Wales does appear to be inconsistent is in the judicial interpretation of the requirement for 'appropriate medical treatment' to be 'available' to the patient in hospital. As set out in Chapter 7, the malleability of this test means that judges can use it at sentencing to deny convicted offenders entry to hospital through the front door on the grounds of untreatability. Yet, a much broader interpretation of the same test can be used post-sentence to bring them into hospital through the back door for preventive detention.

The combination of mental health law and criminal law further raises a problem of fairness. It means that a person who has a mental disorder but who does not qualify for the insanity defence is liable to conviction and punishment on the same basis as a person who has no mental disorder. Yet individuals who do not suffer from any mental disorder cannot be detained post-sentence under mental health law. This differential treatment is a form of discrimination on mental health grounds—a problem I return to below.

Drawing together the discussion so far, there are competing constructions of 'dangerous' offenders with personality disorders in law and policy. The criminal law constructs them as responsible for their past offending, and, in practice, they may be held both culpable and untreatable by judges at sentencing. The use of indeterminate sentences on the grounds of dangerousness suggests that they are also held to be untrustworthy and liable to reoffend. In principle, the process for deciding whether to release such individuals from prison or hospital constructs them as capable of change, whether by learning new skills and improving their attitudes and behaviour, or in the deeper sense of changing their characters. Yet, the labels of dangerousness and personality disorder come with the implication that they are unlikely to change, and likely to try to deceive others. These competing constructions pose risks to their human rights, as set out in the next section.

8.6 Paradoxes of Human Rights

Here, we return to the 'paradox of liberty' (Ashworth and Zedner 2014, 201) and to the paradox created by the 'sword' and 'shield' functions of human rights law in the criminal justice context (Tulkens, 2011). The ECtHR has developed a 'coercive human rights' doctrine that confers positive duties on member states to protect those within its jurisdiction from crimes that violate their human rights (Mavronicola and Lavrysen, 2020).

The ECtHR further recognizes a duty for the state to take measures to protect the public from violent crime, and such measures can include detaining prisoners serving life sentences for as long as they remain dangerous.[8] However, human rights principles also require limits to be set on coercive powers in accordance with the rights of those subject to coercion. This is the important 'shield' function of human rights law, which limits the extent to which the rights of actual or potential victims can be used as a 'sword' against those who are thought to be dangerous.

Former Justice Secretary Robert Buckland's (2020) claim that 'the first duty of any government is to keep the public safe from harm' suggests a continuation of a tendency for governments to present the rights of a nebulous but 'innocent' public as taking priority over 'dangerous' but identifiable subjects (Ramsay, 2012a, 206). As set out in Chapters 6 and 7, this tendency is also reflected in the ECtHR's case law on the right to rehabilitation and the duty to punish. As the case study of the DSPD Programme and the OPD Pathway demonstrates, policies that pursue greater security for the public can have the effect of subjecting individuals to disproportionate punishment. As set out in Chapter 6, the ECtHR's case law on the right to rehabilitation tends to validate and legitimize preventive detention measures by assuming that opportunities for rehabilitation and regular risk assessment will provide a clear route towards release.[9] This assumption tends to preclude scrutiny of the proportionality of the punishment imposed by an indeterminate sentence to the seriousness of the offence. As the evidence considered in Chapters 2–5 demonstrates, the evidence base for the effectiveness of current treatments in reducing risk of reoffending and the weaknesses of recidivism risk assessment instruments when applied to individuals casts doubt on the sufficiency of rehabilitation and risk assessment to act as a brake on punishment.

At first, the ECtHR's coercive human rights doctrine, including on the right to security and the duty to punish, may seem to provide justification for the prioritization of punishment and public protection in sentencing policy and practice. However, as set out in Chapter 7, the state's duty towards real or potential victims cannot entail a duty to violate a convicted or suspected offender's rights under Articles 2 and 3 of the ECHR (see also

---

[8] Recognized in *Mastromatteo v Italy* [2002] ECHR 694 and *Vinter and others v UK* (2016) 63 EHRR 1.
[9] See in particular the ECtHR's decisions in *James, Wells and Lee v UK* and *Murray v Netherlands*, discussed in Chapter 6.

Mavronicola, 2012; 2017a; 2017b). Nor does the state have a duty to punish all offenders who violate the fundamental rights of others (Lavrysen, 2020).

Current sentencing policies tend to overlook the harms that imprisonment can cause to offenders with pre-existing mental disorders and to prioritize punishing culpable offenders and protecting the public from harm. Moreover, current sentencing guidelines downplay the extent of the state's duty to protect the lives and safety of those within its care. While there are positive moves under the OPD Pathway to make staff aware of the shared histories of past trauma that are prevalent amongst prisoners with personality disorders, rehabilitation continues to have a coercive edge. As highlighted in Chapters 4 and 5, rehabilitative interventions in a coercive prison environment that reopen past traumas or force prisoners to confront their own inadequacies can cause distress or even harm to prisoners (see de Motte et al, 2017; Genders and Player, 2022). These risks need to be carefully managed to prevent harm to prisoners' mental health and risks to their physical safety.

8.7 Towards a Rights-respecting Framework

This section sketches out a modest set of proposals for responding to the problem of 'dangerous' offenders while taking into account the risks posed by overreliance on preventive detention and the offer of rehabilitation. Developing a fully-fledged normative framework is beyond the scope of this book. Rather, these suggestions are intended as a starting point for future research. I first consider how law reform could recalibrate the legal concepts of responsibility, dangerousness, and culpability. Then, I set out proposals for a more limited form of preventive detention after conviction. Finally, I turn to consider how reforms to mental health law could place more principled limits on the use of preventive detention.

Recalibrating criminal responsibility

To address the mismatch between findings of criminal responsibility and judgements of dangerousness, the law of insanity requires reform to take into account a broader range of incapacities that can affect a person's ability to conform to the law. This could be done by replacing insanity with a new defence of 'not criminally responsible by reason of recognised medical condition' as recommended by the Law Commission (2013). According to this proposal, a person could be found not criminally responsible where they were affected by a total lack of capacity, arising from a recognized medical condition, to do one or more of the following:

> rationally to form a judgment about the relevant conduct or circumstances; to understand the wrongfulness of what he or she is charged with having done; or to control his or her physical acts in relation to the relevant conduct or circumstances (Law Commission 2013, para 4.126–27).

This reform would bring the law of insanity more in line with diminished responsibility, helping to create a more coherent set of mental incapacity doctrines.

Contrary to the Law Commission's proposal, the definition of 'recognised medical condition' should not exclude disorders that are 'characterised solely or principally by abnormally aggressive or seriously irresponsible behaviour' where 'the evidence for the condition is simply evidence of what might broadly be called criminal behaviour' (Law Commission 2013, para 1.90). Such an exclusion could result in offenders who would otherwise meet the criteria for the new defence being held fully responsible. This distinction would also introduce an undesirable inconsistency with diminished responsibility. Neither should the prior fault doctrine be extended to the new defence, as it is based on questionable assumptions and is likely to be very challenging for juries to apply.[10] Instead, the focus should be on evaluating the impact of a person's condition on their capacity to obey the law at the time of the offence.

Further reforms are necessary to address the inconsistent use of mental incapacity doctrines and findings from the trial stage to assess culpability at sentencing. A reformed plea of diminished *culpability*, available regardless of the offence charged, could replace diminished responsibility and operate in tandem with the new 'not criminally responsible' defence. Where a person totally lacked one or more of the relevant capacities identified by the Law Commission, they could be found not criminally responsible. If the same capacities were substantially impaired but not entirely eclipsed, the person could instead plead diminished culpability at trial. This could form

---

[10] See Chapter 7, Loughnan and Wake (2014) and Mackay and Hughes (2022) for further discussion of prior fault.

the basis for a guilty plea to a less serious offence, if one is available. The plea could also, or alternatively, be submitted at sentencing to form the basis for a more principled and consistent assessment of culpability based on psychiatric evidence. The impact the person's medical condition had on their relevant capacities at the time of the offence could be taken into account when assessing culpability, even where the impairment was not substantial enough to qualify for a lesser offence at the trial stage. This assessment could then be combined with other mitigating or aggravating factors to produce an individualized judgment of the degree of punishment warranted.

Culpability should not, however, be determinative of the disposal when it comes to sentencing an offender with a mental disorder. By combining a more principled assessment of culpability with the flexible four-factor approach in *Vowles*, judges should evaluate whether other important considerations, such as the welfare of the individual, their therapeutic interests, and the suitability of relevant release regimes, should take priority over punishment.

Sentencing courts should further be required to consider the likely impact of imprisonment on the offender by undertaking a robust assessment of whether the prison service can meet their needs. Where suitable and safe prison accommodation is not available, the prison authorities should be required to provide it. Where a prison sentence poses a real and immediate risk to the offender's life or a real risk of exposing them to inhuman and degrading treatment or punishment, sentencing courts should opt for community alternatives or a hospital disposal instead. Policies on transfers from hospital to prison or recalls from release on licence should also be reformed to require an assessment of whether the person's Article 2 and 3 rights will be adequately protected. If a return to prison poses a real risk of breaching Article 2 or 3, alternative arrangements should be made.

Limiting preventive detention after conviction

Under the ECHR, preventive detention is not permissible unless it falls within one of the exceptions to the right to liberty and security of the person. This section considers reforms to detention under Article 5(1)(a). Even if the law of insanity and diminished responsibility were reformed as set out above, some individuals may still be found criminally responsible and liable to punishment despite the presence of a mental disorder. The findings presented in this book suggest that the use of indeterminate prison sentences should be subject to strict limits. The thin evidence base for the effectiveness of current treatments, coupled with risk aversion and scepticism on behalf of decision-makers regarding the possibility for 'dangerous' offenders to change, casts doubt on the possibility for rehabilitation to curb excessive punishments. Below, proposals for a more parsimonious system of punishment and a rights-based system of rehabilitation are set out.

Ashworth and Zedner's (2014; 2019) influential work on preventive justice provides several principles that can be built upon to limit recourse to indeterminate sentences on the grounds of dangerousness. They propose that everyone should have a right to be presumed harmless and that preventive action should only be taken against a person who poses a 'significant risk of serious harm' to others where that person has lost that right through violent offending (Ashworth and Zedner, 2014, 168–69). They further suggest that the burden of proving such a risk should be placed on the state; that judgements of dangerousness should be based on an individual assessment; that decision-makers should be mindful of the contestability of such judgements; and that such judgements should be open to challenge and appeal (Ashworth and Zedner, 2014, 169–70).

Based on these principles, Ashworth and Zedner (2014, 169) suggest that an indeterminate sentence may be considered by a court in exceptional circumstances where an individual who has a previous conviction for a very serious offence is judged to present a 'very serious danger to others'. A principle of parsimony should then apply, requiring the court to determine that no lesser sentence would be effective to protect others from a significant risk of serious harm. Detention beyond a period of proportionate punishment should be served in 'non-punitive conditions with restraints no greater than those required by the imperatives of security' (Ashworth and Zedner, 2014, 169). Where possible, this should be in a facility separate from the prison system and detainees should be entitled to regular reviews of the grounds for their detention (Ashworth and Zedner, 2014, 169).

These requirements are preferable to the ECtHR's willingness to permit indeterminate sentences on broad penological grounds, including punishment, deterrence, public protection, and rehabilitation.[11] As set out Chapter 6, the ECtHR only intervenes where punishment is so disproportionate that it violates Article 3, and it sets a very high threshold for such findings.[12] Given the difficulties involved in demonstrating release from

---

[11] See the cases of *Vinter* (n 8) and *Murray v Netherlands* (2017) 64 EHRR 3, discussed in Chapter 6.
[12] *Weeks v UK* [1987] ECHR 3.

detention, however, a more stringent test of the need for punishment ought to be required before an indeterminate sentence can be imposed. Courts should bear in mind the possibility that a person given an indeterminate sentence may never be released. Indeterminate sentences should therefore be reserved for the most serious offences, including murder, very serious violent or sexual offences, and very serious repeat violent or sexual offending. These sentences should not be automatically imposed by statute but should be based on an individualized assessment of the seriousness of the offence(s). Whole life tariffs should not be permitted given the disillusionment and hopelessness this can instil in prisoners, as highlighted in *Vinter*.[13]

As Ashworth and Zedner (2014) recognize, there are significant difficulties with reliance on risk assessment as a means of determining whether a person poses a 'significant risk of serious harm'. As highlighted in Chapter 2, the deficiencies of actuarial risk assessment instruments (ARAIs) are compounded by the fact that professionals often use their own gut feelings, instinct, and character judgements when assessing risk. While the ECtHR in *Maiorano*[14] seemed to endorse this method of risk assessment, this is clearly problematic. Unstructured professional judgements are a poor predictor of reoffending, and attitudes of character essentialism based on a person's offending history risk foreclosing any possibility of release for offenders convicted of serious offences. This approach is particularly problematic for individuals who are diagnosed with a personality disorder, given that the diagnosis is often associated with stigma, negative character judgements, and pessimism regarding the possibility of change.

For these reasons, assessments of risk should be undertaken cautiously and should never be automatically inferred from a person's past convictions. Instead, decision-makers should place greater weight on up-to-date information about the person, including their recent behaviour, and avoid making intuitive or character-based judgements about risk or their capacity for change. Decision-makers should bear in mind the significant difficulties involved in predicting reoffending, and individuals should have the opportunity to robustly challenge risk assessments at key stages, including both categorization decisions and Parole Board decisions.

Ashworth and Zedner (2014, 169) further suggest that detainees should have access to 'adequately resourced risk-reductive rehabilitative treatment

---

[13] *Vinter* (n 8). See Chapter 6 for further discussion.
[14] App no 28634/06, ECtHR 15 Dec 2009.

and training courses' to enable them to work towards release. Particular caution should, however, be taken not to over-rely on the provision of rehabilitative interventions. The use of such treatments under conditions of coercion may expose offenders to excessive punishment and jeopardize the effectiveness of interventions. The continuing lack of robust evidence for the effectiveness of available treatments for reducing serious recidivism casts further doubt on the prospects for rehabilitative interventions to ensure preventive detention is not overused.

For prisoners serving indeterminate sentences, participation in offending behaviour programmes should be on a voluntary basis. These programmes should be frequently and robustly independently evaluated, including by conducting randomized controlled trials.[15] Prison-based programmes should be linked to community-based aftercare, as there is evidence that this can enhance their effectiveness (Beaudry et al, 2021). Participation in such programmes should only be taken into account in assessing risk for the purposes of progress through the prison system or release where they have been demonstrated to reduce recidivism. In principle, improvements in a life-sentenced prisoner's behaviour should be tested out through a gradual relaxing of security restrictions and day release. There is evidence that participation in day release programmes can also help to reduce recidivism (Cheliotis, 2008; Hillier and Mews, 2018).

This testing out of progress will require greater opportunities for prisoners serving indeterminate sentences to engage with the outside world from the start of their prison sentence. Such opportunities should only be limited by the state's duty to protect the public from real and immediate risks of death or real risks of causing very serious physical or psychological harm.[16] The ECtHR in *Mastromatteo* extended this requirement to include a duty on the state 'to afford *general protection to society* against the *potential* acts of one or of several persons serving a prison sentence for a violent crime'.[17] Nevertheless, the requirement that the risk of the prisoner killing another person should be 'real and immediate' should not be watered down. Similar requirements should apply where the individual is thought to pose a real risk of causing serious harm to others that would violate Article 3. Opportunities for greater social reintegration should only be

---

[15] See Chapters 2 and 5 for a review of the current evidence.
[16] *Osman v UK* [1998] ECHR 101; (2000) 29 EHRR 245.
[17] *Mastromatteo* (n 8), [69]. Emphasis added.

refused where there is up-to-date evidence that the prisoner poses such a risk, and that this risk cannot be adequately mitigated against.

As suggested by Ashworth and Zedner (2014), the preventive part of an indeterminate sentence should be served in a different environment and under a regime that is oriented towards preparation for life in the outside world. Work should also be undertaken to reduce the barriers to social reintegration that long-term prisoners and those who have a record of serious offending face upon release into the community.

In such a system, the vast majority of prisoners would be serving determinate sentences. For these prisoners, release from prison would not be dependent on progress in rehabilitation. Nevertheless, interventions that have been demonstrated to reduce recidivism should be provided on a voluntary basis alongside interventions oriented towards enhancing wellbeing and countering the negative effects of detention. For all prisoners, learning from the OPD Pathway could be drawn upon to facilitate more supportive and trusting relationships between detainees and staff and a more optimistic atmosphere. Wherever possible, all prisoners should enjoy opportunities to engage with the outside world and benefit from day release and community aftercare.

Given the troubled history of attempts to deal with the problem of dangerous offenders discussed in this book, a parsimonious approach towards the deployment of preventive prison sentences for serious offenders may risk provoking public fears if such measures are perceived to be insufficient to ensure public safety. Rational responses to risk that are based on objective evidence are often insufficient to contain public outrage when horrific events occur. Limiting the use of indeterminate sentences would therefore demand much greater political and public tolerance of the risks posed by offenders convicted of serious offences and the limits of the state's power to prevent every instance of violent crime.

Proposals to open up criminal justice policymaking to 'deliberative' (Green, 2006) or 'participatory' (Johnstone, 2000) democracy may go some way towards encouraging more rational decision-making. As Harry Annison (2015, ch 8) suggests, public tolerance of uncertainty could be fostered by making space for continuous dialogue on penal policy between members of the public, policymakers, experts, criminal justice practitioners, and those directly impacted by penal policies. Using such opportunities for dialogue to challenge myths and misconceptions about high profile cases and to honestly present the limits of the state's powers to prevent serious offending and the costs of preventive detention policies could go some way towards reducing public demands for harsher punishments and longer periods of detention.

Limiting detention under mental health law

The looseness of the criteria for detention under Article 5(1)(e) of the ECHR raises the concern that preventive detention statutes can be used to detain people who are unlikely to benefit from treatment under the guise of a therapeutic purpose (Drenkhahn and Morgenstern, 2020). Much stronger safeguards against the retrospective imposition of preventive detention are available under the criminal law than under mental health law. In addition, while detention on the grounds of unsound mind is permissible under Article 5(1)(e), these powers are regarded as discriminatory under the United Nations Convention on the Rights of Persons with Disabilities (CRPD).

The CRPD draws on a social model of disability, 'articulated not in terms of limitations or impairments of disabled people, but as flowing from inadequate social responses to the particular needs of individuals in society' (Bartlett, 2012, 753). Article 14.1 of the CRPD states that:

> States Parties shall ensure that persons with disabilities, on an equal basis with others: a) Enjoy the right to liberty and security of person; b) Are not deprived of their liberty unlawfully or arbitrarily, and that any deprivation of liberty is in conformity with the law, and that the existence of a disability shall in no case justify a deprivation of liberty.

According to the UN High Commissioner for Human Rights, the CRPD forbids 'deprivation of liberty based on the existence of any disability, including mental or intellectual, as discriminatory', including in combination with 'other elements such as dangerousness, or care and treatment' (UN High Commissioner, 2009, para. 48).

The justifications for detaining 'dangerous' individuals tend to rely on the rights of others to be protected from harm. However, it is difficult to justify the preventive detention of people who have a mental disorder when such powers are not available in respect of people who do not have a mental disorder but who pose a similar risk of harm to others. As set out in Chapter 2, the odds of violence amongst drug and alcohol abusers is similar to those who have a diagnosis of ASPD (Yu et al, 2012, 784). It is not, however, possible to detain a person under the MHA 1983 based on dependency on alcohol or drugs alone.[18]

While delinking detention from disability and creating a general law of preventive detention based on dangerousness regardless of mental disorder would avoid overt discrimination (Bartlett, 2012, 773), such a statute would likely fall afoul of Article 5 of the ECHR, unless it followed conviction for a criminal offence. Stricter limits should, however, be imposed before a person who has not been convicted of a criminal offence can be detained under mental health law on the grounds of risk to others.[19]

In principle, a higher threshold should apply for detention on the grounds of risk to others under the MHA 1983 than under an indeterminate sentence, given that punishment is not warranted. Use of detention should be the minimum necessary to meet the state's duty to protect the public. The MHA 1983 should therefore be amended to ensure that preventive detention measures are only taken where the individual poses a real and immediate risk of causing death or a real risk of causing serious harm to others. Otherwise, offending should be dealt with through the criminal justice system, subject to the rights of the offender under Articles 2 and 3. This would set a higher standard than the proposal of the Wessely Review to allow detention where there is 'a substantial likelihood of significant harm' to 'the safety of any other person without treatment' (Department of Health and Social Care, 2018, 113). Sufficient resources should be made available to enable people to receive appropriate mental health treatment on a voluntary basis before they reach such a point of crisis.

A requirement that treatment must be 'necessary', as recommended by Ashworth and Zedner (2014, 219), may not be adequate to limit the use of hospital as a venue for preventive detention. The meaning of 'appropriate medical treatment' in the MHA 1983 has been watered down such that, even though 'mere detention' cannot constitute treatment, it is sufficient for treatment to have a therapeutic 'purpose', even though it may have 'little or no beneficial effect'.[20] A more robust requirement that treatment should not only be necessary to reduce the risk the person poses to the public but must also be expected to confer a therapeutic benefit on the patient should be introduced instead. In determining this question, decision-makers

---

[18] MHA 1983, s 1(3).
[19] Detention on the grounds that a person poses a risk to themselves is beyond the scope of this book. For an in-depth analysis of the role of mental health law in this respect, see Wilson (2021).
[20] *WH v Llanarth Court Hospital (Partnerships in Care)* [2015] UKUT 0695 (AAC), [56].

should have regard to whether treatment would positively contribute to the person's discharge and reintegration into society (Department of Health and Social Care, 2018). This test would fit better with the requirements of detention under Article 5(1)(e) set out by the ECtHR in *Rooman v Belgium*.[21] Treatment should be provided along with opportunities for social reintegration and realistic tests of the patient's progress. In line with the principles above, offending behaviour programmes should be provided on a voluntary basis, and participation should only be taken into account in risk assessment if such programmes have been demonstrated to reduce recidivism.

More robust safeguards against the inappropriate use of hospitals as venues for preventive detention should also be introduced. There should be a requirement for decisions by Justice Secretary to transfer prisoners to hospital chiefly on public protection grounds to be independently scrutinized by the First Tier Tribunal (Mental Health) or the Mental Health Tribunal for Wales. This review could take place within a month after the person has been transferred to hospital to enable prisoners who do require treatment to receive it promptly.

Limiting recourse to detention in this way may again be expected to provoke concerns about the release of 'dangerous' people. Extending deliberative democracy to public health matters, including preventive detention measures, could again help to encourage greater public participation in policy and engagement between policymakers, experts, the media, the public, mental health service users, and practitioners. Coupled with public education campaigns to counteract the stigmatization of people with mental health conditions, public deliberation could help to increase society's tolerance for positive risk-taking. Concerted political efforts to counteract the blame that tends to be attributed to mental health professionals following serious offending by patients before the full facts have been determined could also help to cool down the debate. These strategies could help to move policy and practice forward, and to break away from the paralysing patterns of distrust, coercion and risk aversion seen in the past.

8.8 Conclusion

This chapter has shown that a concern for enhancing individual welfare through rehabilitative efforts has survived the demise of the penal welfare

---

[21] [2019] ECHR 109. See Chapter 2.

era. Policy continues to be influenced by the idea that interventions with offenders are justified on the grounds that they will reduce crime and promote wellbeing. Given the clear priority accorded to security over individual liberty in the 'balance' struck by domestic policy in England and Wales and by human rights law, rehabilitation may be understood as an effort to render coercive preventive measures taken in the pursuit of security more palatable for liberal governments. Reliance on rehabilitative interventions is an inadequate safeguard against disproportionate punishment. It is also inadequate to protect individuals from the harms of preventive detention and coercive treatment. Reserving indeterminate sentences for offenders convicted of very serious offences who pose a significant risk of serious harm to others and ensuring parsimonious use of preventive detention in nonpunitive conditions could be one way forward. Reforms are also required to mental health law to address the discriminatory use of detention motivated by public protection concerns. Any proposals to reform the system must be accompanied by efforts to engage the public, policymakers, experts, and people with lived experience to enable both public participation in policymaking and to cool down the temperature of debates concerning figures who provoke public fears.

Bibliography

Allen, F. A. (1959) 'Legal values and the rehabilitative ideal', *Journal of Criminal Law, Criminology & Police Science*, 50, 226–32.

Almenara, M. A. and van Zyl Smit, D. (2015) 'Human dignity and life imprisonment: The Pope enters the debate', *Human Rights Law Review*, 15(2), 369–76.

Alwin, N., Blackburn, R., Davidson, K., Hilton, M., Logan, C., and Shine, J. (2006) *Understanding Personality Disorder: A Report by the British Psychological Society*. Leicester: British Psychological Society.

American Psychiatric Association (2000) *Diagnostic and Statistical Manual of Mental Disorders: DSM-IV-TR*. 4th edn (text revision). Washington, D.C.: American Psychiatric Association.

American Psychiatric Association (2013) *Diagnostic and Statistical Manual of Mental Disorders: DSM-5*. 5th edn. Washington, D.C.: American Psychiatric Association.

American Psychiatric Association (2022) *Diagnostic and Statistical Manual of Mental Disorders: DSM-5-TR*. 5th edn (text revision). Washington, D.C.: American Psychiatric Association.

American Psychiatric Association (2023) Personality. In: APA Dictionary of Psychology. Available at: https://dictionary.apa.org/personality.

Andrews, D. A. and Bonta, J. (2010) 'Rehabilitating criminal justice policy and practice', *Psychology, Public Policy, and Law*, 16(1), 39–55.

Annison, H. (2014) 'Interpreting the politics of the judiciary: The British senior judicial tradition and the pre-emptive turn in criminal justice', *Journal of Law & Society*, 41(3), 339–66.

Annison, H. (2015) *Dangerous Politics: Risk, Political Vulnerability, and Penal Policy*. Oxford: Oxford University Press.

Annison, H. (2018) 'Tracing the Gordian knot: Indeterminate-sentenced prisoners and the pathologies of English penal politics', *Political Quarterly*, 89(2), 197–205.

Annison, H. and O'Loughlin, A. (2019) 'Fundamental rights and indeterminate sentencing in England and Wales: The value and limits of a right to rehabilitation', in S. Meijer, H. Annison, and A. O'Loughlin (eds) *Fundamental Rights and Legal Consequences of Criminal Conviction*. Oxford: Hart Publishing.

Appelbaum, P. S. and Grisso, T. (1988) 'Assessing patients' capacities to consent to treatment', *New England Journal of Medicine*, 319(25), 1635–38.

Ashworth, A. and Kelly, R. (2022) *Sentencing and Criminal Justice*. 7th edn. Oxford: Hart.

Ashworth, A. and Mackay, R. (2015) 'Case Comment: *R. v Vowles (Lucinda); R. v Barnes (Carl); R. v Coleman (Danielle); R. v Odiowei (Justin Obuza); R. v Irving*

(David Stuart); R. v McDougall (Gordon): Sentencing - guidance where an element of mental disorder exists', *Criminal Law Review*, 7, 542–48.

Ashworth, A. and Player, E. (2005) 'Criminal Justice Act 2003: The sentencing provisions', *Modern Law Review*, 68(5), 822–38.

Ashworth, A. and Zedner, L. (2014) *Preventive Justice*. Oxford: Oxford University Press.

Ashworth, A. and Zedner, L. (2019) 'Some dilemmas of indeterminate sentences: Risk and uncertainty, dignity and hope', in J. W. de Keijser, J. V. Roberts, and J. Ryberg (eds) *Predictive Sentencing: Normative and Empirical Perspectives*. Oxford: Hart Publishing.

Bailey, V. (2019) *The Rise and Fall of the Rehabilitative Ideal, 1895–1970*. London: Routledge.

Baron, J. and Hershey, J. C. (1988) 'Outcome bias in decision evaluation', *Journal of Personality and Social Psychology*, 54(4), 569–79.

Barrett, B., Byford, S., Seivewright, H., Cooper, S., Duggan, C., and Tyrer, P. (2009) 'The assessment of Dangerous and Severe Personality Disorder: Service use, cost, and consequences', *Journal of Forensic Psychiatry and Psychology*, 20(1), 120–31.

Bartlett, A. (2016) *Secure Lives: The Meaning and Importance of Culture in Secure Hospital Care*. Oxford: Oxford University Press.

Bartlett, A. and Kesteven, S. (2010) 'Organizational and conceptual frameworks and the mentally disordered offender', in A. Bartlett and G. McGauley (eds) *Forensic Mental Health: Concepts, Systems and Practice*. Oxford: Oxford University Press.

Bartlett, P. (2012) 'The United Nations Convention on the Rights of Persons with Disabilities and mental health law', *Modern Law Review*, 75, 752–78.

Bateman, A. (2022) 'Mentalizing and group psychotherapy: A novel treatment for antisocial personality disorder', *American Journal of Psychotherapy*, 75, 32–37.

Bateman, A., O'Connell, J., Lorenzini, N., Gardner, T., and Fonagy, P. (2016) 'A randomised controlled trial of mentalization-based treatment versus structured clinical management for patients with comorbid borderline personality disorder and antisocial personality disorder', *BMC Psychiatry*, 16, 1–11.

Beard, J. (2021) *Police, Crime, Sentencing and Courts Bill: Part 7–Sentencing and Release*. House of Commons Briefing Paper no. 9161. London: House of Commons Library. Available at: https://commonslibrary.parliament.uk/research-briefings/cbp-9161/

Beard, J. (2023) *The Parole System of England and Wales: Research Briefing*. London: House of Commons Library. Available at: https://commonslibrary.parliament.uk/research-briefings/cbp-8656/

Beaudry, G., Yu, R., Perry, A. E., and Fazel, S. (2021) 'Effectiveness of psychological interventions in prison to reduce recidivism: a systematic review and meta-analysis of randomised controlled trials', *The Lancet Psychiatry*, 8(9), 759–73.

Beck, J., Broder, F., and Hindman, R. (2016) 'Frontiers in cognitive behaviour therapy for personality disorders', *Behaviour Change*, 33(2), 80–93.

Benefield, N., Joseph, N., Skett, S. Bridgland, S., d'Cruz, L., Goode, I., and Turner, K. (2015) 'The Offender Personality Disorder Strategy jointly delivered by NOMS and NHS England', *Prison Service Journal*, 218, 4–9.

Berger, B. L. (2012) 'Mental disorder and the instability of blame in criminal law', in F. Tanguay-Renaud and J. Stribopoulos (eds) *Rethinking Criminal Law Theory: New Canadian Perspectives in the Philosophy of Domestic, Transnational, and International Criminal Law*. Oxford: Hart Publishing.

Bergner, R. M. (2020) 'What is personality? Two myths and a definition', *New Ideas in Psychology*, 57, 100759.

Blackburn, R. (1988) 'On moral judgements and personality disorders: The myth of psychopathic personality revisited', *British Journal of Psychiatry*, 153(4), 505–12.

Blackburn, R. (2000) 'Treatment or incapacitation? Implications of research on personality disorders for the management of dangerous offenders', *Legal and Criminological Psychology*, 5(1), 1–21.

Blagden, N., Evans, J., Gould, L., Murphy, N., Hamilton, L., Tolley, C., and Wardle, K. (2023) '"The people who leave here are not the people who arrived." A qualitative analysis of the therapeutic process and identity transition in the Offender Personality Disorder Pathway', *Criminal Justice and Behavior*, 50(7), 1035–52.

Blair, T. (1993) 'Tony Blair is tough on crime, tough on the causes of crime', *New Statesman*, 29 January 1993.

Boateng, P. and Sharland, A. (1999) 'Managing dangerous people with severe personality disorder', *Criminal Justice Matters*, 37(1), 4–9.

Bonta, J. and Andrews, D. A. (2007) *Risk-Need-Responsivity Model for Offender Assessment and Rehabilitation 2007–06*. Ottawa, Ontario: Public Safety Canada.

Bottoms, A. E. (1977) 'Reflections on the renaissance of dangerousness', *The Howard Journal of Criminal Justice*, 16, 70–96.

Bowers, L., Carr-Walker, P., Allan, T., Callaghan, P., Nijman, H., and Paton, J. (2006) 'Attitude to personality disorder among prison officers working in a dangerous and severe personality disorder unit', *International Journal of Law and Psychiatry*, 29(5), 333–42.

Bowers, L., Carr-Walker, P., Paton, J. O., Nijman, H., Callaghan, P., Allan, T., and Alexander, J. (2005) 'Changes in attitudes to personality disorder on a DSPD unit', *Criminal Behaviour and Mental Health*, 15(3), 171–83.

Boynton, J. (1980) *Report of the Review of Rampton Hospital*. Cmnd 8073. London: HMSO.

Bradley, K. J. C. (2009) *The Bradley Report: Lord Bradley's Review of people with Mental Health Problems or Learning Disabilities in the Criminal Justice System*. London: Department of Health.

Brinn, A., Preston, J., Costello, R., Opoku, T., Sampson, E., Elliott, I. and Sorbie, A. (2023) *An Impact Evaluation of the Prison-based Thinking Skills Programme (TSP) on Reoffending*. London: Ministry of Justice.

Brooker, C., Sirdifield, C, Blizard, R., Denney, D., and Pluck, G. (2012) 'Probation and mental illness', *Journal of Forensic Psychiatry & Psychology*, 23(4), 522–37.

Brown, M. (2016) 'Risk, dangerousness and violence', in J. Stubbs and S. Tomsen (eds) *Australian Violence: Crime, Criminal Justice and Beyond*. Alexandria, New South Wales, Australia: The Federation Press.

Brown, P., Bakolis, I., Appiah-Kusi, E., Hallett, N., Hotopf, M., and Blackwood, N. (2022) 'Prevalence of mental disorders in defendants at criminal court', *BJPsych Open*, 8(3), e92.

Bibliography

Buchanan, A. and Leese, M. (2001) 'Detention of people with dangerous severe personality disorders: A systematic review', *Lancet*, 358(9297), 1955–59.

Buckland, R. (2020) Lord Chancellor's Speech: White Paper Launch—A Smarter Approach to Sentencing. 16 September 2020. London: Ministry of Justice. Available at: https://www.gov.uk/government/speeches/lord-chancellors-speech-white-paper-launch-a-smarter-approach-to-sentencing.

Burns, T., Yiend, J., Fahy, T., Fazel, S., Fitzpatrick, R., Sinclair, J., Rogers, R., Vasquez Montes, M., and the IDEA Group (2011) *Inclusion for DSPD: Evaluating Assessment and Treatment (IDEA): Final Report to NHS National R&D Programme on Forensic Mental Health*. London: Ministry of Justice.

Butler, R. A. (1975) *Report of the Committee on Mentally Abnormal Offenders*. London: HMSO.

Cairney, P. (2009) 'The "British policy style" and mental health: Beyond the headlines', *Journal of Social Policy*, 38(4), 671–88.

Cairney, P. (2016) *The Politics of Evidence-Based Policy Making*. London: Palgrave McMillan.

Castillo, H. (2003) *Personality Disorder: Temperament or Trauma?* London: Jessica Kingsley Publishers.

Cavadino, M. (2002) 'New mental health law for old—Safety-plus equals human rights minus', *Child and Family Law Quarterly*, 14(2), 175–190.

Cawthra, R. and Gibb, R. (1998) 'Severe personality disorder—Whose responsibility?', *British Journal of Psychiatry*, 173, 8–10.

Cheliotis, L. (2008) Reconsidering the effectiveness of temporary release: A systematic review. Aggression and Violent Behavior, 13(3): 153–68.

Clare, E. and Bottomley, K. (2001) *Evaluation of Close Supervision Centres. Home Office Research Study 219*. London: Home Office Research, Development and Statistics Directorate.

Clark, L. E., Shapiro, J. L., Daly, E. Vanderbleek, E. N., Negrón, M. R., and Harrison, J. (2018) 'Empirically validated diagnostic and assessment methods', in W. J. Livesley and R. Larstone (eds) *Handbook of Personality Disorders*. New York: Guilford Press.

Coid, J. W. (1992) 'DSM-III diagnosis in criminal psychopaths: A way forward', *Criminal Behaviour and Mental Health*, 2(2), 78–94.

Coid, J., Yang, M., Ullrich, S., Roberts, A., and Hare, R. D. (2009a) 'Prevalence and correlates of psychopathic traits in the household population of Great Britain', *International Journal of Law and Psychiatry*, 32(2), 65–73.

Coid, J., Yang, M., Ullrich, S., Roberts, A., Moran, P., Bebbington, P., Brugha, T., Jenkins, R., Farrell, M., Lewis, G., Singleton, N., and Hare, R. (2009b) 'Psychopathy among prisoners in England and Wales', *International Journal of Law and Psychiatry*, 32(3), 134–41.

Cooke, D. J. and Michie, C. (2011) 'Violence risk assessment: Challenging the illusion of certainty', in B. McSherry and P. Keyzer (eds) *Dangerous People: Policy, Prediction, and Practice*. London: Routledge.

Cooke, E., Stephenson, Z., and Rose, J. (2017) 'How do professionals experience working with offenders diagnosed with personality disorder within a prison environment?', *Journal of Forensic Psychiatry and Psychology*, 28(6), 841–62.

Cope, R. (1993) 'A survey of forensic psychiatrists' views on psychopathic disorder', *Journal of Forensic Psychiatry*, 4(2), 215–35.

Corston, J. (2007) *The Corston Report: A Report by Baroness Jean Corston of a Review of Women with Particular Vulnerabilities in the Criminal Justice System.* London: Home Office.

Costa, P. T. and McCrae, R. R. (1992) *Revised NEO Personality Inventory (NEO PI-R tm) and NEO Five-factor Inventory (NEO-FFI): Professional Manual.* Odessa, Florida: Psychological Assessment Resources.

Crewe, B. (2009) *The Prisoner Society: Power Adaptation and Social Life in an English Prison.* Oxford: Oxford University Press.

Criminal Cases Review Commission (2023a) News: No grounds to refer murder and attempted murder convictions back to the Court of Appeal. Available at: https://ccrc.gov.uk/news/stone-application-declined/. Accessed 23 July 2023.

Criminal Cases Review Commission (2023b) News: Fresh review for murder convictions. Available at: https://ccrc.gov.uk/news/fresh-review-for-murder-conv ictions/.

Criminal Justice Joint Inspection (2021a) *A Joint Thematic Inspection of the Criminal Justice Journey for Individuals with Mental Health needs and Disorders.* Manchester: HM Inspectorate of Probation, HM Crown Prosecution Service Inspectorate, HM Inspectorate of Constabulary and Fire & Rescue Services, Care Quality Commission, Healthcare Inspectorate Wales and HM Inspectorate of Prisons. Available at: https://www.justiceinspectorates.gov.uk/hmiprobation/

Criminal Justice Joint Inspection (2021b) *Neurodiversity in the Criminal Justice System: A Review of Evidence.* Manchester: HM Inspectorate of Prisons, HM Inspectorate of Probation and HM Inspectorate of Constabulary and Fire & Rescue Services. Available at: https://www.justiceinspectorates.gov.uk/hmicfrs/publications/neurodiversity-in-the-criminal-justice-system/

Cullen, E. and Newell, T. (1999) *Murderers and Life Imprisonment: Containment, Treatment, Safety and Risk.* Winchester: Waterside Press.

d'Cruz, L. (2015) 'Implementing an offender PD strategy for women', *Prison Service Journal*, 218, 31–34.

D'Silva, K., Duggan, C., and McCarthy, L. (2004) 'Does treatment really make psychopaths worse? A review of the evidence', *Journal of Personality Disorders*, 18(2), 163–77.

Dagan, N. (2020) 'The Janus face of imprisonment: Contrasting judicial conceptions of imprisonment purposes in the European Court of Human Rights and the Supreme Court of the United States', *Criminology & Criminal Justice*, 21(5), 633–49.

Davidson, K. M. and Tyrer, P. (1996) 'Cognitive therapy for antisocial and borderline personality disorders: Single case study series', *British Journal of Clinical Psychology*, 35, 413–29.

Daw, R. (2007) 'The Mental Health Act 2007: The defeat of an ideal', *Journal of Mental Health Law*, 1(16), 131–48.

Dawson, J. B. (2018) 'The Australasian approach to the definition of mental disorder in a Mental Health Act', *Medical Law Review*, 26(4), 610–32.

Day, N. J. S., Hunt, A., Cortis-Jones, L., and Grenyer, B. F. S. (2018) 'Clinician attitudes towards borderline personality disorder: A 15-year comparison', *Personality and Mental Health*, 12(4), 309–20.

de Boer, J. and Gerrits, J. (2007) 'Learning from Holland: the TBS system', *Psychiatry*, 6(11), 459–61.

De Fruyt, F. and De Clercq, B. (2012) 'Childhood antecedents of personality disorders', in T. A. Widiger (ed.) *The Oxford Handbook of Personality Disorders*. Oxford: Oxford University Press.

De Fruyt, F. and De Clercq, B. (2014) 'Antecedents of personality disorder in childhood and adolescence: Toward an integrative developmental model', *Annual Review of Clinical Psychology*, 10, 449–76.

de Motte, C., Bailey, D., Hunter, M., and Bennett, A. L. (2017) 'What is the pattern of self-harm and prison rule-breaking behaviour in personality disordered offenders in a high secure prison?', *Journal of Criminal Psychology*, 7(4), 287–301.

Dell, S. and Robertson, G. (1988) *Sentenced to Hospital: Offenders in Broadmoor*. Oxford: Oxford University Press.

Department for Constitutional Affairs (2007) *Mental Capacity Act 2005 Code of Practice*. London: TSO.

Department of Health (1999) *Review of the Mental Health Act 1983: Report of the Expert Committee*. London: Department of Health.

Department of Health (2000) *Reforming the Mental Health Act: Part II: High Risk Patients*. Cm 5016-II. London: The Stationery Office.

Department of Health (2011) *Personality Disorder Pathway Implementation Plan: Impact Assessment*. London: Department of Health.

Department of Health (2015) *Mental Health Act 1983: Code of Practice*. Norwich: TSO.

Department of Health and Ministry of Justice (2011) *The Offender Personality Disorder Strategy*. London: Department of Health and Ministry of Justice.

Department of Health and NOMS (2011a) *Consultation on the Offender Personality Disorder Pathway Implementation Plan*. London: Department of Health.

Department of Health and NOMS (2011b) *Offender Personality Disorder Strategy for Women: Executive Summary*. London: Department of Health and Ministry of Justice.

Department of Health and Social Care (2018) *Modernising the Mental Health Act: Increasing Choice, Reducing Compulsion. Final Report of the Independent Review of the Mental Health Act 1983 (The Wessely Review)*. London: Department of Health and Social Care. Available at: https://www.gov.uk/government/publications/modernising-the-mental-health-act-final-report-from-the-independent-review.

Department of Health and Social Care and Ministry of Justice (2022) *Draft Mental Health Bill*. Available at: https://www.gov.uk/government/publications/draft-mental-health-bill-2022.

Department of Health, Home Office and HM Prison Service (2001) *DSPD Programme: Dangerous People with Severe Personality Disorder Initiative: Progress Report*. London: Home Office.

Dessecker, A. (2009) 'Dangerousness, long prison terms, and preventive measures in Germany', *Champ Pénal/Penal Field*, VI. GERN Seminar 'Longues peines et peines indéfinies. Punir la dangerosité', Neuchâtel, 3 September 2008. Available at: https://journals.openedition.org/champpenal/7546.

Douglas, T., Pugh, J., Singh, I., Savulescu, J., and Fazel, S. (2017) 'Risk assessment tools in criminal justice and forensic psychiatry: The need for better data', *European Psychiatry*, 42, 134–37.

Drenkhahn, K. and Morgenstern, C. (2020) 'Preventive detention in Germany and Europe', in A. R. Felthous and H. Saß (eds) *The Wiley International Handbook on Psychopathic Disorders and the Law*. 2nd edn. Hoboken, New Jersey: Wiley-Blackwell.

DSPD Programme, Department of Health and Ministry of Justice (2008) *Forensic Personality Disorder Medium Secure and Community Pilot Services Planning & Delivery Guide*. London: Ministry of Justice and Department of Health.

DSPD Programme, Department of Health, Home Office, and HM Prison Service (2006) *Dangerous and Severe/Complex Personality Disorder High Secure Services Planning and Delivery Guide for Women's DSPD Services (Primrose Programme)*. London: Home Office.

DSPD Programme, Department of Health, Ministry of Justice, and HM Prison Service (2008) *Dangerous and Severe Personality High Secure Services for Men Planning & Delivery Guide*. London: Ministry of Justice and Department of Health.

Duggan, C. (2011) 'Dangerous and severe personality disorder', *British Journal of Psychiatry*, 198(6), 431–33.

Duggan, C. and Howard, R. (2009) 'The "functional link" between personality disorder and violence: A critical appraisal', in M. McMurran and R. Howard (eds) *Personality, Personality Disorder and Violence: An Evidence-Based Approach*. Chichester: John Wiley & Sons.

Dyer, A. (2016) 'Irreducible life sentences: What difference have the European Convention on Human Rights and the United Kingdom Human Rights Act made?', *Human Rights Law Review*, 16(3), 541–84.

Eastman, N. (1999) 'Public health psychiatry or crime prevention?', *British Medical Journal*, 318(7183), 549–50.

Eigen, J. P. (1995) *Witnessing Insanity: Madness and Mad-Doctors in the English Court*. New Haven; London: Yale University Press.

Eigen, J. P. (1999) 'Lesion of the will: Medical resolve and criminal responsibility in Victorian insanity trials', *Law & Society Review*, 33(2), 425–59.

Ericson, R. V. (2007) *Crime in an Insecure World*. Cambridge: Polity Press.

European Committee for the Prevention of Torture and Inhuman or Degrading Treatment or Punishment (2020) *Report to the United Kingdom Government on the visit to the United Kingdom carried out by the European Committee for the Prevention of Torture and Inhuman or Degrading Treatment or Punishment (CPT) from 13 to 23 May 2019*. Strasbourg: Council of Europe.

Fallon, P., Bluglass, R., Edwards, B., and Daniels, G. (1999a) *Report of the Commitee of Inquiry into the Personality Disorder Unit, Ashworth Special Hospital: Volume I*. Cm 4194-ii. London: The Stationery Office.

Fallon, P., Bluglass, R., Edwards, B., and Daniels, G. (1999b) *Report of the Commitee of Inquiry into the Personality Disorder Unit, Ashworth Special Hospital. Volume*

II: Expert Evidence on Personality Disorder. CM4195. London: The Stationery Office.

Favril, L., Yu, R., Hawton, K., and Fazel, S. (2020) 'Risk factors for self-harm in prison: a systematic review and meta-analysis', *Lancet Psychiatry*, 7, 682–91.

Favril, L., Yu, R., Uyar, A., Sharpe, M., and Fazel, S. (2022) 'Risk factors for suicide in adults: systematic review and meta-analysis of psychological autopsy studies', *Evid Based Ment Health*, 25(4), 148–55.

Fazel, S. and Danesh, J. (2002) 'Serious mental disorder in 23000 prisoners: A systematic review of 62 surveys', *Lancet*, 359(9306), 545–50.

Fazel, S., Singh, J. P., Doll, H., and Grann, M. (2012) 'Use of risk assessment instruments to predict violence and antisocial behaviour in 73 samples involving 24 827 people: Systematic review and meta-analysis', *British Medical Journal*, 345(7868), 1–12.

Feeley, M. M. and Simon, J. (1992) 'The new penology: Notes on the emerging strategy of corrections and its implications', *Criminology*, 30(4), 449–74.

Felthous, A. R. and Saß, H. (eds) (2020) *The Wiley International Handbook on Psychopathic Disorders and the Law*. 2nd edn. Hoboken, New Jersey: Wiley-Blackwell.

Ferguson, E. A. (2021) *'A Sentence of Last Resort': The Order for Lifelong Restriction and the Sentencing of Dangerous Offenders in Scotland*. PhD thesis. University of Glasgow.

Fine, C. and Kennett, J. (2004) 'Mental impairment, moral understanding and criminal responsibility: Psychopathy and the purposes of punishment', *International Journal of Law and Psychiatry*, 27(5), 425–43.

First, M. B., Bell, C. C., Cuthbert, B., Krystal, J. H., Malison, R., Offord, D. R., Reiss, D. Shea, T., Widiger, T., and Wisner, K. L. (2002) 'Personality disorders and relational disorders: A research agenda for addressing crucial gaps in DSM', in: D. J. Kupfer, M. B. First, and D. A. Regier (eds) *A Research Agenda for DSM-V*. Washington, D.C.: American Psychiatric Association.

Fischhoff, B. (1975) 'Hindsight is not equal to foresight: The effect of outcome knowledge on judgment under uncertainty', *Journal of Experimental Psychology: Human Perception and Performance*, 1(3), 288–99.

Fox, S. (2010) 'The role of the prison officer (Dangerous and Severe Personality Disorder in the prison system)', in N. Murphy and D. McVey (eds) *Treating Personality Disorder: Creating Robust Services for People with Complex Mental Health Needs*. London: Routledge.

Francis, R., Higgins, J., and Cassam, E. (2006) *Report of the Independent Inquiry into the Care and Treatment of Michael Stone*. South East Coast Strategic Health Authority, Kent County Council and Kent Probation.

Freckelton, I. and Keyzer, P. (2010) 'Indefinite detention of sex offenders and human rights: The intervention of the human rights committee of the United Nations', *Psychiatry, Psychology and Law*, 17(3), 345–54.

García-Gutiérrez, M. S., Navarrete, F., Sala, F., Gasparyan, A., Austrich-Olivares, A., and Manzanares, J. (2020) 'Biomarkers in psychiatry: concept, definition, types and relevance to the clinical reality', *Frontiers in Psychiatry*, 11, 432.

Garland, D. (1985) *Punishment and Welfare: A History of Penal Strategies*. Aldershot: Gower.
Garland, D. (1996) 'The limits of the sovereign state: Strategies of crime control in contemporary society', *British Journal of Criminology*, 36(4), 445–71.
Garland, D. (1997) '"Governmentality" and the problem of crime: Foucault, criminology, sociology', *Theoretical Criminology*, 1(2), 173–214.
Garland, D. (2001) *The Culture of Control: Crime and Social Order in Contemporary Society*. Oxford: Oxford University Press.
Garrington, C. and Boer, D. P. (2020) 'Structured professional judgement in violence risk assessment', in J. S. Wormith, L. A. Craig, and T. E. Hogue (eds) *The Wiley Handbook of What Works in Violence Risk Management: Theory, Research and Practice*. Hoboken, New Jersey: Wiley-Blackwell.
Gartlehner, G., Crotty, K., Kennedy, S., Edlund, M. J., Ali, R., Siddiqui, M., Fortman, R., Wines, R., Persad, E., and Viswanathan, M. (2021) 'Pharmacological treatments for borderline personality disorder: A systematic review and meta-analysis', *CNS Drugs*, 35(10), 1053–67.
Genders, E. and Player, E. (1995) *Grendon: A Study of a Therapeutic Prison*. Oxford: Clarendon Press.
Genders, E. and Player, E. (2010) 'Therapy in prison: Revisiting Grendon 20 years on', *The Howard Journal*, 49(5), 431–50.
Genders, E. and Player, E. (2014) 'Rehabilitation, risk management and prisoners' rights', *Criminology and Criminal Justice*, 14(4), 434–57.
Genders, E. and Player, E. (2022) 'Long sentenced women prisoners: Rights, risks and rehabilitation', *Punishment & Society*, 24(1), 3–25.
Gendreau, P. and Ross, R. R. (1987) 'Revivification of rehabilitation: Evidence from the 1980s', *Justice Quarterly*, 4(3), 349–407.
Gibbens, T. C. N. and Jennings, R. (1960) 'The Mental Health Act, 1959', *The Modern Law Review*, 23(4), 410–24.
Gibbon, S., Khalifa, N. R., Cheung, N. H., Völlm, B. A., and McCarthy, L. (2020) 'Psychological interventions for antisocial personality disorder', *Cochrane Database of Systematic Reviews*, 9, Art. No.: CD007668.
Giddens, A. (1998) *The Third Way: The Renewal of Social Democracy*. Cambridge: Polity Press.
Glannon, W. (2008) 'Moral responsibility and the psychopath', *Neuroethics*, 1, 158–66.
Glaser, W. (1990) 'Morality and medicine', *Legal Service Bulletin*, 15(3), 114–16.
Glenn, A. L. and Raine, A. (2014) 'Neurocriminology: Implications for the punishment, prediction and prevention of criminal behaviour', *Nature Reviews: Neuroscience*, 15(1), 54–63.
Gostin, L. (1983) 'Contemporary social historical perspectives on mental health reform', *Journal of Law and Society*, 10(1), 47–70.
Grant, B. F., Chou, S. P., Goldstein, R. B., Huang, B., Stinson, F. S., Saha, T. D., Smith, S. M., Dawson, D. A., Pulay, A. J., Pickering, R. P., and Ruan, W. J. (2008) 'Prevalence, correlates, disability, and comorbidity of DSM-IV borderline personality disorder: Results from the Wave 2 National Epidemiologic

Survey on Alcohol and Related Conditions', *Journal of Clinical Psychiatry*, 69(4), 533–45.

Grant, B. F., Stinson, F. S., Dawson, D. A., Chou, S. P., and Ruan, W. J. (2005) 'Co-occurrence of DSM-IV personality disorders in the United States: results from the National Epidemiologic Survey on Alcohol and Related Conditions', *Comprehensive Psychiatry*, 46(1), 1–5.

Gray, J. E., McSherry, B. M., O'Reilly, R. L., and Weller, P. J. (2010) 'Australian and Canadian Mental Health Acts compared', *Australian and New Zealand Journal of Psychiatry*, 44(12), 1126–31.

Green, D. (2006) 'Public opinion versus public judgment about crime: Correcting the "comedy of errors"', *British Journal of Criminology*, 46(1), 131.

Guiney, T. (2019) 'Marginal gains or diminishing returns? Penal bifurcation, policy change and the administration of prisoner release in England and Wales', *European Journal of Probation*, 11(3), 139–52.

Gutiérrez, F., Vall, G., Peri, J. M., Baillés, E., Ferraz, L., Gárriz, M., and Caseras, X. (2012) 'Personality disorder features through the life course', *Journal of Personality Disorders*, 26(5), 763–74.

Habermeyer, E., Tribolet-Hardy, F., Felthous, A. R., and Motov, V. (2020) 'Hospitalization and civil commitment of individuals with psychopathic disorders in Germany and Switzerland, Russia, and the United States', in A. R. Felthous and H. Saß (eds) *The Wiley International Handbook on Psychopathic Disorders and the Law*. 2nd edn. Hoboken, New Jersey: Wiley-Blackwell.

Hadden, J. M., Thomas, S., Jellicoe-Jones, L., and Marsh, Z. (2016) 'An exploration of staff and prisoner experiences of a newly commissioned personality disorder service within a category B male establishment', *Journal of Forensic Practice*, 18(3), 216–28.

Haddock, A., Snowden, P., Dolan, M., Parker, J., and Rees, H. (2001) 'Managing dangerous people with severe personality disorder: A survey of forensic psychiatrists' opinions', *Psychiatric Bulletin*, 25(8), 293–96.

Hancock, P. and Jewkes, Y. (2011) 'Architectures of incarceration: The spatial pains of imprisonment', *Punishment & Society*, 13(5), 611–29.

Hannah-Moffat, K. (2005) 'Criminogenic needs and the transformative risk subject: Hybridizations of risk/need in penality', *Punishment & Society*, 7(1), 29–51.

Hannah-Moffat, K. (2015a) 'Needle in a haystack: Logical parameters of treatment based on actuarial risk-needs assessments', *Criminology and Public Policy*, 14(1), 113–20.

Hannah-Moffat, K. (2015b) 'The uncertainties of risk assessment: Partiality, transparency, and just decisions', *Federal Sentencing Reporter*, 27, 244–47.

Hannah-Moffat, K. (2016) 'A conceptual kaleidoscope: Contemplating "dynamic structural risk" and an uncoupling of risk from need', *Psychology, Crime & Law*, 22(1-2), 33–46.

Hannah-Moffat, K. (2019) 'Algorithmic risk governance: Big data analytics, race and information activism in criminal justice debates', *Theoretical Criminology*, 23(4), 453–70.

Hannah-Moffat, K., Maurutto, P., and Turnbull, S. (2009) 'Negotiated risk: Actuarial illusions and discretion in probation', *Canadian Journal of Law and Society*, 24(3), 391–409.

Hare, R. D. (1991) *The Psychopathy Checklist—Revised (PCL-R)*. Toronto, Canada: Multi-Health Systems.

Hare, R. D. (1998) 'The Hare PCL-R: Some issues concerning its use and misuse', *Legal and Criminological Psychology*, 3(1), 99–119.

Hare, R. D. (2020) 'The PCL-R Assessment of Psychopathy', in A. R. Felthous and H. Saß (eds) *The Wiley International Handbook on Psychopathic Disorders and the Law*. 2nd edn. Hoboken, New Jersey: Wiley-Blackwell.

Hayward, M. and Moran, P. (2008) 'Comorbidity of personality disorders and mental illnesses', *Psychiatry*, 7(3), 102–04.

Hebenton, B. and Seddon, T. (2009) 'From dangerousness to precaution: Managing sexual and violent offenders in an insecure and uncertain age', *British Journal of Criminology*, 49(3), 343–62.

Hemphill, J. F., Hare, R. D., Wong, S. (1998) 'Psychopathy and recidivism: A review', *Legal and Criminological Psychology*, 3, 139–70.

Henderson, D. K. (1942) 'Psychopathic states', *Journal of Mental Science*, 88(373), 485–90.

Henfrey, S. A. (2018) 'Kaizen: Working responsively with psychopathic traits', *Journal of Criminological Research, Policy and Practice*, 4(3), 199–211.

Herpertz, S. C., Huprich, S. K., Bohus, M., Chanen, A., Goodman, M., Mehlum, L., Moran, P., Newton-Howes, G., Scott, L., and Sharp, C. (2017) 'The challenge of transforming the diagnostic system of personality disorders', *Journal of Personality Disorders*, 31(5), 577–89.

Hillier, J. and Mews, A. (2018) *The Reoffending Impact of Increased Release of Prisoners on Temporary Licence. Analytical Summary 2018*. London: Ministry of Justice.

HM Chief Inspector of Prisons (2000) *Inspection of Close Supervision Centres August– September 1999. A Thematic Review by HM Chief Inspector of Prisons for England and Wales*. London: HM Inspectorate of Prisons.

HM Inspectorate of Prisons (2006) *Extreme Custody: A Thematic Inspection of Close Supervision Centres and High Security Segregation*. London: HM Inspectorate of Prisons.

HM Inspectorate of Prisons (2019) *HM Chief Inspector of Prisons for England and Wales. Annual Report 2018-2019*. London: HMSO.

HM Inspectorate of Prisons (2023) *HM Chief Inspector of Prisons for England and Wales. Annual Report 2022-2023*. London: HMSO.

HM Prison and Probation Service and NHS (2023) *The Offender Personality Disorder Pathway: A Joint Strategy for 2023 to 2028*. London: HM Prison and Probation Service and NHS.

Home Affairs Committee (2000) *Session 1999-2000 First Report: Managing Dangerous People With Severe Personality Disorder. Volume 1: Report and Proceedings of the Committee*. London: The Stationery Office.

Home Office (2000) *Memorandum by the Home Office*, in Home Affairs Committee, Session 1999-2000 First Report: Managing Dangerous People With Severe Personality Disorder. Volume II: Minutes of Evidence and Appendices. Appendix 1. London: The Stationery Office.

Home Office and Department of Health (1999) *Managing Dangerous People with Severe Personality Disorder: Proposals for Policy Development*. London: Home Office.

Hood, R. and Shute, S. (2000) *The Parole System at Work: A Study of Risk Based Decision-Making. Home Office Research Study 202*. London: Home Office.

Hood, R., Shute, S., Feilzer, M., and Wilcox, A. (2002) 'Sex offenders emerging from long-term imprisonment: A study of their long-term reconviction rates and of Parole Board members' judgements of their risk', *British Journal of Criminology*, 42(2), 371–94.

Horn, N., Johnstone, L., and Brooke, S. (2007) 'Some service user perspectives on the diagnosis of Borderline Personality Disorder', *Journal of Mental Health*, 16(2), 255–69.

Hough, M., Jacobson, J., and Millie, A. (2003) *The Decision to Imprison: Sentencing and the Prison Population*. London: Prison Reform Trust.

House of Commons Committee of Public Accounts (2017) *Mental Health in Prisons: Eighth Report of Session 2017–19. HC 400*. London: House of Commons.

House of Commons Health and Social Care Committee (2018) *Prison Health. Twelfth Report of Session 2017–19*. London: House of Commons.

House of Commons Justice Committee (2022) *IPP sentences. Third Report of Session 2022–23. HC 266*. London: House of Commons.

Howard, H. (2015) 'Diminished responsibility, culpability and moral agency: The importance of distinguishing the terms', in B. Livings, A. Reed, and N. Wake (eds) *Mental Condition Defences and the Criminal Justice System: Perspectives from Law and Medicine*. Newcastle: Cambridge Scholars.

Howard, R. (2006) 'How is personality disorder linked to dangerousness? A putative role for early-onset alcohol abuse', *Medical Hypotheses*, 67(4), 702–08.

Howard, R. (2015) 'Personality disorders and violence: What is the link?', *Borderline Personality Disorder and Emotion Dysregulation*, 2(1), 1–11.

Howells, K. and Day, A. (2007) 'Readiness for treatment in high risk offenders with personality disorders', *Psychology, Crime and Law*, 13(1), 47–56.

Howells, K., Jones, L., Harris, M., Wong, S., Daffern, M., Tombs, D., Kane, E., Gallager, J., Ijomah, J., Krishnan, G., Milton, J., and Thornton, D. (2011) 'The baby, the bathwater and the bath itself: A response to Tyrer *et al.*'s review of the successes and failures of dangerous and severe personality disorder', *Medicine, Science and the Law*, 51(3), 129–33.

Howells, K., Krishnan, G. and Daffern, M. (2007) 'Challenges in the treatment of dangerous and severe personality disorder', *Advances in Psychiatric Treatment*, 13(5), 325–32.

Hutchinson, S. (2006) 'Countering catastrophic criminology: Reform, punishment and the modern liberal compromise', *Punishment & Society*, 8(4), 443–67.

Hutton, N. (2005) 'Beyond populist punitiveness?', *Punishment & Society*, 7(3), 243–58.

Jacobson, J. and Hough, M. (2010) *Unjust Deserts: Imprisonment for Public Protection*. London: Prison Reform Trust.

Jeffcote, N., Gerko, K. Van, and Nicklin, E. (2018) 'Meaningful service user participation in the pathway', in C. Campbell and J. Craissati (eds) *Managing Personality Disordered Offenders: A Pathways Approach*. Oxford: Oxford University Press.

Johnstone, G. (2000) 'Penal policy making: Elitist, populist or participatory?', *Punishment & Society*, 2(2), 161–80.

Bibliography

Jolliffe, D., Cattell, J., Raza, A., and Minoudis, P. (2017a) 'Evaluating the impact of the London Pathway Project', *Criminal Behaviour and Mental Health*, 27, 238-53.

Jolliffe, D., Cattell, J., Raza, A., and Minoudis, P. (2017b) 'Factors associated with progression in the London Pathway Project', *Criminal Behaviour and Mental Health*, 27, 222-37.

Jones, D. W. (2016) *Disordered Personalities and Crime: An Analysis of the History of Moral Insanity*. London: Routledge.

Jones, L. (2015) 'The Peaks Unit: From a pilot for "untreatable" psychopaths to trauma informed milieu therapy', *Prison Service Journal*, 218, 17-23.

Jones, L. (2018) 'Trauma-informed care and "good lives" in confinement', in G. Akerman, A. Needs, and C. Bainbridge (eds) *Transforming Environments and Rehabilitation*. London: Routledge.

Jones, L. (2020) 'Violence risk formulation: The move towards collaboratively produced, strengths-based safety planning', in J. S. Wormith, L. A. Craig, and T. E. Hogue (eds) *The Wiley Handbook of What Works in Violence Risk Management: Theory, Research and Practice*. Chichester: Wiley.

Jones, M. S. (1952) *Social Psychiatry. A Study of Therapeutic Communities*. London: Tavistock Publications.

Kane, J. M., Agid, O., Baldwin, M. L., Howes, O., Lindenmayer, J. P., Marder, S., Olfson, M., Potkin, S. G., and Correll, C. U. (2019) 'Clinical guidance on the identification and management of treatment-resistant schizophrenia', *Journal of Clinical Psychiatry*, 80(2), 18com12123.

Kant, I. (1960) *Religion within the Limits of Reason Alone*. T. M. Greene and H. H. Hudson (trans.), New York: Harper and Row.

Kearns, G. and Mackay, R. (1999) 'More fact(s) about the insanity defence', *Criminal Law Review*, Sep, 714-25.

Kemshall, H. and Maguire, M. (2001) 'Public protection, partnership and risk penality: The multi-agency risk management of sexual and violent offenders', *Punishment & Society*, 3(2), 237-64.

Kemshall, H. and Weaver, B. (2012) 'The sex offender public disclosure pilots in England and Scotland: Lessons for "marketing strategies" and risk communication with the public', *Criminology & Criminal Justice*, 12(5), 549-65.

Kendell, R. E. (2002) 'The distinction between personality disorder and mental illness', *British Journal of Psychiatry*, 180, 110-15.

Keyzer, P. (2011) 'The international human rights parameters for the preventive detention of serious sex offenders', in B. McSherry and P. Keyzer (eds) *Dangerous People: Policy, Prediction, and Practice*. London: Routledge.

Keyzer, P. and McSherry, B. (2015) 'The preventive detention of sex offenders: Law and practice', *University of New South Wales Law Journal*, 38(2), 792-822.

Khalifa, N. R., Gibbon, S., Völlm, B. A., Cheung, N. H., and McCarthy, L. (2020) 'Pharmacological interventions for antisocial personality disorder', *Cochrane Database of Systematic Reviews*, 9, Art. No.: CD007667.

Khan, Z. (2022) 'A typology of prisoner compliance with the Incentives and Earned Privileges scheme: Theorising the neoliberal self and staff-prisoner relationships', *Criminology & Criminal Justice*, 22(1), 97-114.

Kirkpatrick, T., Draycott, S., Freestone, M., Cooper, S., Twiselton, K., Watson, N., Evans, J., Hawes, V., Jones, L. Moore, C., Andrews, K., and Maden, T. (2010) 'A descriptive evaluation of patients and prisoners assessed for dangerous and severe personality disorder', *Journal of Forensic Psychiatry and Psychology*, 21(2), 264–82.

Kommers, D. P. and Miller, R. A. (2012) *The Constitutional Jurisprudence of the Federal Republic of Germany*. 3rd edn. Durham, North Carolina: Duke University Press.

Kubiak, S., Fedock, G., Kim, W. J., and Bybee, D. (2016) 'Long-term outcomes of a RCT intervention study for women with violent crimes', *Journal of the Society for Social Work and Research*, 7(4), 661–79.

Kuester, L., Freestone, M., Seewald, K., Rathbone, R., and Bui, K. (2022) *Evaluation of Psychologically Informed Planned Environments (PIPEs): Assessing the First Five Years*. Ministry of Justice Analytical Series. London: Ministry of Justice. Available at: https://www.gov.uk/government/publications/evaluation-of-psychologically-informed-planned-environments

La Fond, J. Q. (2011) 'Sexual offender commitment laws in the USA: The inevitable failure of misusing civil commitment to prevent future sex crimes', in B. McSherry and P. Keyzer (eds) *Dangerous People: Policy, Prediction, and Practice*. London: Routledge.

Lacey, N. (2001) 'Responsibility and modernity in criminal law', *Journal of Political Philosophy*, 9(3), 249–76.

Lacey, N. (2011) 'The resurgence of character: Responsibility in the context of criminalization', in R. A. Duff and S. Green (eds) *Philosophical Foundations of Criminal Law*. Oxford: Oxford University Press.

Lacey, N. (2012) 'Political systems and criminal justice: The prisoners' dilemma after the Coalition', *Current Legal Problems*, 65(1), 203–39.

Lacey, N. (2016) *In Search of Criminal Responsibility: Ideas, Interests, and Institutions*. Oxford: Oxford University Press.

Lacombe, D. (2008) 'Consumed with sex: The treatment of sex offenders in risk society', *British Journal of Criminology*, 48(1), 55–74.

Lam, D. C. K., Poplavskaya, E. V., Salkovskis, P. M., Hogg, L. I., and Panting, H. (2016) 'An experimental investigation of the impact of personality disorder diagnosis on clinicians: Can we see past the borderline?', *Behavioural and Cognitive Psychotherapy*, 44(3), 361–73.

Lamph, G., Dorothy, J., Jeynes, T., Coak, A., Jassat, R., Elliott, A., McKeown, M., and Thornton, T. (2022) 'A qualitative study of the label of personality disorder from the perspectives of people with lived experience and occupational experience', *Mental Health Review*, 27(1), 31–47.

Larsen, R. R., Jalava, J., and Griffiths, S. (2020) 'Are Psychopathy Checklist (PCL) psychopaths dangerous, untreatable, and without conscience? A systematic review of the empirical evidence', *Psychology, Public Policy, and Law*, 26(3), 297–311.

Lavrysen, L. (2020) 'Positive obligations and the criminal law: A bird's-eye view on the case law of the European Court of Human Rights', in L. Lavrysen and N. Mavronicola (eds) *Coercive Human Rights: Positive Duties to Mobilise the Criminal Law under the ECHR*. Oxford: Hart.

Bibliography 231

Law Commission (2012) *Insanity and Automatism: Supplementary Material to the Scoping Paper.* London: Law Commission.

Law Commission (2013) *Criminal Liability: Insanity and Automatism. A Discussion Paper.* London: Law Commission.

Lazarus, L. (2007) 'Mapping the right to security', in B. J. Goold and L. Lazarus (eds) *Security and Human Rights.* Oxford: Hart Publishing.

Lazarus, L. (2012a) 'Positive obligations and criminal justice: Duties to protect or coerce?' in L. Zedner and J. V. Roberts (eds) *Principles and Values in Criminal Law and Criminal Justice: Essays in Honour of Andrew Ashworth.* Oxford: Oxford University Press.

Lazarus, L. (2012b) 'The right to security–Securing rights or securitising rights?', in R. Dickinson, E. Katselli, C. Murray, and O. W. Pedersen (eds) *Examining Critical Perspectives on Human Rights.* Cambridge: Cambridge University Press.

Lazarus, L. (2015) 'The right to security', in R. S. Cruft, M. Liao, and M. Renzo (eds) *Philosophical Foundations of Human Rights.* Oxford: Oxford University Press.

Lazarus, L. (2020) 'Preventive obligations, risk and coercive overreach', in L. Lavrysen and N. Mavronicola (eds) *Coercive Human Rights: Positive Duties to Mobilise the Criminal Law under the ECHR.* Oxford: Hart.

Lewis, A. (1963) 'Medicine and the affections of the mind', *The British Medical Journal,* 2(5372), 1549–57.

Lewis, G. and Appleby, L. (1988) 'Personality disorder: The patients psychiatrists dislike', *British Journal of Psychiatry,* 153, 44–49.

Lewis, S. (2018) 'A campaign for climate change: The role of therapeutic relationships within a climate of control', in G. Akerman, A. Needs, and C. Bainbridge (eds) *Transforming Environments and Rehabilitation.* London: Routledge.

Lidlington, D. (2017) Speech on Parole Board 50th Anniversary. Available at: https://www.ukpol.co.uk/david-lidington-2017-speech-on-parole-board-50th-anniversary/

Liebling, A. (2011) 'Moral performance, inhuman and degrading treatment and prison pain', *Punishment & Society,* 13(5), 530–50.

Liebling, A. (2013) '"Legitimacy under pressure" in high security prisons', in J. Tankebe and A. Liebling (eds) *Legitimacy and Criminal Justice.* Oxford: Oxford University Press.

Liebling, A. (2016) 'High security prisons in England and Wales: Principles and practice', in Y. Jewkes, J. Bennett, and B. Crewe (eds) *Handbook on Prisons.* 2nd edn. Cullompton: Routledge.

Liebling, A. and Maruna, S. (2005) *The Effects of Imprisonment.* Cullompton: Willan.

Liebling, A., Arnold, H. and Straub, C. (2011) *An Exploration of Staff–Prisoner Relationships at HMP Whitemoor: 12 years on. Revised Final Report.* London: Ministry of Justice.

Lilienfeld, S. O. (2005) 'Longitudinal studies of personality disorders: Four lessons from personality psychology', *Journal of Personality Disorders,* 19(5), 547–56.

Linehan, M. M., Armstrong, H. E., Suarez, A., Allmon, D., and Heard, H. L. (1991) 'Cognitive–behavioral treatment of chronically parasuicidal borderline patients', *Archives of General Psychiatry,* 48, 1060–64.

Linehan, M. M., Heard, M. L., and Armstrong, H. E. (1993) 'Naturalistic follow-up of a behavioral treatment for chronically parasuicidal borderline patients', *Archives of General Psychiatry*, 50, 971–74.

Linehan, M. M. (1993) *Cognitive Behavioral Treatment of Borderline Personality Disorder*. New York: Guilford Press.

Lloyd, M. and Bell, R. (2015) 'Editorial comment: Personality disorder in offenders then and now', *Prison Service Journal*, 218, 2–3.

Loader, I. (2006) 'Fall of the "Platonic Guardians": Liberalism, criminology and political responses to crime in England and Wales', *British Journal of Criminology*, 46(4), 561–86.

Loader, I. and Walker, N. (2007) *Civilizing Security*. Cambridge: Cambridge University Press.

Loughnan, A. (2007) 'Manifest madness: Towards a new understanding of the insanity defence', *Modern Law Review*, 70(3), 379–401.

Loughnan, A. (2012) *Manifest Madness: Mental Incapacity in the Criminal Law*. Oxford: Oxford University Press.

Loughnan, A. and Wake, N. (2014) 'Of blurred boundaries and prior fault: Insanity, automatism and intoxication', in A. Reed and M. Bohlander (eds) *General Defences in Criminal Law: Domestic and Comparative Perspectives*. Farnham: Ashgate.

Loughnan, A. and Ward, T. (2014) 'Emergent authority and expert knowledge: Psychiatry and criminal responsibility in the UK', *International Journal of Law and Psychiatry*, 37(1), 25–36.

Lynch, M. (2000) 'Rehabilitation as rhetoric: The ideal of reformation in contemporary parole discourse and practices', *Punishment & Society*, 2(1), 40–65.

Lynch, N. (2023) 'Levi Bellfield confesses to murders of Lin and Megan Russell, lawyer says', *Sky News*, 27 April. Available at: https://news.sky.com/story/levi-bellfield-confesses-to-murders-of-lin-and-megan-russell-lawyer-says-12867678. Accessed 23 July 2023.

Lynch, T. R., Trost, W. T., Salsman, N., and Linehan, M. M. (2007) 'Dialectical behavior therapy for borderline personality disorder', *Annual Review of Clinical Psychology*, 3, 181–205.

Mackay, R. (1990) 'Fact and fiction about the insanity defence', *Criminal Law Review*, 247–55.

Mackay, R. (2018) 'The impairment factors in the new diminished responsibility plea', *Criminal Law Review*, (6), 462–71.

Mackay, R. and Hughes, D. (2021) 'Explaining the "explanation" requirement in the new diminished responsibility plea', *Criminal Law Review*, (6), 461–77.

Mackay, R. and Hughes, D. (2022) 'Insanity and blaming the mentally ill–A critique of the prior fault principle in the Law Commission's discussion paper', *Criminal Law Review*, (1), 21–40.

Mackay, R. and Mitchell, B. (2017) 'The new diminished responsibility plea in operation: Some initial findings', *Criminal Law Review*, (1), 18–35.

Mackay, R. D. (1995) *Mental Condition Defences in the Criminal Law*. Oxford: Clarendon Press.

Mackay, R. D., Mitchell, B. J. and Howe, L. (2006) 'Yet more facts about the insanity defence', *Criminal Law Review*, May, 399–411.

Bibliography 233

Maden, A. (2007) 'Dangerous and Severe Personality Disorder: Antecedents and origins', *British Journal of Psychiatry*, 190 (supp. 49), s8–s11.

Maden, T. and Tyrer, P. (2003) 'Dangerous and Severe Personality Disorders: A new personality concept from the United Kingdom', *Journal of Personality Disorders*, 17(6), 489–96.

Marshall, L. E. (2019) 'Effective sex offender treatment in correctional settings: A strengths-based approach', In D. L. L. Polaschek, A. Day, and C. R. Hollin (eds) *The Wiley International Handbook of Correctional Psychology*. Chichester: Wiley.

Martens, W. H. J. (2000) 'Antisocial and psychopathic personality disorders: Causes, course, and remission–A review article', *International Journal of Offender Therapy and Comparative Criminology*, 44(4), 406–30.

Martufi, A. (2018) 'The paths of offender rehabilitation and the European dimension of punishment: New challenges for an old ideal?', *Maastricht Journal of European and Comparative Law*, 25(6), 672–88.

Maruna, S. (2001) *Making Good: How Ex-Convicts Reform and Rebuild their Lives*. Washington, D.C.: American Psychological Association.

Maurutto, P. and Hannah-Moffat, K. (2006) 'Assembling risk and the restructuring of penal control', *British Journal of Criminology*, 46(3), 438–54.

Mavronicola, N. (2012) 'What is an "absolute right"? Deciphering absoluteness in the context of Article 3 of the European Convention on Human Rights', *Human Rights Law Review*, 12(4), 723–58.

Mavronicola, N. (2014) 'Inhuman and degrading punishment, dignity, and the limits of retribution', *Modern Law Review*, 77(2), 292–307.

Mavronicola, N. (2015) 'Crime, punishment and Article 3 ECHR: Puzzles and prospects of applying an absolute right in a penal context', *Human Rights Law Review*, 15(4), 721–43.

Mavronicola, N. (2017a) 'Is the prohibition against torture and cruel, inhuman and degrading treatment absolute in international human rights law? A reply to Steven Greer', *Human Rights Law Review*, 17, 479–98.

Mavronicola, N. (2017b) 'Taking life and liberty seriously: Reconsidering criminal liability under Article 2 of the ECHR', *Modern Law Review*, 80(6), 1026–51.

Mavronicola, N. (2020) 'Coercive overreach, dilution and diversion: Potential dangers of aligning human rights protection with criminal law (enforcement)', in L. Lavrysen and N. Mavronicola (eds) *Coercive Human Rights: Positive Duties to Mobilise the Criminal Law under the ECHR*. Oxford: Hart.

Mavronicola, N. and Lavrysen, L. (2020) 'Coercive human rights: Introducing the sharp edge of the European Convention on Human Rights', in L. Lavrysen and N. Mavronicola (eds) *Coercive Human Rights: Positive Duties to Mobilise the Criminal Law under the ECHR*. Oxford: Hart.

McAnallen, A. and McGinnis, E. (2021) 'Trauma-informed practice and the criminal justice system: A systematic narrative review', *Irish Probation Journal*, 18, 109–28.

McBride, R.-S. (2017) 'On the advancement of therapeutic penality: Therapeutic authority, personality science and the therapeutic community', *Sociology of Health & Illness*, 39(7), 1258–72.

McCartan, K. F., Hoggett, J., and Kemshall, H. (2018) 'Risk assessment and management of individuals convicted of a sexual offence in the UK', *Sexual Offender Treatment*, 13(2).

McGuire, J. (2018) 'Implementing prison-based treatment programs', in J. Wooldredge and P. Smith (eds) *The Oxford Handbook of Prisons and Imprisonment*. Oxford: Oxford University Press.

McLaughlin, E., Muncie, J., and Hughes, G. (2001) 'The permanent revolution: New Labour, new public management and the modernization of criminal justice', *Criminal Justice*, 1(3), 301–18.

McManus, S., Bebbington, P., Jenkins, R., and Brugha, T. (eds) (2016) *Mental Health and Wellbeing in England: Adult Psychiatric Morbidity Survey 2014*. Leeds: NHS Digital.

McMurran, M. and Delight, S. (2017) 'Processes of change in an offender personality disorder pathway prison progression unit', *Criminal Behaviour and Mental Health*, 27(3), 254–64.

McNeill, F. (2012) 'Four forms of "offender" rehabilitation: Towards an interdisciplinary perspective', *Legal and Criminological Psychology*, 17(1), 18–36.

McNeill, F., Burns, N., Halliday, S., Hutton, N., and Tata, C. (2009) 'Risk, responsibility and reconfiguration: Penal adaptation and misadaptation', *Punishment & Society*, 11(4), 419–42.

McRae, L. (2013) 'Rehabilitating antisocial personalities: Treatment through self-governance strategies', *Journal of Forensic Psychiatry and Psychology*, 24(1), 48–70.

McRae, L. (2015) 'The Offender Personality Disorder Pathway: Risking rehabilitation?', *Medical Law Review*, 23(3), 321–47.

McSherry, B. and Keyzer, P. (eds) (2011) *Dangerous People: Policy, Prediction, and Practice*. London: Routledge.

Meijer, S. (2017) 'Rehabilitation as a positive obligation', *European Journal of Crime, Criminal Law and Criminal Justice*, 25(2), 145–62.

Mews, A., Di Bella, L., and Purver, M. (2017) *Impact evaluation of the prison-based Core Sex Offender Treatment Programme. Ministry of Justice Analytical Series*. London: Ministry of Justice.

Ministry of Justice (2010) *Breaking the Cycle: Effective Punishment, Rehabilitation and Sentencing of Offenders*. London: Ministry of Justice.

Ministry of Justice (2011) *The Early Years of the DSPD (Dangerous And Severe Personality Disorder) Programme: Results of Two Process Studies*. Research Summary 4/11. London: Ministry of Justice.

Ministry of Justice (2018a) *A Review of Self-inflicted Deaths in Prison Custody in 2016*. London: Ministry of Justice.

Ministry of Justice (2018b) *Female Offender Strategy*. London: Ministry of Justice. Available at: https://www.gov.uk/government/publications/female-offender-strategy.

Ministry of Justice (2020) *Safety in Custody Statistics, England and Wales: Deaths in Prison Custody to March 2020. Assaults and Self-harm to December 2019*. London: Ministry of Justice.

Ministry of Justice (2023a) *Safety in Custody Statistics, England and Wales: Deaths in Prison Custody to December 2022 Assaults and Self-harm to September 2022.* London: Ministry of Justice.

Ministry of Justice (2023b) *Offender Management Statistics: Prison releases 2022.* London: Ministry of Justice.

Ministry of Justice and HM Prison & Probation Service (2017) *Mentally Disordered Offenders - The Restricted Patient System: Background Briefing.* London: Ministry of Justice and HM Prison & Probation Service. Available at: https://www.gov.uk/government/publications/mentally-disordered-offenders-the-restricted-patient-system.

Ministry of Justice and HM Prison & Probation Service (2022) *Early Release on Compassionate Grounds (ERCG).* London: Ministry of Justice and HM Prison & Probation Service. Available at: https://assets.publishing.service.gov.uk/government/uploads/system/uploads/attachment_data/file/1075155/early-release-compassionate-grounds-pf.pdf.

Ministry of Justice and HM Prison & Probation Service (2023) *Recall, Review and Re-Release of Recalled Prisoners Policy Framework.* London: Ministry of Justice and HM Prison & Probation Service.

Ministry of Justice and NOMS (2010) *Guidance for Working with MAPPA and Mentally Disordered Offenders.* London: Ministry of Justice.

Moffitt, T. E. (1993) 'Adolescence-limited and life-course-persistent antisocial behavior: A developmental taxonomy', *Psychological Review*, 100(4), 674–701.

Mokros, A., Hare, R. D., Neumann, C. S., and Habermeyer, E. (2020) 'Subtypes and variations of psychopathic disorders', in A. R. Felthous and H. Saß (eds) *The Wiley International Handbook on Psychopathic Disorders and the Law.* 2nd edn. Hoboken, New Jersey: Wiley-Blackwell.

Monahan, J., Steadman, H. J., Appelbaum, P. S., Robbins, P. C., Mulvey, E. P., Silver, E., Roth, L. H., and Grisso, T. (2000) 'Developing a clinically useful actuarial tool for assessing violence risk', *British Journal of Psychiatry*, 176, 312–19.

Moore, D. and Hannah-Moffat, K. (2005) 'The liberal veil: Revisiting Canadian penality', in Pratt, J., Brown, D., Brown, M., Hallsworth, S., and Morrison, W. (eds) *The New Punitiveness: Trends, Theories, Perspectives.* Cullompton: Willan.

Moran, P., Fortune, Z., Barrett, B., Spence, R., Rose, D., Armstrong, D., Slade, M., Mudd, D., Coid, J., Crawford, M., and Tyrer, P. (2008) *An Evaluation of Pilot Services for People with Personality Disorder in Adult Forensic Settings. Final Report Submitted to National Coordinating Centre for NHS Service Delivery & Organisation R & D.* National Institute for Health and Care Research. Available at: https://njl-admin.nihr.ac.uk/document/download/2027499.

Moran, P., Jarrett, M, Vamvakas, G., Roberts, S., Barrett, B., Campbell, C., Khondoker, M, Trebilcock, J., Weaver, T., Walker, J., Crawford, M., and Forrester, A. (2022) *National Evaluation of the Male Offender Personality Disorder Pathway Programme (NEON).* Ministry of Justice Analytical Series. London: Ministry of Justice. Available at: https://www.gov.uk/government/publications/national-evaluation-of-the-male-opd-pathway.

Morse, S. J. (1998) 'Fear of danger, flight from culpability', *Psychology, Public Policy, and Law*, 4(1–2), 250–67.

Morse, S. J. (1999) 'Craziness and criminal responsibility', *Behavioral Sciences & the Law*, 17(2), 147–64.

Morse, S. J. (2008a) 'Determinism and the death of folk psychology: Two challenges to responsibility from neuroscience', *Minnesota Journal of Law, Science & Technology*, 9, 1–36.

Morse, S. J. (2008b) 'Psychopathy and criminal responsibility', *Neuroethics*, 1(3), 205–12.

Mullen, P. (1999) 'Dangerous people with severe personality disorder', *British Medical Journal*, 319, 1146–47.

Mullen, P. E. (2007) 'Dangerous and severe personality disorder and in need of treatment', *British Journal of Psychiatry*, 190 (SUPPL. 49), 3–7.

Murphy, N. and McVey, D. (2010) *Treating Personality Disorder: Creating Robust Services for People with Complex Mental Health Needs*. London: Routledge.

National Audit Office (2017) *Mental Health in Prisons*. London: National Audit Office.

National Collaborating Centre for Mental Health (2009) *Borderline Personality Disorder: The NICE Guideline on Treatment and Management*. National Clinical Practice Guideline Number 78. August 2018 update. London: British Psychological Society and Royal College of Psychiatrists.

National Collaborating Centre for Mental Health (2010) *Antisocial Personality Disorder: Treatment, Management and Prevention*. National Clinical Practice Guideline Number 77. August 2018 update. London: British Psychological Society and Royal College of Psychiatrists.

National Confidential Inquiry into Suicide and Safety in Mental Health (2022) *Annual Report 2022: England, Northern Ireland, Scotland and Wales*. Manchester: University of Manchester.

National Institute for Mental Health in England (2003) *Personality Disorder: No Longer a Diagnosis of Exclusion. Policy Implementation Guidance for the Development of Services for People with Personality Disorder*. London: Department of Health.

NOMS (2013) *Category A Function: The Review of Security Category—Category A / Restricted Status Prisoners*. PSI 08/2013. Available at: https://assets.publishing.service.gov.uk/government/uploads/system/uploads/attachment_data/file/910233/PSI-08-2013-The-Review-of-Security-Category-Category-A-Restricted-Status-Prisoners-Revised-June-2016.pdf.

NOMS (2014) *Prison Service Order 19/2014*. Available at: https://www.gov.uk/government/publications/sentence-planning-psi-192014-pi-132014.

NOMS and NHS England (2015) *The Offender Personality Disorder Pathway Strategy 2015*. London: NOMS and NHS England.

O'Loughlin, A. (2014) 'The Offender Personality Disorder Pathway: Expansion in the face of failure?', *Howard Journal of Criminal Justice*, 53(2), 173–92.

O'Loughlin, A. (2019) 'De-constructing risk, therapeutic needs and the dangerous personality disordered subject', *Punishment & Society*, 21(5), 616–38.

O'Loughlin, A. (2020) 'Continuity and change in penal policy towards personality disordered offenders', in P. Taylor, S. Morley, and J. L. Powell (eds) *Mental Health and Punishments*. London: Routledge.

Bibliography

O'Loughlin, A. (2021a) 'Risk reduction and redemption: An interpretive account of the right to rehabilitation in the jurisprudence of the European Court of Human Rights', *Oxford Journal of Legal Studies*, 41(2), 510–38.

O'Loughlin, A. (2021b) 'Sentencing mentally disordered offenders: Towards a rights-based approach', *Criminal Law Review*, (2), 98–112.

O'Loughlin, A. and Peay, J. (2023) 'Mental health, mental disabilities, and crime', in A. Liebling, S. Maruna, and L. McAra (eds) *The Oxford Handbook of Criminology*. 7th edn. Oxford: Oxford University Press.

O'Loughlin, A., Gormley, J., Willmott, L., Bild, J., Roberts, J., and Draper, A. (2022) *Mental Health and Sentencing: Literature Review*. Edinburgh: Scottish Sentencing Council.

O'Malley, P. (1999) 'Volatile and contradictory punishment', *Theoretical Criminology*, 3(2), 175–96.

Ogloff, J. R. P. and Davis, M. R. (2020) 'From predicting dangerousness to assessing and managing risk for violence: A journey across four generations', in J. S. Wormith, L. A. Craig, and T. E. Hogue (eds) *The Wiley Handbook of What Works in Violence Risk Management: Theory, Research and Practice*. Hoboken, New Jersey: Wiley-Blackwell.

Padfield, N. (2022) 'Sentencing reform 2022-style', *Archbold Review*, 6, 4–6.

Paris, J. (2015) *The Intelligent Clinician's Guide to the DSM-V*. Oxford: Oxford University Press.

Peay, J. (1999) 'Proposals for the dangerous severely personality disordered: Well or ill-intentioned?', *Criminal Justice Matters*, 37(1), 23–24.

Peay, J. (2011a) *Mental Health and Crime*. Abingdon: Routledge.

Peay, J. (2011b) 'Personality disorder and the law: Some awkward questions', *Philosophy, Psychiatry, & Psychology*, 18(3), 231–44.

Peay, J. (2015) 'Sentencing mentally disordered offenders: Conflicting objectives, perilous decisions and cognitive insights', *LSE Law, Society and Economy Working Papers*. 1/2015.

Peay, J. (2016) 'Responsibility, culpability and the sentencing of mentally disordered offenders: Objectives in conflict', *Criminal Law Review*, (3), 152–64.

Peay, J. and Player, E. (2018) 'Pleading guilty: Why vulnerability matters', *Modern Law Review*, 81, 929–57.

Penney, S. (2012) 'Impulse control and criminal responsibility: Lessons from neuroscience', *International Journal of Law and Psychiatry*, 35(2), 99–103.

Percy Commission (1957) *Report of the Royal Commission on the Law Relating to Mental Illness and Mental Deficiency (the Percy Commission)*. London: H.M.S.O.

Pettit, P. (2002) 'Is criminal justice politically feasible?', *Buffalo Criminal Law Review*, 5(2), 427–50.

Pickard, H. (2015) 'Choice, deliberation, violence: Mental capacity and criminal responsibility in personality disorder', *International Journal of Law and Psychiatry*, 40, 15–24.

Pickersgill, M. (2013) 'How personality became treatable: The mutual constitution of clinical knowledge and mental health law', *Social Studies of Science*, 43(1), 30–53.

Pifferi, M. (2016) *Reinventing Punishment: A Comparative History of Criminology and Penology in the Nineteenth and Twentieth Centuries*. Oxford: Oxford University Press.

Pilgrim, D. (2007) 'New "mental health" legislation for England and Wales: Some aspects of consensus and conflict', *Journal of Social Policy*, 36(1), 79–95.

Pinto, M. (2020) 'Sowing a "culture of conviction": What shall domestic criminal justice systems reap from coercive human rights?', in L. Lavrysen and N. Mavronicola (eds) *Coercive Human Rights: Positive Duties to Mobilise the Criminal Law under the ECHR*. Oxford: Hart.

Player, E. (2017) 'The offender personality disorder pathway and its implications for women prisoners in England and Wales', *Punishment & Society*, 19(5), 568–89.

Pollack, S. (2005) 'Taming the shrew: Regulating prisoners through women-centered mental health programming', *Critical Criminology*, 13(1), 71–87.

Pratt, J. (2007) *Penal Populism*. London: Routledge.

Radzik, L. (2009) *Making Amends: Atonement in Morality, Law, and Politics*. New York: Oxford University Press.

Ramsay, P. (2012a) 'Imprisonment under the precautionary principle', in G. R. Sullivan and I. Dennis (eds) *Seeking Security: Pre-Empting the Commission of Criminal Harms*. Oxford: Hart.

Ramsay, P. (2012b) *The Insecurity State: Vulnerable Autonomy and the Right to Security in the Criminal Law*. Oxford: Oxford University Press.

Ramsden, J., Joyes, E., Gordon, N., and Lowton, M. (2016) 'How working with psychologists has influenced probation practice: Attempting to capture some of the impact and the learning from the Offender Personality Disorder Pathway project', *Probation Journal*, 63(1), 54–71.

Raynor, P. and Robinson, G. (2005) *Rehabilitation, Crime and Justice*. Basingstoke: Palgrave Macmillan.

Raynor, P. and Robinson, G. (2009) 'Why help offenders? Arguments for rehabilitation as a penal strategy', *European Journal of Probation*, 1(1), 3–20.

Reed, J. (1994) *Report of the Department of Health and Home Office Working Group on Psychopathic Disorder*. London: Department of Health.

Registrar of the European Court of Human Rights (2009) Press release issued by the Registrar: Chamber Judgment Case of *Maiorano and Others v. Italy* (Application no. 28634/06). Available at: https://hudoc.echr.coe.int/app/conversion/pdf/?library = ECHR&id = 003-2969914-3270642&filename = 003-2969914-3270642.pdf

Reidy, K. and Kelly, B. (2021) 'Involuntary status and mental capacity for treatment decisions under sections 4, 3, and 57 of Ireland's Mental Health Act, 2001: Analysis and recommendations for reform', *Irish Journal of Psychological Medicine*, 1–6.

Rice, M. E., Harris, G. T., and Cormier, C. A. (1992) 'An evaluation of a maximum security therapeutic community for psychopaths and other mentally disordered offenders', *Law and Human Behavior*, 16(4), 399–412.

Robinson, C., Sorbie, A., Huber, J., Teasdale, J., Scott, K., Purver, M., and Elliott, I. (2021) *Reoffending Impact Evaluation of the Prison-based RESOLVE Offending Behaviour Programme*. London: Ministry of Justice.

Robinson, G. (2008) 'Late-modern rehabilitation: The evolution of a penal strategy', *Punishment & Society*, 10(4), 429–45.

Rogan, M. (2018) 'Discerning penal values and judicial decision making: The case of whole life sentencing in Europe and the United States of America', *Howard Journal of Crime and Justice*, 57(3), 321–38.

Rose, D. (2021) 'Violent inmates are MORE likely to reoffend after going through "rehabilitation" programmes, reveals shock study kept secret by ministers for three years', *The Daily Mail*, 19 March.

Rose, N. (2000) 'Government and control', *British Journal of Criminology*, 40(2), 321–39.

Rotman, E. (1986) 'Do criminal offenders have a constitutional right to rehabilitation?', *Journal of Criminal Law and Criminology*, 77(4), 1023–68.

Rotman, E. (1990) *Beyond Punishment: A New View on the Rehabilitation of Criminal Offenders*. New York: Greenwood Press.

Royal College of Nursing (2000a) 'Memorandum by the Royal College of Nursing of the United Kingdom', in Home Affairs Committee *Session 1999–2000 First Report: Managing Dangerous People With Severe Personality Disorder. Volume II: Minutes of Evidence and Appendices*. London: The Stationery Office.

Royal College of Nursing (2000b) 'Memorandum by the Royal College of Nursing of the United Kingdom', in Select Committee on Health *Fourth Report: Provision of NHS Mental Health Services. Volume II: Minutes of Evidence and Appendices to the Minutes of Evidence*. London: House of Commons.

Royal College of Psychiatrists (2000) 'Memorandum by the Royal College of Psychiatrists', in Select Committee on Health *Fourth Report: Provision of NHS Mental Health Services. Volume II: Minutes of Evidence and Appendices to the Minutes of Evidence*. London: House of Commons.

Rutherford, A. (1997) 'Criminal policy and the eliminative ideal', *Social Policy and Administration*, 31(5 SUPPL.), 116–35.

Rutherford, A. (2006) 'Dangerous people: Beginnings of a New Labour Proposal', in T. Newburn and P. Rock (eds) *The Politics of Crime Control: Essays in Honour of David Downes*. Oxford: Oxford University Press.

Rutherford, M. (2009) 'Imprisonment for public protection: An example of "reverse diversion"', *Journal of Forensic Psychiatry and Psychology*, 20, S46–S55.

Ryan, M. J. (2015) 'Science and the New Rehabilitation', *Virginia Journal of Criminal Law*, 3(2), 261–341.

Sadlier, G. (2010) *Evaluation of the Impact of the HM Prison Service Enhanced Thinking Skills Programme on Reoffending Outcomes of the Surveying Prisoner Crime Reduction (SPCR) Sample*. Ministry of Justice Research Series 19/10. London: Ministry of Justice.

Samele, C., McKinnon, I., Brown, P., Srivastava, S., Arnold, A., Hallett, N., and Forrester, A. (2021) 'The prevalence of mental illness and unmet needs of police custody detainees', *Criminal Behaviour and Mental Health*, 31(2), 80–95.

Saradjian, J., Murphy, N., and McVey, D. (2010) 'Delivering integrated treatment to people with personality disorder', in N. Murphy and D. McVey (eds) *Treating Personality Disorder: Creating Robust Services for People with Complex Mental Health Needs*. London: Routledge.

Saradjian, J., Murphy, N., and McVey, D. (2013) 'Delivering effective therapeutic interventions for men with severe personality disorder within a high secure prison', *Psychology, Crime and Law*, 19(5–6), 433–47.

Sariaslan, A., Arseneault, L., Larsson, H., Lichtenstein, P., and Fazel, S. (2020) 'Risk of subjection to violence and perpetration of violence in persons with psychiatric disorders in Sweden', *JAMA Psychiatry*, 77(4), 359–67.

Saß, H. and Felthous, A. R. (2020) 'History and conceptual development of psychopathic disorders', in A. R. Felthous and H. Saß (eds) *The Wiley International Handbook on Psychopathic Disorders and the Law*. 2nd edn. Hoboken, New Jersey: Wiley-Blackwell.

Seddon, T. (2007) *Punishment and Madness: Governing Prisoners with Mental Health Problems*. London: Routledge.

Seddon, T. (2008) 'Dangerous liaisons: Personality disorder and the politics of risk', *Punishment & Society*, 10(3), 301–17.

Select Committee on Health (2000) *Fourth Report: Provision of NHS Mental Health Services. Volume II: Minutes of Evidence and Appendices to the Minutes of Evidence*. London: House of Commons.

Sentencing Council of England and Wales (2019) *General Guideline: Overarching Principles*. London: Sentencing Council of England and Wales. Accessible at: https://www.sentencingcouncil.org.uk/overarching-guides/magistrates-court/item/general-guideline-overarching-principles/

Sentencing Council of England and Wales (2020) *Sentencing Offenders with Mental Disorders, Developmental Disorders, or Neurological Impairments*. London: Sentencing Council of England and Wales. Available at: https://www.sentencingcouncil.org.uk/overarching-guides/magistrates-court/item/sentencing-offenders-with-mental-disorders-developmental-disorders-or-neurological-impairments/.

Shaw, J., Higgins, C., and Quartey, C. (2017) 'The impact of collaborative case formulation with high risk offenders with personality disorder', *Journal of Forensic Psychiatry and Psychology*, 28(6), 777–89.

Sheehan, L., Nieweglowski, K., and Corrigan, P. (2016) 'The stigma of personality disorders', *Current Psychiatry Reports*, 18(1), 11.

Simon, J. (1998) 'Managing the monstrous: Sex offenders and the new penology', *Psychology, Public Policy, and Law*, 4(1–2), 452–67.

Singh, J. P., Grann, M., and Fazel, S. (2011) 'A comparative study of violence risk assessment tools: A systematic review and metaregression analysis of 68 studies involving 25,980 participants', *Clinical Psychology Review*, 31(3), 499–513.

Singleton, N., Gatward, R., and Meltzer, H. (1998) *Psychiatric Morbidity among Prisoners: Summary Report*. London: Stationery Office.

Sisti, D. A. and Caplan, A. L. (2012) 'Accommodation without exculpation? The ethical and legal paradoxes of borderline personality disorder', *Journal of Psychiatry & Law*, 40(1), 75–92.

Skett, S. and Lewis, C. (2019) 'Development of the Offender Personality Disorder Pathway: A summary of the underpinning evidence', *Probation Journal*, 66(2), 167–80.

Skett, S., Goode, I., and Barton, S. (2017) 'A joint NHS and NOMS offender personality disorder pathway strategy: A perspective from 5 years of operation', *Criminal Behaviour and Mental Health*, 27(3), 214–21.

Smith, K. J. M. (1998) *Lawyers, Legislators and Theorists: Developments in English Criminal Jurisprudence 1800–1957*. Oxford: Oxford University Press.

Sparks, R. (2002) 'Out of the "Digger": The warrior's honour and the guilty observer', *Ethnography*, 3(4), 556–81.

Stanton-Ife, J. (2012) 'Preventive detention at the margins of autonomy', in G. R. Sullivan and I. Dennis (eds) *Seeking Security: Pre-Empting the Commission of Criminal Harms*. Oxford: Hart.

Stevenson, A. (2015) Oxford Dictionary of English. 3rd edn. Oxford: Oxford University Press.

Stinson, F. S., Dawson, D. A., Goldstein, R. B., Chou, S. P., Huang, B., Smith, S. M., Ruan, W. J., Pulay, A. J., Saha, T. D., Pickering, R. P., and Grant, B. F. (2008) 'Prevalence, correlates, disability, and comorbidity of DSM-IV Narcissistic Personality Disorder: Results from the Wave 2 National Epidemiologic Survey on Alcohol and Related Conditions', *Journal of Clinical Psychiatry*, 69(7), 1033–45.

Stoffers, J., Völlm, B. A., Rücker, G., Timmer, A., Huband, N., and Lieb, K. (2010) 'Pharmacological interventions for borderline personality disorder', *Cochrane Database of Systematic Reviews*, 6, Art. No.: CD005653.

Storebø, O. J., Stoffers-Winterling, J. M., Völlm, B. A., Kongerslev, M. T., Mattivi, J. T., Jørgensen, M. S., Faltinsen, E., Todorovac, A., Sales, C. P., Callesen, H. E., Lieb, K., and Simonsen, E. (2020) 'Psychological therapies for people with borderline personality disorder', *Cochrane Database of Systematic Reviews*, 5, Art. No.: CD012955.

Szmukler, G. (2000) 'Homicide inquiries: what sense do they make?', *Psychiatric Bulletin*, 24, 6–10.

Szmukler, G. (2003) 'Risk assessment: "numbers" and "values"', *Psychiatric Bulletin*, 27, 205–07.

Szmukler, G., Daw, R., and Callard, F. (2014) 'Mental health law and the UN Convention on the Rights of Persons with Disabilities', *International Journal of Law and Psychiatry*, 37(3), 245–52.

Tadros, V. (2007) *Exemptions from Criminal Responsibility: Natural, Social and Political*. Oxford: Oxford University Press.

Tata, C. (2019) 'Humanising punishment? Mitigation and "case-cleansing" prior to sentencing', *Oñati Socio-Legal Series*, 9(5), 659–83.

Taylor, C. (2011) 'Nothing left to lose? Freedom and compulsion in the treatment of dangerous offenders', *Psychodynamic Practice*, 17(3), 291–306.

Taylor, P., Leese, M., Williams, D., Butwell, M., Daly, R., and Larkin, E. (1998) 'Mental disorder and violence. A special (high security) hospital study', *British Journal of Psychiatry*, 172, 218–26.

Tennant, A. and Howells, K. (2010) *Using Time, Not Doing Time: Practitioner Perspectives on Personality Disorder and Risk*. Chichester: Wiley-Blackwell.

Tew, J. and Atkinson, R. (2013) 'The Chromis programme: From conception to evaluation', *Psychology, Crime and Law*, 19(5–6), 415–31.

Bibliography

The Law Society (2000) 'Memorandum by the Law Society', in Home Affairs Committee *Session 1999–2000 First Report: Managing Dangerous People With Severe Personality Disorder. Volume II: Minutes of Evidence and Appendices.* London: The Stationery Office.

Trebilcock, J. and Weaver, T. (2010a) *Multi-method Evaluation of the Management, Organisation and Staffing (MEMOS) in High Security Treatment Services for People with Dangerous and Severe Personality Disorder (DSPD) Final Report.* London: Ministry of Justice.

Trebilcock, J. and Weaver, T. (2010b) *Study of the Legal Status of Dangerous and Severe Personality Disorder (DSPD) Patients and Prisoners, and the Impact of DSPD Status on Parole Board and Mental Health Review Tribunal Decision-making.* London: Ministry of Justice.

Trebilcock, J. and Weaver, T. (2012a) '"Everybody knows that the prisoner is going nowhere": Parole Board members' views about Dangerous and Severe Personality Disorder in England and Wales', *International Journal of Criminology and Sociology*, 29, 141–50.

Trebilcock, J. and Weaver, T. (2012b) '"It doesn't have to be treatable": Mental Health Review Tribunal (MHRT) members' views about Dangerous and Severe Personality Disorder (DSPD)', *Journal of Forensic Psychiatry and Psychology*, 23(2), 244–60.

Trebilcock, J., Jarrett, M., Weaver, T., Campbell, C., Forrester, A., Walker, J., and Moran, P. (2019) 'A more promising architecture? Commissioners' perspectives on the reconfiguration of personality disorder services under the Offender Personality Disorder (OPD) pathway', *Mental Health Review Journal*, 24(4), 306–16.

Trull, T. J. and Durrett, C. A. (2005) 'Categorical and dimensional models of personality disorder', *Annual Review of Clinical Psychology*, 1(1), 355–80.

Truss, L. (2017) A Speech on Criminal Justice Reform by the Secretary of State for Justice. London: Ministry of Justice. Available at: https://www.gov.uk/government/speeches/a-speech-on-criminal-justice-reform-by-the-secretary-of-state-for-justice.

Tulich, T. (2017) 'Critical reflections on preventive justice', in T. Tulich, R. Ananian-Welsh, S. Bronitt, and S. Murray (eds) *Regulating Preventive Justice: Principle, Policy and Paradox.* London: Routledge.

Tulkens, F. (2011) 'The paradoxical relationship between criminal law and human rights', *Journal of International Criminal Justice*, 9(3), 577–95.

Tyler, N., Miles, H. L., Karadag, B., and Rogers, G. (2019) 'An updated picture of the mental health needs of male and female prisoners in the UK: prevalence, comorbidity, and gender differences', *Social Psychiatry and Psychiatric Epidemiology*, 54(9), 1143–52.

Tyrer, P. and Mulder, R. (2018) 'Dissecting the elements of borderline personality disorder', *Personality and Mental Health*, 12(2), 91–92.

Tyrer, P. and Mulder, R. (2022) *Personality Disorder: From Evidence to Understanding.* Cambridge: Cambridge University Press.

Tyrer, P., Barrett, B., Byford, S., Cooper, S., Crawford, M., Cicchetti, D., Duggan, C., Joyce, E., Kirkpatrick, T., Maier, M., O'Sullivan, S., Maden, T., Rogers, R.,

Rutter, D., and Seivewright, H. (2007) *Evaluation of the Assessment Procedure at Two Pilot Sites in the DSPD Programme (IMPALOX Study)*. London: Ministry of Justice.

Tyrer, P., Cooper, S., Rutter, D., Seivewright, H., Duggan, C., Maden, T., Barrett, B., Joyce, E, Rao, B., Nur, U., Cicchetti, D., Crawford, M., and Byford, S. (2009) 'The assessment of dangerous and severe personality disorder: Lessons from a randomised controlled trial linked to qualitative analysis', *Journal of Forensic Psychiatry and Psychology*, 20(1), 132–46.

Tyrer, P., Crawford, M., Mulder, R., Blashfield, R., Farnam, A., Fossati, A., Kim, Y.-R., Koldobsky, N., Lecic-Tosevski, D., Ndetei, D., Swales, M., Clark, L. A., and Reed, G. M. (2011) 'The rationale for the reclassification of personality disorder in the 11th revision of the International Classification of Diseases (ICD-11)', *Personality and Mental Health*, 5(4), 246–59.

Tyrer, P., Duggan, C., Cooper, S., Crawford, M., Seivewright, H., Rutter, D., Maden, T., Byford, S., and Barrett, B. (2010) 'The successes and failures of the DSPD experiment: The assessment and management of severe personality disorder', *Medicine, Science and the Law*, 50(2), 95–99.

Tyrer, P., Duggan, C., Cooper, S., Tyrer, H., Swinson, N., and Rutter, D. (2015) 'The lessons and legacy of the programme for dangerous and severe personality disorders', *Personality and Mental Health*, 9, 96–106.

Tyrer, P., Mulder, R., Kim, Y. R., and Crawford, M. J. (2019) 'The development of the ICD-11 classification of personality disorders: An amalgam of science, pragmatism, and politics', Annual Review of Clinical Psychology, 7(15), 481–502.

UN High Commissioner for Human Rights (2009) *Annual Report*. A/HRC/10/48 (26 January 2009).

van der Wolf, M. J. F. and Herzog-Evans, M. (2015) 'Mandatory measures: "Safety measures". Supervision and detention of dangerous offenders in France and the Netherlands: A comparative and human rights' perspective', in M. Herzog-Evans (ed) *Offender Release and Supervision: The Role of Courts and the Use of Discretion*. Nijmegen: Wolf Legal Publishers.

van Marle, H. J. C. (2002) 'The Dutch Entrustment Act (TBS): Its principles and innovations', *International Journal of Forensic Mental Health*, 1(1), 83–92.

van Zyl Smit, D. and Appleton, C. (2019) *Life Imprisonment: A Global Human Rights Analysis*. Harvard University Press.

van Zyl Smit, D., Weatherby, P., and Creighton, S. (2014) 'Whole life sentences and the tide of European human rights jurisprudence: What is to be done?', *Human Rights Law Review*, 14(1), 59–84.

Vannier, M. (2016) 'A right to hope? Life imprisonment in France', in D. van Zyl Smit and C. Appleton (eds) *Life Imprisonment and Human Rights*. Oxford: Hart Publishing.

Verheul, R. and Widiger, T. A. (2004) 'A meta-analysis of the prevalence and usage of the personality disorder not otherwise specified (PDNOS) diagnosis', *Journal of Personality Disorders*, 18(4), 309–19.

Völlm, B. and Konappa, N. (2012) 'The dangerous and severe personality disorder experiment—Review of empirical research', *Criminal Behaviour and Mental Health*, 22, 165–80.

Bibliography

Ward, T. (1997) 'Law, common sense and the authority of science: Expert witnesses and criminal insanity in England, Ca. 1840–1940', *Social & Legal Studies*, 6(3), 343–62.

Ward, T. (2006) 'English law's epistemology of expert testimony', *Journal of Law and Society*, 33(4), 572–95.

Ward, T. (2017) 'Expert testimony, law and epistemic authority', *Journal of Applied Philosophy*, 34(2), 263–77.

Ward, T. and Fortune, C.-A. (2013) 'The Good Lives Model: Aligning risk reduction with promoting offenders' personal goals', *European Journal of Probation*, 5(2), 29–46.

Warren, F., McGauley, G., Norton, K., Dolan, B., Preedy-Fayers, K., Pickering, A., and Geddes, J. R. (2003) *Review of Treatments for Severe Personality Disorder (Home Office Online Report 30/03)*. London: Home Office.

Wasik, M. (2014) 'Sentencing–the last ten years', *Criminal Law Review*, 7, 477–91.

Wasik, M. (2021) 'The Police, Crime, Sentencing and Courts Bill: Changes to sentencing and early release', *Criminal Law Review*, (12), 1051–70.

Whiting, D., Lichtenstein, P., and Fazel, S. (2021) 'Violence and mental disorders: A structured review of associations by individual diagnoses, risk factors, and risk assessment', *The Lancet Psychiatry*, 8(2), 150–61.

Whooley, O. (2016) 'Measuring mental disorders: The failed commensuration project of DSM-5', *Social Science & Medicine*, 166, 33–40.

Widiger, T. A. and Costa, P. T. (2012) 'Integrating normal and abnormal personality structure: The Five-Factor Model', *Journal of Personality*, 80(6), 1471–506.

Widiger, T. A., Livesley, W. J., and Clark, L. A. (2009) 'An integrative dimensional classification of personality disorder', *Psychological Assessment*, 21(3), 243–55.

Wiener, M. J. (2003) *Reconstructing the Criminal: Culture, Law and Policy in England, 1830–1914*. Cambridge: Cambridge University Press.

Williams, I. and Glasby, J. (2010) 'Making "what works" work: The use of knowledge in UK health and social care decision-making', *Policy and Society*, 29(2), 95–102.

Wilson, K. E. (2021) *Mental Health Law: Abolish or Reform?* Oxford: Oxford University Press.

Winsper, C. (2018) 'The aetiology of borderline personality disorder (BPD): Contemporary theories and putative mechanisms', *Current Opinion in Psychology*, 21, 105–10.

Wong, S. C. P. and Gordon, A. (2006) 'The validity and reliability of the Violence Risk Scale: A treatment-friendly violence risk assessment tool', *Psychology, Public Policy, and Law*, 12(3), 279–309.

Wootton, B. (1981) *Crime and Criminal Law: Reflections of a Magistrate and Social Scientist*. London: Stevens.

World Health Organization (2022) *ICD-11 2022 Release*. Available at: https://www.who.int/news/item/11-02-2022-icd-11-2022-release.

Wormith, J. S. (2017) 'Automated offender risk assessment', *Criminology & Public Policy*, 16, 281–303.

Wortley, N. (2023) 'Case Comment: R. v Byrne [2022] EWCA Crim 1630', *Criminal Law Week*, CLW/23/01/8.

Bibliography 245

Yang, M., Wong, S. C., and Coid, J. (2010) 'The efficacy of violence prediction: A meta-analytic comparison of nine risk assessment tools', *Psychological Bulletin*, 136, 740–67.

Yu, R., Geddes, J. R., and Fazel, S. (2012) 'Personality disorders, violence, and antisocial behavior: A systematic review and meta-regression analysis', *Journal of Personality Disorders*, 26(5), 775–92.

Zachar, P., Krueger, R. F., and Kendler, K. S. (2016) 'Personality disorder in DSM-5: An oral history', *Psychological Medicine*, 46(1), 1–10.

Zachar, Peter (2014) *A Metaphysics of Psychopathology*. Cambridge, Massachusetts: MIT Press.

Zanarini, M. C, Frankenburg, F. R, Hennen, J., and Silk, K. R. (2003) 'The longitudinal course of borderline psychopathology: 6-Year prospective follow-up of the phenomenology of borderline personality disorder', *American Journal of Psychiatry*, 160(2), 274–83.

Zedner, L. (1994) 'Reparation and retribution: Are they reconcilable?', *Modern Law Review*, 57(2), 228–50.

Zedner, L. (2002), 'Dangers of dystopias in penal theory', *Oxford Journal of Legal Studies*, 22(2), 341–66.

Zedner, L. (2003) 'The concept of security: An agenda for comparative analysis', *Legal Studies*, 23(1), 153–75.

Zedner, L. (2006) 'Neither safe nor sound? The perils and possibilities of risk', *Canadian Journal of Criminology and Criminal Justice*, 48(3), 423–34.

Zedner, L. (2010) 'Security, the state, and the citizen: The changing architecture of crime control', *New Criminal Law Review*, 13(2), 379–403.

Zedner, L. (2016) 'Penal subversions: When is a punishment not punishment, who decides and on what grounds?', *Theoretical Criminology*, 20(1), 3–20.

Zedner, L. and Ashworth, A. (2019) 'The rise and restraint of the Preventive State', *Annual Review of Criminology*, 2(1), 429–50.

Index

For the benefit of digital users, indexed terms that span two pages (e.g., 52–53) may, on occasion, appear on only one of those pages.

Annison, H 78, 211–12
antisocial personality disorder (ASPD)
  circularity 35–36
  definition 28–29, 34
  and self-harm 38
  and suicide 38
  treatment *see* treatments for personality disorder
  and violence 37–38
appropriate medical treatment test
  definition 184–85, 213–14
  introduction of 7, 50, 85
  and the Draft Mental Health Bill 2022 54
  and preventive detention 185–86, 191, 203, 213–14
  and sentencing 183–86, 203
Ashworth Hospital 68, 71–73
Ashworth, A. 198–99, 201, 208–11
autonomy 74, 107–8, 126–27, 163–67

Belmont Hospital 66–67
bias
  hindsight bias 153–56
  outcome bias 153–56
  in risk assessment 48–49
Blair, T 5, 88
blame culture 6, 73, 76, 81–82, 85, 102–3, 106, 131, 214
Blunkett, D 78
Boateng, P 14, 76–77, 90
borderline pattern 34
borderline personality disorder (BPD)
  and character 140–41
  definition 29, 33–34, 140–41
  and self-harm 38, 91
  and suicide 38
  treatment *see* treatments for personality disorder

Boyle, M 60, 80, 151–52
Broadmoor Hospital 69, 72, 84, 95–96
Butler Committee (Committee on Mentally Disordered Offenders) 69–70, 71, 74

character
  and criminal responsibility 140, 198–200
  essentialism 140, 142, 153–56, 197–98
  and offending 146–51, 197–200
  and personality disorder 26–27, 52, 66–67, 140–42, 197–98
  and retributive punishment 146–51
  and risk assessment 46–48, 142–45, 153–56, 197–99, 209
civil commitment 52–53, 201–2
close supervision centres (CSCs) 91–92, 97
coercion 45, 92–93, 117, 130–31, 138–39, 151, 156–58, 209–10
coercive human rights doctrine 5, 14–15, 161, 186–90, 193, 203–5
Committee on Mentally Disordered Offenders *see* Butler Committee
community sentence / order 129, 168
consent 74, 92, 117, 162, 169, 210
Conservative-led governments 9, 71
Conservative-Liberal Democrat Coalition Government 111
Convention on the Rights of Persons with Disabilities (UN) 212–13
counter-law 61–62
criminal responsibility 160–67, 206–7 *see also* personality disorder and criminal responsibility
culpability 22–23, 160–68, 171–82, 183–84, 185, 190–91, 198, 200

Department of Health 5, 57, 62–65, 69, 75–81, 88–71, 111

depression 29, 38
desert 65 *see also* disproportionate punishment
determinate prison sentences, perceived problem of 5–6, 7–8, 57–58, 69–70, 74, 76–79, 81–82, 117
dialectical behaviour therapy *see* treatments for personality disorder
diminished culpability 165–66, 206–7
diminished responsibility 162–63, 164–67, 171–77, 178–81, 190–91, 199–200, 206–8
discharge from hospital 10–16, 53–54, 58–59, 102–6, 170–73, 182–85, 193–94, 213–14
discretionary life sentence 58–59, 62, 135
disproportionate punishment 16, 106–9, 135–39, 156–58, 204, 207–11
disruptive prisoners or patients 13, 21–22, 69–73, 77–82, 83–84, 91–93, 94–97, 100–1, 110–16, 130–31, 137, 193–96
disruptive prisoners, pathologization of 112–15, 130–31
dissocial personality disorder *see* antisocial personality disorder
Draft Mental Health Bill 2022 54
duty to criminalize / duty to punish 188–90, 204–5
Dyer, A. 147–48

Eastman, N 29
emotionally unstable personality disorder *see* borderline personality disorder
Ericson, R 61
evidence-based medicine 41, 87–88, 98–100
Expert Committee on the Review of the Mental Health Act 1983 *see* Richardson Committee
experts, decline of faith in 61–62, 70–71, 75

Fallon Inquiry 70–75, 77, 78–79, 92, 95
Fallon, P 71–72
false negatives 47–48
false positives 3, 37, 47–48, 49, 54–55, 142–43
First-Tier Tribunal (Mental Health) *see* mental health tribunal

Garland, D 11, 61–62
Grendon Prison 69

Hannah-Moffat, K 108

Hebenton, B 61
Henderson, D 27, 65–66
HMP Frankland 84, 86, 97
HMP Low Newton 19, 84, 111–12
HMP Whitemoor 40–41, 84, 86, 91, 94–95, 104–5, 122, 123
Home Office 5, 14, 57, 60, 62–65, 69, 75–81, 88–93, 99, 133–34, 151–52
hospital and limitation direction (hybrid order) 4, 7, 160, 168–69, 170, 174, 183–84
hospital orders 4, 9, 51, 70, 73–74, 160–61, 166, 167–77, 178–86, 190
Howells, K. 99
human rights *see also* Convention on the Rights of Persons with Disabilities
absolute right (ECHR) 132–33, 187–91
'balancing rights' metaphor 56–57, 60, 67, 78–82, 105, 109, 133–34, 156–57
and criminal law 14–15, 186, 203–4
and mental health law 53–54, 81, 212–14
prohibition of torture or inhuman or degrading treatment or punishment (ECHR, Art 3) 106–7, 132–37, 144–46, 149, 152, 157–58, 186–90, 191, 204–5, 207, 208–9, 210–11, 213
right to liberty and security of person (ECHR, Art 5) 6–7, 17–18, 52–53, 58–59, 81, 132–36, 207–11, 212–14
right to life (ECHR, Art 2) 80, 106–7, 132, 152–56, 157–58, 186–90, 204–5, 207, 210–11, 213
'right to rehabilitation' 2, 16, 78–80, 132–39, 144–46, 151, 155–59, 189, 197, 204
'right to security' 16, 79–80, 132–34, 151–58, 204–5
hybrid order *see* hospital and limitation direction

impact of imprisonment 178–83, 186–90, 205–7
imprisonment for public protection (IPP) 7–8, 9–11, 53, 78, 79–80, 133–39, 140–42, 146, 158
improvement science 98–100
Independent Review of the Mental Health Act 1983 (Wessely Review) 54, 97–98, 213
insanity 26–27, 160–68, 178–81, 190–91, 198–203, 205–8
interviewees 19
intoxication 167

joint working group on personality
disorder 57, 62–64, 69, 70–71, 74–
81, 88–93
judges 48, 58–59, 153–56, 159, 160–61,
162–63, 164, 166–69, 171–72, 173, 174,
176–81, 183–84, 185–86, 190–91, 200,
203, 207

labelling 17, 31–32, 34, 46, 101, 102–6, 109,
114–16, 192, 203 *see also* personality
disorder and stigma
Lacey, N 139–40, 149
Lacombe, D 104
late transfers from prison to hospital 72,
92–93, 97, 107–8, 194
Lavrysen, L 189
Lazarus, L 152
less eligibility 122–23
Lewis, A 51–52, 121
liberalism 56, 65–66, 68, 194
Liebling, A 94–95
Loader, I 70–71
Loughnan, A 160–61

Maden, T 62–63
Major, J 71–72
Mavronicola, N 146
McRae, L 104
media 6, 11, 63–64, 73, 76, 88, 90, 214
medication 30–31, 175, 176, 179–80, 185–86
medium secure unit 84, 90, 91, 93, 104
mental capacity
and care and treatment 74, 162, 169, 202
and criminal law 160–61, 163, 165–66,
179, 180–81, 192, 199–203, 205–7
mental disorder, definition of 25–26
mental health tribunal 102–4, 142, 170–73,
184–85, 214
mental illness 29–31, 51–52, 103–4,
116, 183–84
Ministry of Justice 44–45, 97, 111, 118
moral defectives 64–66
Moran, P 118
Morse, SJ 163, 201–2
multi-agency public protection
arrangements (MAPPA) 124

New Labour Government 2, 5, 7–8, 50, 56–
57, 60–61, 62–63, 65, 71, 75–82, 88–93

offender assessment system
(OASyS) 8, 113–14

offender's duty to engage in
rehabilitation 138–39, 156–58
offenders with personality disorder
as manipulative or untrustworthy
subjects 101, 103–5, 196–203
as monsters 12, 60–62, 193–95
as rational and responsible subjects 101,
110, 122–23, 125–27, 193–95, 196–203
as traumatized subjects 110, 122–23, 195
offending behaviour programmes 43–45,
53, 104, 123–24, 129–30, 137–38, 141–
42, 143–44, 210, 213–14
order for lifelong restriction (Scotland) 50–51

paradox of liberty 1, 192–93, 203–5
paradox of security 4, 192–93, 203–5
Parole Board 8–11, 15–16, 48, 53, 102–4,
128–29, 142, 157, 175, 182–83, 197, 209
parsimony 208–9
Peay, J 29, 174
penal welfarism 12–13, 61–62, 74–76,
193, 214–15
Percy Commission (Royal Commission
on the Law Relating to Mental Illness
and Mental Deficiency) 64–67, 70,
74–75, 80–81
personality disorder
cognitive, emotional and/or volitional
deficits 161–62, 165–66, 206–7
and criminal responsibility 17, 161–67,
198–203
definition and diagnosis 25–31, 33–35
double bind 17, 83–84, 100–9, 196–98
double disadvantage 4, 16–17, 161, 183,
191, 201–3
and exclusion from hospital 68–69, 73,
77, 81–82
history 26–27
and offending 36–38, 88–89
prevalence 35–37
and psychopathy 27
and self-harm 38, 91, 97, 106–7, 114–
15, 116
and stigma 3, 21–22, 31–33, 34–35,
101, 106, 114–15, 121, 125, 130–31,
141, 209
and suicide or attempted suicide 38, 116
and trauma / abuse 30, 37, 39, 116
treatment *see* treatments for personality
disorder
Pinto de Albuquerque, Judge 136–37,
138, 143

Pinto, M 189
populist punitiveness 61–63, 78
post-sentence preventive
    detention 51, 52–53
preventive detention in hospital 4, 58–59,
    72–73, 92–93, 117, 212–14 see also civil
    commitment
prior fault doctrine 167
prison, compatibility with rehabilitation 13,
    93–95, 122–27, 195–96
probation 35–36, 48, 110, 111–12,
    113, 195–96
psychiatric evidence 162–63, 166, 167–68,
    176–84, 190–91, 200, 206–7
psychiatrists
  and blame culture 6, 73, 214
  criticism of DSPD construct and
    proposals 7, 59, 91
  and medical ethics 7, 49–50, 51–52, 59
  negative views of people diagnosed
    with personality disorder /
    psychopaths 67–68
  refusal to take on personality disorder
    patients 62–63, 73, 76
  and social control 51–52, 59
  views on hospital detention on the
    grounds of personality disorder 51–52,
    67–68, 73–74
  views on treatability of personality
    disorder 5–6, 20–21, 39, 57, 58, 67–
    69, 72, 76
psychologically informed planned
    environments (PIPEs) 124–25
psychologists
  negative views of people diagnosed with
    personality disorder 104–5
  and treatment of personality
    disorder 69, 70–71
  views on treatability of personality
    disorder 72
psychopathic disorder (legal category) 5–6,
    7, 50, 51–52, 56–57, 58, 67–70, 71–75,
    95–96, 103–4
psychopathic personalities 26–27, 28, 65–
    66, 95–96
psychopathy
  circularity 35–36
  diagnosis 36
  historical concept or category 26–27, 28,
    64–70, 72, 81–82

modern definition 36
and offending 37–38
prevalence 36
relationship to personality
    disorder 27, 36
treatment 41, 66–70 see also treatment
    for personality disorder
psychosis 51, 116, 162–63, 178, 190–91
public fears about dangerous people 11,
    62–63, 69, 70–71, 110, 194,
    211, 214–15
punitiveness 5, 15–16, 107–8, 124–25, 159

Radzik, L 148, 149–50
Rampton Hospital 40–41, 84, 99
Ramsay, P 138–39
recall to hospital 168–69, 170–71, 173
recall to prison 9–10, 43, 119–20, 168–69,
    171, 173–74, 185–86, 207
Reed Review 64, 70–71
Reed, J 71
rehabilitation
  meaning 16
  as a management tool 13
  as redemption 16, 133–35, 144–
    51, 158–59
  as risk reduction 16, 133–44, 158–59
  survival of 12–13
rehabilitative ideal 11–13, 61–62, 75–76,
    78–79, 194
release from prison 7–9, 53, 74–75, 76–77,
    101–6, 128–30, 182–83, 211
reviewable sentences 70, 74
Richardson Committee (Expert Committee
    on the Review of the Mental Health Act
    1983) 70–71, 74–75, 79
Richardson, G 74
rights-based model of rehabilitation 18,
    79–80, 130, 207–11
risk assessment 46–49
risk-need-responsivity (RNR) model 16,
    46–47, 124, 126–27, 133, 137–44
Robinson, G 79–80
Rose, N 61
Rotman, E 18, 79–80, 130
Royal Commission on the Law Relating to
    Mental Illness and Mental Deficiency
    see Percy Commission
rule of law 56, 61, 66, 70, 81–82, 194
Rutherford, A 61–63, 64

schizophrenia 29–31, 37–38, 166–67, 178, 198
security, compatibility with therapy or rehabilitation 93–98, 122–27
security categorization (prisons) 101–6
Seddon, T 60–61
segregation 73, 91, 97, 100–1, 115
separate service for the DSPD group *see* third service
sexually violent predators 52, 81
Simon, J 12
staff
  burnout and retention 91, 108–9, 194
  cultures 95, 125–26
  relationships with prisoners / patients 10, 91, 94–95, 115, 118, 120–22, 124–27, 195–96, 211
Stanton-Ife, J 107–8
Stone, M 6, 62–64, 76, 77, 90, 97–98
Straw, J 57, 63–64, 69, 70–71, 75, 78, 79, 88
structural factors and offending 115, 124, 127
subjective benefits from treatment 96, 120–21

Tadros, V 163
terbeschikkingstelling (TBS) system 81
third service 6–7, 58–59, 74, 81, 84, 98
third way 56–57
training units 69–70
transfer direction 4, 58, 72, 74, 92–93, 97, 100–2, 160, 168, 170–71, 183–85, 196, 214
treatability
  legal test 5–6, 7, 22–23, 50–51, 58–59, 62, 67–70, 80–81, 193–94 *see also* appropriate medical treatment

of personality disorder / psychopathy / psychopathic disorder 4, 5–6, 22–23, 51–52, 66–70, 71–75, 96–97, 193–94
role in sentencing 183–86, 203
treatments for personality disorder
  cognitive behavioural therapy (CBT) 40, 43–44
  dialectical behaviour (or behavioural) therapy (DBT) 40
  effectiveness 41, 43–45, 87–88, 89, 98–100, 105–6, 118–22, 129–30, 143–44, 209–10
  history 66–70
  maturation 68, 69–70, 95–96, 105–6
  mentalization-based therapy 40
  offending behaviour programmes 43–45
  and risk of harm 97, 106–7, 127–28, 205
  therapeutic community 43–44, 66–67, 69, 89, 157
  trauma-based or trauma-informed 40–42, 110, 122, 123–27
  treatment guidelines 42–43

Ward, T 160–61
warehousing 83, 85–87, 99
Wessely Review *see* Independent Review of the Mental Health Act 1983
Wessely, S. 54, 97–98
whole life orders 133, 134, 144–51, 189, 208–9
women's services 5, 7, 8, 19, 42–43, 84, 90, 111–13, 116, 123

Zedner, L 107, 149–50, 157, 198–99, 201, 208–10, 211